Collective Preference and Choice

Collective decision making is a familiar feature of our social, political, and economic lives. It ranges from the relatively trivial (e.g. the choice of the next family car) to the globally significant (e.g. whether or not a country should go to war). Yet, whether trivial or globally significant, such decisions involve a number of challenging problems. These problems arise in the standard social choice setting, where individuals differ in their preferences. They also arise in the standard decision-making setting, where individuals share the same preferences, but differ in their decisional capabilities. The distinctive feature of *Collective Preference and Choice* is that it looks at classical aggregation problems that arise in three closely related areas: social choice theory, voting theory, and group decision making under uncertainty. Using a series of exercises and examples, the book explains these problems with reference to a number of important contributions to the study of collective decision making.

SHMUEL NITZAN is Sir Issac Wolfson Professor of Economics at Bar-Ilan University, Israel. He is the author (with Jacob Paroush) of *Collective Decision Making* (1986) and (with Gil Epstein) of *Endogenous Public Policy and Contests* (2007). His research focuses on political economy, social choice, collective decision making, public economics, and voting theory.

Collective Preference and Choice

SHMUEL NITZAN

CAMBRIDGE
UNIVERSITY PRESS

CAMBRIDGE
UNIVERSITY PRESS

Shaftesbury Road, Cambridge CB2 8EA, United Kingdom

One Liberty Plaza, 20th Floor, New York, NY 10006, USA

477 Williamstown Road, Port Melbourne, VIC 3207, Australia

314–321, 3rd Floor, Plot 3, Splendor Forum, Jasola District Centre, New Delhi – 110025, India

103 Penang Road, #05–06/07, Visioncrest Commercial, Singapore 238467

Cambridge University Press is part of Cambridge University Press & Assessment, a department of the University of Cambridge.

We share the University's mission to contribute to society through the pursuit of education, learning and research at the highest international levels of excellence.

www.cambridge.org
Information on this title: www.cambridge.org/9780521722131

First published 2010

A catalogue record for this publication is available from the British Library

ISBN   978-0-521-89725-9   Hardback
ISBN   978-0-521-72213-1   Paperback

Dedicated to the memory of my mother and father

Contents

Figures

Preface

The study of *collective preference and choice* involves exposure to
a number of interesting and challenging problems. Clarifying these
problems and their significance is the main objective of this book.

The problems of collective decision making arise in the standard
social choice setting, where individuals differ in their preferences.
They also occur in the standard team or committee decision-making
setting, where individuals share the same preferences, but differ in
their decisional capabilities in an uncertain environment. The issues
of collective preference and choice are relevant and of significance to
many disciplines in the social sciences.

The term "social preference" relates to the description of the
system of tastes or preferences of society. The term "social choice"
relates to behavior; that is, the selection of one of the feasible actions
or alternatives faced by society. The book presents the classical aggregation problems of (i) social choice theory, (ii) voting theory and
(iii) group decision making under uncertainty, and discusses their
implications.

The social choice problem is clarified by Arrow's impossibility
theorem, Sen's paretian liberal paradox and Gibbard–Satterthwaite
impossibility theorem. The basic problems of voting theory are examined by focusing on Condorcet's voting paradox and on the comparison between the voting rules proposed by Condorcet, Dodgson and
Borda. The problem of judgment aggregation is studied using the
framework of Condorcet's jury theorem.

The book also presents three more recent approaches to the resolution of the problems in these three fields. These are, respectively,
the metric approach to social compromise, the attempt to ameliorate

majority decisiveness (tyranny) by using scoring rules, and the identification of the optimal group decision rule in the context of uncertain dichotomous choice.

There are relatively few textbooks focusing on social choice, on voting theory or on collective decision making under uncertainty. To the best of my knowledge, none of these relates to the main problems in **all** three (related) fields. This book provides such coverage, while not attempting to treat the three themes comprehensively.

The book has twelve chapters. The first part of the book (Chapters 1–3) has three objectives: to explain the basic reasons for the problematic nature of preference and decision aggregation (Chapter 1); to provide a brief overview of the problems presented in the book (Chapter 2); and to clarify the relationship between preferences and choice (Chapter 3). This relationship is relevant in discussions of both individual and social preferences and choices.

The second part of the book (Chapters 4–10) deals with individuals – voters, decision makers – who have different preferences. In this part, we discuss the main problems of social choice under non-strategic behavior (Chapters 4, 5 and 6), and some basic problems of voting theory (Chapters 7 and 8). The last two chapters in this part, Chapters 9 and 10, deal with strategic behavior.

The third part of the book (Chapters 11–12) deals with individuals who share the same preferences, but differ in their decisional skills. The analysis in this part uses the uncertain dichotomous choice model.

Unlike in other areas of economic theory and political thought, no book has to date presented issues of collective preferences and choice in a simple, relatively brief and yet profound way, accessible even to those who are not close to the field. The reason for this is twofold. First, the treatment of the topic in the literature has been based on intensive use of mathematical tools and consequently the presentation of the material to a relatively broad readership in "soft" non-technical language is difficult. Second, the topic is interdisciplinary and therefore tends to "fall between the cracks."

The study of the problems of collective preferences and choice has gathered momentum in the past fifty years, though some of the main problems were already being discussed in the eighteenth and nineteenth centuries. The findings obtained began to play an important role in sub-disciplines such as Political Theory, Public Economics and Welfare Economics, and contributed to the development of new sub-disciplines such as Social Choice, Public Choice, Voting Theory and Collective Decision Making. A noteworthy indication of increased recognition in the significance of the subject is the fact that since 1972, six of the recipients of the Nobel prize in Economics – Paul Samuelson, Kenneth Arrow, John Nash, John Harsanyi, Amartya Sen, and William Vickrey – achieved their high recognition partly because of their contribution to the clarification of the problematic nature of social choice, or their contribution to the resolution of some of the problems associated with collective decision making.

In summary, this book does not aim to systematically and comprehensively cover the numerous topics related to collective preferences and choice. Its objective is to clarify the main problems of collective decision making and arouse the interest of the reader to further and deeper study of the fascinating problems of social choice theory, voting theory and group decision making under uncertainty.

Finally, the presentation of the material in this book has been influenced by my considerable experience of teaching these topics. In particular, I have included a relatively large number of problems together with their detailed answers. I hope this will help readers and students to better understand the material, be able to apply it – and perhaps even enjoy it!

Acknowledgments

I would like to thank Eyal Baharad, Ruth Ben Yashar, Itzhak Gilboa, Marc Gradstein, and Eyal Winter for their most useful substantive and editorial suggestions. Barbara Grant provided very careful professional editing services on the entire manuscript for which I am most grateful. I am also grateful to Julian Bates, Jamie Hood, and Philip Good for their very effective assistance in the production of the book. I owe Anat Lavon-Alexandron and Eitan Lavon a special debt for their help in the design of the book cover. Finally, I would like to thank the Open University of Israel for funding the preparation of this book.

Some of the material in the book is based on research, my own and others', contained in papers that have been published in professional journals. I am grateful to the copyright holders who granted their permission to use these papers. Specifically:

May, K., *Independent Necessary and Sufficient Conditions for Simple Majority Decision*, Econometrica, 1952, 680–684. With kind permission of the Econometric Society. (Used in Section 5.1.)

Farkas, D. and S. Nitzan, The Borda Rule and Pareto Stability: A Comment, *Econometrica*, 47, 1979, 1305–1306. With kind permission of the Econometric Society. (Used in Chapter 6.)

Baharad, E. and S. Nitzan, "The Cost of Implementing the Majority Principle: The Golden Voting Rule", *Economic Theory*, 2007, Vol. 31(1), 69–84. With kind permission of Springer Science+Business Media. (Used in Chapter 8.)

Reny, P. J., "Arrow's Theorem and the Gibbard-Satterthwaite Theorem: A Unified Approach", *Economics Letters*, 2001, Vol. 70(1), 99–105. With kind permission of Elsevier. (Used in Section 10.2.)

Ben-Yashar, R. and S. Nitzan, The Invalidity of Condorcet Jury Theorem under Endogenous Decisional Skills, *Economics of Governance*, 2, 2001, 143–152. With kind permission of Springer Science+Business Media. (Used in section 11.5.)

Ben-Yashar, R. and S. Nitzan, The Optimal Decision Rule for Fixed Size Committees in Dichotomous Choice Situations: The General Result, *International Economic Review*, 38(1), 1997, 175–187. With kind permission of *Wiley-Blackwell*. (Used in Chapter 12.)

Part I Introduction

I The reason for the problems

The term *preferences* or *system of preferences* relates to tastes defined on a set of alternatives. The term *choice* refers to a pattern of behavior that takes the form of choice from a set of alternatives. In the context of collective choice, that is, choice by a number of individuals, the alternatives can be possible decisions of a group of judges or of a jury, the possible modes of action faced by a board of directors, different policies considered by a government, local community, committee of experts, a political party that wishes to win an election, or a group of civil servants. The use of the terms *social preferences* or *social choice* is common in social contexts in which the chosen alternatives affect several individuals (some or all members of society). These terms play an important role in areas of economics and political science that are concerned with decisions that affect different individuals. Not only are these individuals affected by the social decision, they or their representatives are often directly involved in making the decision. In economics, for example, decisions on family consumption are made by family members, decisions on the business strategy of a company are made by members of the board of directors and decisions on government policy are reached by members of a committee of experts. In political science, decisions that determine the form of government, identity of the ruler, the laws of the state or its policy are made by the eligible citizens or their representatives in the legislature and the government.

The first question that will be dealt with in Chapter 3 concerns the relationship between preferences and choice. This is a general question that arises on both the social and the individual levels; that is, in the context of collective and individual decision making. In contrast, questions that will be dealt in Chapters 4 onward arise only in the context of social preferences or social choice. One needs to consider the basic reasons for the emergence of these problems. Why are problems expected in the social context?

A multi-person society naturally needs a rule to transform individual preferences or choices into a social preference or social choice. Such a rule is referred to as an *aggregation rule*. It aggregates the individual preferences and transforms them into social preferences or aggregates individual choices and transforms them into social choice. In society, there are usually conflicts of interest among members. The need for an aggregation rule and the existence of conflicts of interest are the two basic reasons for the problematic nature of social preferences and social choice. Let us clarify them and their relationship to four types of fundamental problem that arise in the social context.

When there is only a single individual, it is plausible to assume that the preference relation of the single-member society is the preference relation of that member and that such a society chooses the alternative preferred by that individual. When society consists of more than one individual, a plausible social preference relation and a natural social choice do not exist. This situation raises the need for an aggregation rule that transforms the individual preference relations into a social preference relation or the individual choices into a social choice.

Technically, the social choice model can be applied to the case of individual choice. However, qualitatively, there is a significant difference between social and individual choice. An individual's choice usually affects only that individual and the complexity of that choice is relatively limited. In addition, when the individual's preferences are well defined, an alternative usually exists that is the best according to his or her preferences. In the social context, the alternatives are more complex and, in particular, affect the welfare of several and, possibly, all the individuals. Since individuals have different preferences, they prefer or wish to choose different alternatives. This means that in the social context there is a *conflict of interests* among the individuals that has no counterpart and, in fact, is meaningless when there is only a single individual. In the social context, usually no single alternative is considered best by all individuals.

As already mentioned, the need for an aggregation rule and the existence of conflicts of interest cause four types of problem. Under individual decision making, the choice is controlled by the individual who can behave as he or she wishes. In contrast, in collective decision making, the chosen alternative depends on the different preferences or choices of the individuals; however, it also depends on the aggregation rule (the social choice function). Individuals wishing to choose different alternatives will want to apply different choice functions. For this reason, in the social context, the first problem is how to reach agreement on the social choice function: the problem of securing agreement on the aggregation rule.

Two additional general questions that arise in the social context relate to the functioning or performance of the aggregation rule, the rule that transforms the individual preferences (choices) into social preferences (choice). The first question is whether the aggregation rule preserves the existing desirable properties of the individual preference relations or choices. The second question is whether this rule satisfies new, desirable properties that are regarded as plausible in the social context. The performance of the aggregation rule can be considered deficient if it does not preserve some existing desirable properties of the individual preference relations or of their choices. Another general problem that arises in the social context relates to deficient functioning of this sort. The performance of the aggregation rule can also be considered deficient if it does not satisfy properties that are deemed desirable in the social context. The second type of general problem that arises in the social context relates to deficient functioning of this sort.

Finally, strategic incentives do not exist in the context of a single individual, because the behavior of a single-member society hinges only on the preferences or the behavior of that member. In contrast, in a multi-member society, an individual may be aware of the relationship between the preferences or the behavior of other individuals and the social choice and, consequently, behave strategically, taking into account the expected behavior (decisions, voting, choices) of the other individuals. In such a situation there are two types of strategic incentive that can harm the functioning of the social decision rule. First, the individual may have an incentive not to take part in the collective decision (the elections). On one hand, he or she may believe that participation in the collective decision has only a negligible effect on his or her welfare. On the other hand, such participation involves non-negligible costs. Second, the individual may have an incentive not to reveal his or her true preferences because such truthful preference revelation is not advantageous. Problems of the fourth type are due to the existence of such strategic incentives.

I.I EXERCISES

Question 1a
Using a schematic diagram, explain why the problem of the relationship between preferences and choice is a general problem that arises both in the individual and in the social context.

Answer
The following simple diagram (Figure 1.1) clarifies that the question of the relationship between preferences and choice is meaningful in both contexts.

Question 1b
Explain why social choice can be viewed as a "game."

Answer
The social choice problem has a typical structure of a non-cooperative strategic game in normal form. Such a game has three components: a set of players, a strategy set for every player, and the players' pay-off functions. The players in the social choice game are the individual members of society. The strategy of a player is the answer to two

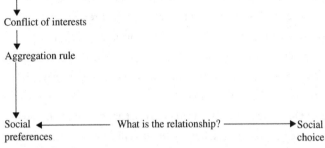

FIGURE I.I The relationship between preferences and choice

questions: shall I take part in the game or not; and if the answer to the first question is positive, then what preferences to report?

The aggregation rule transforms the individual strategies into a social choice, which is the outcome of the game. The payoff (utility, numerical representation of preferences) of every individual thus depends on the strategies chosen by that individual and by other individuals.

I.2 SUMMARY

- The first question that we will deal with is: What is the relationship between preferences and choice? This is a general question that arises on the social as well as the individual level.

- In the context of social preferences and choice, the need for an aggregation rule and the existence of conflicts of interest cause four types of problem.

- The existence of conflicts of interest implies that different individuals prefer different alternatives. Since different aggregation rules result in different social preferences, an individual prefers an aggregation rule that yields social preferences that coincide with his or her own preferences. The existence of conflicts of interest is therefore a basic reason for the difficulty involved in reaching an agreement on the aggregation rule applied by society.

- **First problem: The problem of securing agreement on the aggregation rule (the social preferences).**
- The second and third problems relate to the nature of the aggregation rule. This rule determines the properties of the social preferences and the question is whether or not these preferences satisfy certain plausible properties.
- **Second problem: Does the aggregation rule preserve existing desirable properties of the individual preferences?**
- **Third problem: Does the aggregation rule ensure that the social preferences satisfy some properties that are regarded as plausible in the social context?**
- The fourth type of problem relates to strategic incentives; namely, the possibility of viewing the social choice problem as a strategic game in normal form. In particular, one can ask the following question:
- **Fourth problem: Can individuals choose not to take part in the game or not to reveal their true preferences?**

2 Brief overview of the problems

In formal models, the individual preferences or the preferences of a group of individuals (family, society, economy, board of directors, committee of experts, government, general staff, etc.) are often represented by a *preference relation*. Individual or group behavior is represented by a function called a *choice function* or a *decision rule*. Naturally, one may think that there exists a firm relationship between preferences and behavior. In other words, it is natural to assume that a chosen alternative is the preferred one. The common attempt to derive the individual's preference relation from his or her behavior is based on the assumption that such a relationship indeed exists. The basic problem dealt with in Chapter 3 is that a strong connection between preferences and choice does not necessarily exist.

In this chapter, the student is first exposed to the basic concepts that relate to individual or social preferences and choice. We then examine two questions. On one hand, what properties does a preference relation have to satisfy in order to guarantee the existence of a well-defined choice function that is consistent with that preference relation? On the other hand, what properties does the choice function have to satisfy in order to ensure that it can be viewed as intrinsically and naturally related to some preference relation?

The demeanor of people, the resources available to them, their background, nature, attitudes, beliefs and wishes are different. Recognition of these differences raises a serious doubt regarding the assumption that individuals who take part in a social choice share the same preferences. If people were identical, the study of the social choice could be based on the analysis of a representative individual's choice, that of one of the homogeneous members of society. The reason for this is that in such a situation, the choice of a representative individual could be expected to be the same as the choice of society. In this simple case, one can make the common assumption in economics that the individual is rational. That is, the individual can be assigned a reasonable preference relation, such that he or she always chooses the best feasible alternative according to this preference relation. If individuals differ in their tastes, one can still ask whether it is possible to relate to social choice, like to an individual's choice, on the basis of the assumption that the social choice is rationalizable by some preference relation. Such a preference relation is usually called a *social preference relation* or the preference relation of an individual who represents society. The existence of a plausible social preference relation and of a corresponding *social choice function* ensures rational social behavior and is of major methodological significance. In particular, it enables the achievement of the positive objectives (explanation and prediction) of the theory that focuses on the study of social choice, employing the standard paradigmatic methodology in economics. In the normative social context, the existence of such a relation raises the question of what is the "desirable" or "appropriate" social preference relation. The answer to this question can be based on agreement regarding the properties that the desirable social preference relation should satisfy. Such an agreement may lead to the identification of a desirable social choice function that enables society to overcome the difficulty of taking action in situations characterized by conflicts of interest among individuals.

For this reason, this question is crucial for every society that seeks to adopt a decision rule that represents its preferences. Clearly, coping with this question is a major challenge of the theory of social choice and, in fact, of any theory that deals with the study of social behavior or attempts to come up with a recommendation regarding an appropriate social decision-making method.

The agreement on certain plausible properties of the social preference relation may result in a dead end if it turns out that the properties are logically inconsistent. Such a situation means that the search for a social preference relation has failed, because a social preference relation that satisfies *all* the agreed-upon desirable properties does not exist. Alternately, one can argue that in such a situation, if the social preference relation satisfies some of the properties, then it must violate at least one of the remaining properties. Chapter 4 is devoted to a discussion of the non-existence of a plausible or desirable social preference relation. In that chapter, we present the two best-known problems of this type. The first is Arrow's impossibility theorem, sometimes referred to as Arrow's possibility theorem. The second is Sen's impossibility theorem, usually referred to as the Paretian liberal paradox (the efficiency notion in the theorem was proposed by the Italian sociologist-economist Wilfredo Pareto, 1848–1923).

Consensus on the desirable properties of the social preference relation may enable axiomatization of the social preference relation. Axiomatization implies identification of the only social preference relation that satisfies the desirable properties. Such a situation means that the search for a social preference relation has succeeded; not only does there exist a social preference relation that satisfies *all* the agreed-upon desirable properties, but no other relation satisfies these properties. Chapter 5 is devoted to the identification of the proper social preference relation or the appropriate social choice function by axiomatization. In that chapter, we will present two examples of this type of solution to the social choice problem: axiomatization of the simple majority rule and axiomatization of the Borda rule.

Agreement on the desirable properties of the social preference relation may lead to a third possibility: identification of a few, or many, social preference relations or social decision rules that satisfy the desirable properties. Such a situation means that the search for a social preference relation has resulted in "over success"; such success does enable selection of a desirable rule, but it nevertheless raises the question of which rule should be selected, out of the set of appropriate rules. Chapter 6 deals with this problem and proposes to resolve it by compromising with the unanimity criterion.

Arrow's impossibility theorem implies that an anthropomorphic approach to society is problematic. More precisely, there is no way to transform the individual preference profile into a plausible, non-dictatorial social preference relation that ensures the existence of a well-defined consistent social choice that resembles the rational choice of every member of society. This problem casts doubt on the meaning and use of notions such as the *public interest*, the *national goal* or the *reasonable man/citizen*. Since no social decision rule can be rationalized by a plausible non-dictatorial social preference relation, one may expect that the use of different decision rules will result in "paradoxes," namely in the violation of some desirable properties. Chapter 7 illustrates such paradoxes. As already noted, different individuals usually prefer different decision rules. Therefore, a democratic political system faces the basic difficulty of reaching an agreement on the applied voting rule. The examples presented in Chapter 7 point to another difficulty: the paradoxical nature of the outcome of voting rules.

The use of (simple or special) majority rules that do not enable expression of preference intensity is very common in economic-political environments. A distinctive drawback of such rules is their vulnerability to the tyranny of the majority. This disadvantage is a major issue in the 'political thought' literature. The first part of Chapter 8 is devoted to the resolution of this problem by the use of scoring rules. Such voting rules grant the minority some ability to express its preferences effectively. The second part of the chapter is devoted to the identification of the "golden voting rule," the rule that in a balanced way takes into account the need to provide the minority with some effective ability to express its preferences by preventing majority tyranny, as well as the need to prevent erosion in the implementation of the majority principle; namely, the need to respect the majority's right to be decisive.

The discussion in Chapters 4, 5, 6, 7 and 8 disregards strategic considerations; that is, it ignores the possibility that individuals are aware of the relationship between their behavior and the collective choice, and take into account the expected actions (voting, decisions) of other individuals. It can be argued that in these chapters, the social choice is "mechanical"; the decision rule transforms the individual decisions into a social decision assuming that individuals are naïve: The behavior of every individual is consistent with his or her preferences, but is not the outcome of strategic considerations. Chapter 9 focuses on the problem of the inefficiency of the collective decision rule and clarifies, first, in a non-strategic setting, why the social choice is usually inefficient. It then clarifies that even under strategic behavior, although every individual chooses the optimal action from his or her point of view, the social choice is inefficient. The problem of inefficiency of collective action is studied in this chapter in the economic context of the provision of a public good, assuming that the collective decision is made by applying the simple majority rule, the Borda rule, the unanimity rule, the dictatorial rule or the market-like decentralized mechanism that is based on the voluntary provision of the public good (every individual decides how much of the public good he or she wishes to purchase).

When some of the goods are public goods, the competitive-market mechanism cannot ensure the selection of an efficient allocation of resources. This example of market failure serves as an important argument to justify government intervention aimed to secure the attainment of efficiency; efficiency of the allocation of resources (the consumption patterns and production plans) in the economy. The success of government intervention hinges on the ability of the government to acquire reliable information on individual preferences. The problem dealt with in Chapter 10 is that such ability is dubious, because individuals have an effective incentive not to reveal their preferences. In other words, sincere revelation of preferences does not serve the individuals' interests and therefore one cannot expect such sincere preference revelation. Furthermore, the vulnerability of the social decision rule to manipulations when individuals report their preferences is a basic general problem, as implied by the Gibbard–Satterthwaite impossibility theorem. In the simple case where society makes a decision on whether to produce or not to produce some public good, under some restrictive assumptions on individual preferences, there exist mechanisms that reveal the true preferences of the individuals. In the last part of Chapter 10, we present the demand-revealing process offered by Groves and Clarke, and discuss its merits and disadvantages.

Although the source of the problems mentioned so far is the difference in individual preferences and the conflict of interests this implies, the question of the appropriate way to transform the decisions (votes) of individuals into a collective decision may also arise when individual preferences are the same, but their decisional skills are different. In a world where individual decisions are not necessarily fully consistent with their preferences; that is, in situations where individuals can err, it is meaningful and important to evaluate and compare different collective decision rules. Chapter 11 is devoted to a comparison between individual decisions and decisions based on simple majority rule. This comparison is carried out in the context of an uncertain dichotomous choice, assuming that when individuals share the same preferences and the same decisional skills, they may err. Condorcet's theorem clarifies why, from the point of view of every individual, the simple majority rule is the superior collective decision rule.

In the simple setting of dichotomous choice with heterogeneous individuals, the simple majority rule and the expert rule are just two of the (usually many) possible collective decision rules. The last chapter focuses on the question of the optimal collective decision rule from the point of view of group members who share identical preferences, but differ in their decisional capabilities.

This book focuses on different problems related to the aggregation of preferences, decisions and judgments, but there is no pretension to cover in an exhaustive way the problems dealt with in the social choice, voting theory or group decision-making literature. Let us conclude this chapter with a remark on one significant application of social choice theory not included in this book. The axiomatic approach presented in Chapter 5 can be applied to the characterization of alternative social utility functions (social welfare functions) that represent the social preference relation (in these cases, the social preference relation does not satisfy all the desirable properties that appear in Arrow's impossibility theorem). The first notable example is the axiomatic characterization of the utilitarian social welfare function. This axiomatization was first proposed by Harsanyi (1955). The second prominent example is the axiomatic characterization of the maximin rule, the social welfare function implied by the justice principles proposed by John Rawls (1971). The first axiomatization of this rule was proposed by Hammond (1976). The third noteworthy example is the axiomatization of the multiplicative social welfare function proposed by John Nash (1950). These social welfare functions are of major significance in public economics, in discussions of distributive justice, and in bargaining theory. A very useful comprehensive survey of the relevant literature appears in Sen (1986); see also Yaari (1981).

2.1 EXERCISES

Question 2a

Explain briefly the axiomatic approach to social choice.

Answer

The axiomatic approach attempts to identify the desirable social preference relation or the appropriate social choice function by reaching agreement on their desirable properties, hoping that these properties uniquely characterize the social preference relation or the social choice function.

Question 2b

What two difficulties are associated with the axiomatic approach to social choice?

Answer

The first difficulty is that agreement on the plausible properties of the social preference relation may result in a dead end, if it turns out that these properties are logically inconsistent. Such a situation implies that no social preference relation can satisfy *all* the agreed-upon desirable properties.

The second difficulty is that the axiomatization may result in several, and perhaps many, desirable social preference relations. This situation means that it is then necessary to cope with the question of which rule should be selected out of the set of desirable rules.

Question 2c

How can one cope with the first difficulty associated with the axiomatic approach to social choice?

Answer

The difficulty can be resolved if one or some of the desirable properties are weakened or relinquished. Restricting the incidence of a required property is one possible way of weakening it.

2.2 SUMMARY

- The first problem that will be dealt with in Chapter 3 is the relationship between preferences and choice. In particular, on one hand we will clarify what properties a preference relation has to satisfy in order to guarantee the existence of a well-defined choice function consistent with that preference relation. On the other hand, we will clarify what properties the choice function has to satisfy in order to ensure that it can be viewed as intrinsically and naturally related to some preference relation.

- In this chapter we presented a brief overview of the nine problems associated with collective decision making, namely, the aggregation of preferences, decisions and judgments. This brief exposure to the problems does not enable deep understanding of the problems. Its purpose is a preliminary acquaintance with the specific problems, separately and together, that can be referred to as "the problematic nature of collective preferences and collective choice." Despite the superficiality of the acquaintance to this entirety, it enables orderly classification of the problems according to clear criteria.

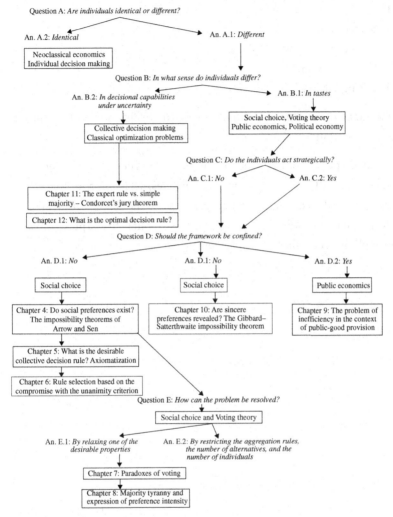

FIGURE 2.1 The classification of the problems and their disciplinary relevance

- The following three questions are used as the main criteria for classification:
  a. Are individuals identical or different?
  b. In what sense do individuals differ?
  c. Do individuals act strategically?

- The problems are classified into four fields:
  a. Social Choice
  b. Collective Decision Making
  c. Public Economics
  d. Voting Theory.

It should be noted that problems dealt with are also relevant to Public Choice and Political Economy.

- The main part of the book includes nine chapters devoted to problems associated with the aggregation of preferences, decisions and judgments. The flow diagram in Figure 2.1 presents the classification of the problems according to the three criteria applied. It also presents the disciplinary relevance of the problems.

3 The relationship between preferences and choice

The assumption that there exists a firm relationship between the preferences of the economic unit and its behavior (choice from the set of the feasible alternatives it faces) is very common in economic theory. In fact, the exclusive working supposition in the analysis of the economic unit's behavior is that it can be assigned a system of preferences, such that its choice is the best alternative according to that system of preferences. It should be noted that under this assumption, which is often called the **rationality principle**, the system of preferences assigned to the economic unit is conceived as a device (theoretical construction) that enables explanation and prediction of its behavior. The existence of such a tight relationship between preferences and choice is not necessary. The system of preferences need not be well defined, and still a meaningful choice may exist. It is also possible that the system of preferences is well defined, but is inconsistent with the observed choice of the economic unit. And it is also possible that the notion of preferences is questionable or even meaningless as, for example, when it is assigned to a group of individuals who face the task of making a collective choice. This chapter is devoted to a formal presentation of the concepts of **preference** and **choice** and to a clarification of the relationship between them. In particular, we wish to answer the following two questions:

1. What are the necessary properties of a system of preferences that ensure the existence of choice consistent with that system of preferences? The challenge here is the identification of the properties of preferences that ensure the existence of rational choice.

This chapter draws on and adapts material from Chapter 1 in Austen-Smith and Banks (1998).

2. What are the necessary properties of choice that ensure that it can be conceived as consistent with some system of preferences? The challenge here is the identification of the properties of choice that ensure its rationalizability.

3.1 PREFERENCE-DRIVEN CHOICE

In the context of preference and choice, the basic concepts or primitives are the set of alternatives X and the preference relation R, which is defined on it. In this chapter we assume that X is a finite set and its elements are denoted by x, y, z, etc. The binary preference relation R, the relation "preferred or indifferent to," enables comparison between pairs (not necessarily all pairs) of alternatives by the economic unit; an individual, or a group of individuals. We write xRy when alternative x is preferred or indifferent to alternative y from the perspective of the individual or the group. The strict preference relation P and the indifference relation I are defined using R as follows:

$$xPy \leftrightarrow xRy \,\&\, {\sim}yRx$$

$$xIy \leftrightarrow xRy \,\&\, yRx$$

${\sim}yRx$ means that yRx is not satisfied. xPy and xIy mean, respectively, that "x is preferred to y" and "x is indifferent to y."

Let χ denote the set of all non-empty subsets of X.

$$\chi = \{S \subseteq X : S \neq \phi\}$$

Given the preference relation R and the subset of alternatives S that belongs to χ, let us define the **maximal set** M associated with (R, S) as follows:

$$M(R, S) = \{x \varepsilon S : \forall y \varepsilon S, \, xRy\}$$

$M(R, S)$ includes the best or top-ranked alternatives in S according to the preference relation R. Usually, $M(R, S)$ is called the **choice set** corresponding to R and S, because it is natural to assume that, given S and R, the chosen alternatives are those included in $M(R, S)$. That is, the decision maker selects from the feasible alternatives that he faces the best alternative from his point of view. This assumption, which is common in economics and to some extent in other social sciences, is called the **rationality principle**. The behavioral pattern that it implies is called **rational behavior**.

The first question that we examine is: What are the necessary properties of a preference relation R that ensure, for any given subset of alternatives S, that the choice set $M(R, S)$ is non-empty?

Reflexivity

A preference relation R is reflexive if every alternative x is preferred or indifferent to itself, that is, xRx.

Completeness

A preference relation R is complete if for every two distinct alternatives x and y, x is preferred or indifferent to y, or y is preferred or indifferent to x, that is, xRy or yRx.

Verify that reflexivity and completeness of R are necessary properties for ensuring that the choice set $M(R, S)$ is non-empty for every subset S.

Transitivity

A preference relation R is transitive if for every three alternatives x, y and z in X,

$$xRy \ \& \ yRz \rightarrow xRz$$

Acyclicity

A preference relation R is acyclic if for every series of alternatives in X,

$$\{x, \ y, \ z \ldots u, \ v\},$$

$$xPy \ \& \ yPz \ldots \& \ uPv \rightarrow xRv$$

Notice that acyclicity is a weaker requirement than transitivity; transitivity implies acyclicity, but acyclicity does not imply transitivity.

A relation R is called an **ordering** if it is reflexive, complete and transitive. If R is an ordering, then $M(R, S)$ is non-empty, for any given subset of alternatives S that belongs to χ. In other words, reflexivity, completeness, and transitivity are sufficient conditions for the existence of a non-empty choice set under all circumstances (any given S). This claim follows from the following result, which clarifies what are the necessary and sufficient conditions for the existence of a non-empty choice set for any S in χ.

Theorem 3.1: Let R be reflexive and complete. Then the choice set $M(R, S)$ is not empty given any subset of alternatives S in χ, if and only if R is acyclic.

Proof:[1] (sufficiency) For any $S \subset X$, choose $x \in S$. If for all $s \in S$, xRs, then the proof is complete; otherwise, since R is complete and reflexive, there must exist an alternative y, $y \in S \setminus \{x\}$, such that yPx. If for all $s \in S$, yRs, then again the proof is complete. Otherwise there must exist z, $z \in S \setminus \{x, y\}$, such that zPy. Since R is acyclic, in such a case it follows that zPx. Since X (and therefore S) is a finite set, the same argument can be reapplied to conclude that there must exist an alternative that is preferred or indifferent to any other alternative in S.

(necessity) Suppose that $x_1 P x_2 P x_3 \ldots P x_{n-1} P x_n$. We have to prove that $x_1 R x_n$. Let $S = \{x_1, \ldots, x_n\}$ and suppose that $M(R, S) \neq \phi$. Since $x_{i-1} P x_i$, $i = 2, \ldots, n$, we get that $x_i \notin M(R, S)$, $i = 2, \ldots, n$. Therefore, since $M(R, S) \neq \phi$, it must be that $x_1 \in M(R, S)$, which implies that alternative x_1 is preferred or indifferent to any alternative in S, and in particular, $x_1 R x_n$, as we wish to prove. **Q.E.D.**

---

[1] This chapter is part of the introduction to the book. To avoid excessive cumbersomeness and digression from the main topic of the book, we chose to include in this chapter only the central results that deal with the relationship between preference and choice. With the exception of the proof of Theorem 3.1, we do not present proofs of the results. A more comprehensive discussion that includes the proofs of the results presented in this chapter as well as additional results appears in Chapter 1 of Austen-Smith and Banks (1998).

A function $C(.)$ that specifies for any set of alternatives S in χ a non-empty subset of alternatives in S, $C(S) \subset S$, is called a **choice function**. The chosen subset can include one or several alternatives. If the chosen subset always includes a single alternative, the choice function is called **resolute**. By Theorem 3.1, if R is a reflexive, complete and transitive (and therefore acyclic) relation on X, that is, if R is an ordering on the set of alternatives X, then $C(S) = M(R, S)$ is a well-defined choice function. This function is referred to as the **rational choice function corresponding to R, or the choice function driven by R**.

3.2 RATIONALIZABLE CHOICE

Let us turn to the properties of choice, observable properties that can be verified empirically, that ensure the rationalizability of choice by a reflexive, complete, and transitive relation. Namely, we consider the possibility of relating to actual choice as driven by some preference ordering R. For any subset of alternatives S, this ordering would generate the chosen alternatives as its maximal set $M(R, S)$.

A choice function is **rationalizable** if there exists a relation R on X such that for any S in χ, $C(S) = M(R, S)$. A natural candidate to provide rationalization to $C(.)$ is the relation R_c, which is derived from the choice function $C(.)$ as follows:

$$\forall x, y \in X, x R_c y \Leftrightarrow x \in C(\{x, y\})$$

The relation R_c is called the **base relation** of $C(.)$. It can be easily verified that

Proposition 3.1: A choice function $C(.)$ is rationalizable if and only if it is rationalizable by its base relation. That is, if and only if for any S in χ, $C(S) = M(R_c, S)$.

The following example clarifies that not every choice function is rationalizable.

Example 3.1

Suppose that $X = \{x, y, z\}$, $C(\{x\}) = \{x\}$, $C(\{y\}) = \{y\}$, $C(\{z\}) = \{z\}$, $C(\{x, y\}) = C(\{x, z\}) = \{x\}$ and $C(\{y, z\}) = C(\{x, y, z\}) = \{y\}$.

By Proposition 3.1, since $C(\{x, y\}) = \{x\}$ and $C(\{x, y, z\}) = \{y\}$, every relation R that rationalizes the choice function $C(.)$ and, in particular, the base relation R_c must satisfy the impossible requirement: xPy and yPx. This means that $C(.)$ is not rationalizable. ∎

Two properties of a choice function are presented below. The first property α is called consistency in contraction. The other property β is called consistency in expansion. Consistency in contraction (expansion) is stated in terms of permissible changes in choice following contraction (expansion) in the set of alternatives.

A choice function satisfies **property** α if and only if for any S and T in χ,

$$S \subseteq T \Rightarrow C(T) \cap S \subseteq C(S)$$

Property α implies that if alternative x is chosen from T and T is contracted to S by eliminating some alternatives that differ from x, then x must be among the chosen elements from the contracted set of alternatives S. It can be easily verified that the choice function in Example 3.1 does not satisfy property α. The choice function in this example is not exceptional. Some commonly used choice functions violate this property. For example, the plurality rule $C^{PL}(.)$ is inconsistent in contraction. According to this choice function, when a group of individuals selects a candidate from a set of candidates, every individual indicates who is his most preferred candidate and the chosen candidates are those who are most preferred by the largest number of individuals (of course, with a large number of voters the chosen candidate is usually unique). The following example clarifies that indeed the plurality rule violates property α.

Example 3.2

Suppose that $T = \{x, y, z\}$ and the transitive preference relations of five voters are as follows: Two individuals prefer x to y and y to z. Two individuals prefer y to z and z to x. The fifth individual prefers z

to x and x to y. In this case, candidates x and y are chosen from $T = \{x, y, z\}$; however, only candidate x is chosen from the contracted set $S = \{x, y\}$. The fact that candidate y is not chosen from the contracted set $S = \{x, y\}$ means that the plurality rule violates property α. ∎

A choice function satisfies **property** β if, and only if, for any S and T in χ,

$$S \subseteq T \,\&\, C(S) \cap C(T) \neq \phi \Rightarrow C(S) \subseteq C(T)$$

Property β implies that if alternative x is chosen from S and from T that contains S, then any other alternative that is chosen from S is also chosen from T. It can be easily proved that a resolute choice function satisfies property β and that the plurality rule does not satisfy property β.

Properties α and β are necessary and sufficient conditions for the rationalizability of a choice function $C(.)$ by an ordering.

Theorem 3.2: A choice function $C(.)$ is rationalizable by an ordering if, and only if, it satisfies properties α and β.

By Proposition 3.2 and the fact that a resolute choice function satisfies property β, it follows that property α is a necessary and sufficient condition for the rationalizability of a resolute choice function by an ordering.

The consistency properties α and β are equivalent to the weak axiom of revealed preference (WARP) that is usually encountered in the context of consumer theory. A choice function satisfies the **weak axiom of revealed preference (WARP)** if, and only if, for any S and T in χ,

$$x \in C(S), y \in S \setminus C(S) \,\&\, y \in C(T) \Rightarrow x \notin T$$

That is, if alternative x is revealed preferred to alternative y (if x is chosen from S and y is contained in S, but not chosen), then alternative y cannot be revealed preferred to alternative x (the fact that y is chosen from T implies that x does not belong to T).

Proposition 3.2: A choice function $C(.)$ satisfies properties α and β if, and only if, it satisfies the weak axiom of revealed preference (WARP).

The concluding result of this chapter is obtained from Proposition 3.2 and Theorem 3.2.

Theorem 3.3: A choice function $C(.)$ is rationalizable by an ordering if, and only if, it satisfies the weak axiom of revealed preference (WARP).

3.3 EXERCISES

Chapter 1 in Austen-Smith and Banks (1998) presents a comprehensive discussion of the relationship between preference and choice. In this chapter we have presented the basic concepts and five important results relevant to this discussion.

3.1 Preference-driven choice

Question 3.1
1. What is the choice set in the theory of the consumer?
2. What is the choice set in the theory of the producer?

Answers
1. In consumer theory the choice set includes affordable bundles of commodities that are preferred or indifferent to any bundle of commodities in the consumer's budget set.
2. In producer theory the choice set consists of feasible production plans (activities) that yield maximal profit.

Question 3.2
Explain why reflexivity and completeness of R are necessary properties for the choice set $M(R, S)$ to be non-empty for any S.

Answer
Reflexivity is a necessary property for ensuring the existence of a non-empty choice set in those cases where S consists of a single alternative. Completeness is a necessary property for ensuring the

existence of a non-empty choice set in those cases where S includes two alternatives.

Question 3.3
Explain why reflexivity, completeness, and transitivity ensure the realization of the rationality principle.

Answer
These three properties ensure that in any subset of alternatives there exists a "best" (most preferred) alternative. This means that the rationality principle can be realized.

3.2 Rationalizable choice

Question 3.4
Prove Proposition 3.1, namely that a choice function $C(.)$ is rationalizable if and only if it is rationalizable by its base relation. That is, if and only if for any S in χ, $C(S) = M(R_c, S)$.

Answer
The sufficiency part is simple; if the base relation of $C(.)$ rationalizes $C(.)$, then by definition, $C(.)$ is rationalizable. To prove the necessity part, suppose that $C(.)$ is rationalizable by some relation R and let us prove that R_c must be such an R. For any two alternatives x and y in X, by definition of $M(R,.)$, $xRy \Leftrightarrow x \in M(R, \{x, y\})$. Since R rationalizes $C(.)$,

$$x \in M(R, \{x, y\}) \Leftrightarrow x \in C(\{x, y\}).$$

But, by definition of R_c,

$$x \in C(\{x, y\} \Leftrightarrow xR_c y$$

Hence, for any two alternatives x and y in X, $xRy \Leftrightarrow xR_c y$, that is, $R = R_c$.

Question 3.5

Prove that a resolute choice function is consistent in expansion, that is, it satisfies the property β.

Answer

If the choice function $C(.)$ is resolute, then the fact that the intersection of the choice sets $C(S)$ and $C(T)$ is non-empty implies that $C(S) = C(T)$. This means that $C(.)$ satisfies property β.

Question 3.6

A group of voters selects a candidate from a group of candidates by applying the plurality rule. According to this rule, every voter indicates who is his most preferred candidate and the chosen candidate is the one who is most preferred by the largest number of voters. Discuss the following claim: "It is clear that the plurality rule satisfies property α. If a certain candidate is chosen from a group of candidates T, then he is also chosen from any sub-group of candidates S which is contained in T, because in both cases the same candidate is the most preferred one for the same number of voters."

Answer

The claim is false. It is true that if a certain candidate is chosen from the group T, then he is the most preferred candidate in T for the largest number of voters. But when T is reduced to the sub-group S, it is perfectly possible that the same candidate is no longer the one who is most preferred by the largest number of voters, as illustrated in Example 3.2.

Question 3.7

Prove that the plurality rule is inconsistent in expansion, that is, it violates property β.

Answer

Suppose that $T = \{x, y, z, w\}$ and the transitive preference relations of five voters are as follows. Two voters prefer x to y, y to w and w to z. Two voters prefer w to y, y to z and z to x. The fifth voter prefers

z to x, x to w and w to y. In this case candidates x and y are chosen from $S = \{x, y, z\}$, but x and w are chosen from $T = \{x, y, z, w\}$. The fact that candidate y is not chosen from T implies that the plurality rule violates property β.

Question 3.8
Prove that the plurality rule does not satisfy the weak axiom of revealed preference (WARP).

Answer
In Example 3.2, $x \in C(S)$, $y \in S \setminus C(S) \,\&\, y \in C(T)$, but $x \in T$, that is, the plurality rule violates WARP.

Question 3.9
Suppose that C(S) is a choice function driven by the preference relation R, $C(S) = M(R,S)$. Prove that $C(.)$ satisfies the consistency properties α and β.

Answer
Suppose that $S \subseteq T$. By definition, $C(T) = \{x \in T : \forall y \in T, xRy\}$. Hence, if $z \in C(T) \cap S$, then $\forall y \in S, zRy$, that is, $z \in C(S)$. We have therefore obtained that the choice function $C(.)$ satisfies the consistency property α,

$$S \subseteq T \Rightarrow C(T) \cap S \subseteq C(S).$$

Now suppose that $S \subseteq T$ and that $C(S) \cap C(T) \neq \phi$. Hence, if $z \in C(S)$, then $\forall y \in T, zRy$, that is, $z \in C(T)$. We have therefore obtained that the choice function $C(.)$ satisfies the consistency property β,

$$S \subseteq T \,\&\, C(S) \cap C(T) \neq \phi \Rightarrow C(S) \subseteq C(T)$$

Question 3.10
1. Is a choice function which is driven by a preference relation R necessarily resolute?
2. Is the plurality rule a resolute choice function?

Answer

1. No. It is certainly possible that the maximal set corresponding to a particular set of alternatives contains more than a single alternative. Such examples are frequently encountered in the theory of the consumer.

2. No. See example 3.2.

3.4 SUMMARY

- In the context of preference and choice, the basic concepts or primitives are the **set of alternatives** X and the **preference relation** R, which is defined on it.

- Given the preference relation R and the subset of alternatives S, the **maximal set** $M(R, S)$ includes the best alternatives in S according to R.

- The assumption that given S and R, the chosen alternatives are those included in $M(R, S)$ is called the **rationality principle**. This assumption is common in economics and therefore $M(R, S)$ is also called the **choice set** corresponding to R and S.

- **Theorem 3.1:** Let R be reflexive and complete. Then the choice set $M(R, S)$ is not empty given any subset of alternatives S in χ, if and only if R is acyclic.

- A relation R is called an **ordering** if it is reflexive, complete and transitive.

- A **choice function** $C(.)$ specifies for any set of alternatives S a non-empty subset of alternatives in S, $C(S) \subset S$.

- A choice function is **rationalizable** if there exists a relation R on X such that for any S in χ, $C(S) = M(R, S)$.

- The **base relation** R_c of a choice function $C(.)$ is defined as follows:
  $\forall x, y \in X, x R_c y \Leftrightarrow x \in C(\{x, y\})$.

- **Proposition 3.1:** A choice function $C(.)$ is rationalizable if, and only if, it is rationalizable by its base relation.

- **Property** α (consistency in contraction): A choice function satisfies **property** α if, and only if, for any S and T in χ,

$$S \subseteq T \Rightarrow C(T) \cap S \subseteq C(S)$$

- **Property** β (consistency in expansion): A choice function satisfies **property** β if, and only if, for any S and T in χ,

$$S \subseteq T \ \& \ C(S) \cap C(T) \neq \phi \Rightarrow C(S) \subseteq C(T)$$

- **Theorem 3.2:** A choice function $C(.)$ is rationalizable by an ordering if, and only if, it satisfies properties α and β.
- A choice function satisfies the **weak axiom of revealed preference (WARP)** if, and only if, for any S and T in χ,

$$x \in C(S), \ y \in S \backslash C(S) \ \& \ y \in C(T) \Rightarrow x \notin T$$

- **Proposition 3.2:** A choice function $C(.)$ satisfies properties α and β if, and only if, it satisfies the weak axiom of revealed preference (WARP).
- **Theorem 3.3:** A choice function $C(.)$ is rationalizable by an ordering if, and only if, it satisfies the weak axiom of revealed preference (WARP).

Part II Different Preferences

4 Do social preferences exist? Arrow's and Sen's impossibility theorems

In the context of social choice, the concepts of **social preference relation** and **social choice function** must be examined. The relationship between these concepts and the preference relations of the individuals in society must then be clarified. The central normative question is: what is the "desirable" social preference relation? One answer to this question is based on agreement regarding the desirable properties of the appropriate social preference relation, because such agreement can result in the unequivocal identification of this relation, and in turn, the appropriate social choice function. This approach is called the **axiomatic approach**. Its success may enable society to take action, even in situations where there is a conflict of interests among its members. This is a key normative issue, of major concern to any society that seeks to adopt a decision rule that reflects its preferences. Clearly, coping with this issue is a major challenge for social choice theory and in fact, for any theory that is concerned with the study of social behavior or with the search for an appropriate method of social choice.

A fundamental positive question, that was of major concern to researchers of social choice, is whether social choice, like individual choice, can be rationalized by some reasonable preference relation. The existence of such a relation, and of a social choice function that can be rationalized by this relation, guarantees rational social behavior. This is very significant methodologically, because it enables achievement of the positive objectives (explanation and prediction) of the theory of social choice, applying the fertile methodology paradigmatic in economics.

This chapter is devoted to a formal presentation of the concepts of social preference and social choice, and to the study of the relationship between individual and social preferences. The main question that will be explored is whether there exists a reasonable, appropriate or desirable social preference relation. As mentioned above, this question is of major normative and positive significance. The first part of the chapter introduces Arrow's impossibility theorem, which provides one possible negative answer to this central question. The second part of the chapter presents Sen's impossibility theorem, the Paretian liberal paradox, which provides another possible negative answer to this question. The two theorems demonstrate the conceptual difficulties associated with social choice. In particular, they clarify the difficulty of preserving the desirable properties of individual preference relations, the difficulty of ensuring the fulfillment of properties of the social preference relation that are deemed desirable, and the difficulty of securing consensus regarding the social choice.

4.1 THE SOCIAL CHOICE MODEL

The social choice model has three components:

a. A **set of alternatives** X.
b. A **preference profile** $R = (R_1, \ldots, R_n)$ that includes the preference relations of the n individuals in society. R_i is the preference relation of individual i.
c. A preferences aggregation rule, in short, an **aggregation rule** f, that specifies for given preference profiles a social preference relation.

In this chapter we make the following assumptions:

- The set of alternatives X is finite and includes at least three alternatives.
- The set of individuals $N = \{1, \ldots, n\}$ includes at least two members.
- The preference relation of every individual R_i is an ordering.
- The social preference relation is reflexive and complete, that is, the range of the aggregation rule f is the set B that includes all binary relations that are reflexive and complete.

Denote by R the **social preference relation**, "socially preferred or indifferent to" that corresponds to the preference profile $\boldsymbol{R}$, $R = f(\boldsymbol{R})$. The relation P, "socially preferred to", and the relation I, "socially indifferent to", are obtained from R as follows:

$$\forall x, y \in X, xPy \Leftrightarrow xRy \& (not)yRx$$

$$\forall x, y \in X, xIy \Leftrightarrow xRy \& yRx$$

Denote by $\mathfrak{R}$ the set of all possible orderings on X and by $\mathfrak{R}^n$ the set of all possible profiles of preference orderings. When indifference between alternatives is not allowed, that is, when the preference relation of every individual is anti-symmetric, the preference relation of every individual P_i will be called a **strict ordering**. Given some preference profile $\boldsymbol{R}$, $\boldsymbol{R} \in \mathfrak{R}^n$, and two alternatives x and y in X, let us denote by $P(x, y, \boldsymbol{R})$ the set of individuals who prefer x to y:

$$P(x, y, \boldsymbol{R}) = \{i \in N : xP_iy\}$$

Similarly, we define the sets:

$$R(x, y, \boldsymbol{R}) = \{i \in N : xP_iy\}, \quad I(x, y, \boldsymbol{R}) = \{i \in N : xI_iy\}$$

The aggregation rule f^{maj}, which is called the **simple majority rule**, because it is based on the use of the simple majority principle, is defined as follows:

$$\forall x, y \in X, xR^{maj}y \Leftrightarrow \left| R(x, y, \boldsymbol{R}) \right| \geq n/2$$

$R^{maj} = f^{maj}(\boldsymbol{R})$, the **simple majority relation**, is the social preference relation which is obtained by f^{maj}, given $\boldsymbol{R}$.

The aggregation rule f^B, the **Borda aggregation rule**, that takes into account the relative ranking of every alternative from the viewpoint of every individual, is defined as follows:

Suppose that the individual preference relations are strict orderings, and denote by $r_i(x)$ the relative ranking of alternative x in individual i's preference relation on X. Then,

$$\forall x, y \in X, \quad xR^By \Leftrightarrow \sum_N r_i(x) \leq \sum_N r_i(y)$$

$R^B = f^B(P)$ is the **Borda social preference relation,** which is obtained by f^B, given P.

Example 4.1

Suppose that $N = \{1, 2, 3\}$, $X = \{w, x, y, z\}$ and the preference profile is $P = (P_1, P_2 P_3)$:

$$P_1 : w P_1 x P_1 y P_1 z$$
$$P_2 : y P_2 z P_2 x P_2 w$$
$$P_3 : z P_3 y P_3 w P_3 x$$

Let us determine the simple majority relation R^{maj} and the Borda social preference relation R^B corresponding to the profile P:

$$|R(y, z; R)| = 2, \quad |R(z, w; R)| = 2, \quad |R(w, x; R)| = 2|$$

Therefore, by definition,

$$y \, R^{maj} z \, R^{maj} w \, R^{maj} x$$

Since

$$\sum_N r_i(w) = 8, \quad \sum_N r_i(x) = 9, \quad \sum_N r_i(y) = 6, \quad \sum_N r_i(z) = 7$$

we get that

$$y \, R^B z \, R^B w \, R^B x$$

The two aggregation rules, the simple majority rule and the Borda aggregation rule transform P to the same social preference relation. ∎

Example 4.2

Suppose that $N = \{1, 2, 3\}$, $X = \{w, x, y, z\}$ and the preference profile is $P = (P_1, P_2 P_3)$:

$$P_1 : y P_1 z P_1 w P_1 x$$
$$P_2 : x P_2 y P_2 z P_2 w$$
$$P_3 : z P_3 y P_3 w P_3 x$$

Let us determine the simple majority relation R^{maj} and the Borda social preference relation R^B corresponding to the profile P:

$$|R(y, z; R)| = 2, |R(z, w; R)| = 3, |R(w, x; R)| = 2$$
$$y\ R^{maj}\ z\ R^{maj}\ w\ R^{maj}\ x$$
$$\sum_N r_i(w) = 10, \quad \sum_N r_i(x) = 9,$$
$$\sum_N r_i(y) = 5, \quad \sum_N r_i(z) = 6$$

Therefore, by definition,

$$y\ R^B z\ R^B x\ R^B w$$

The two aggregation rules transform P to different social preference relations. ∎

4.2 ARROW IMPOSSIBILITY THEOREM

Five desirable properties of a preference aggregation rule f are introduced below.

a. The first property is *unrestricted domain*. It ensures that the aggregation rule specifies a social preference relation to any society, that is, to any possible preference profile.

U – Unrestricted Domain:

The domain of the aggregation rule f includes all possible preference profiles. In other words, the domain of f is $\mathfrak{R}^n$, $f : \mathfrak{R}^n \rightarrow B$.

b. The second property is *transitivity* of every social preference relation in the range of the aggregation rule f. The significance of this property has been clarified in the preceding chapter.

T – Transitivity:

For any preference profile R in $\mathfrak{R}^n$, $R = f(R)$ is transitive.

Since we have assumed that every social preference relation in the range of the aggregation rule f is reflexive and complete, the requirement of transitivity implies that every relation in the range of the aggregation rule is an ordering, that is, the range of f is $\mathfrak{R}$, the set of orderings on X. The properties U and T imply that $f : \mathfrak{R}^n \rightarrow \mathfrak{R}$. Such an aggregation rule is often called a **social welfare function**.

c. The third property is the *Pareto principle*. This property ensures that, when all individuals share the same strict preferences regarding two alternatives, the social preference respects the individual preferences. The Pareto principle is a plausible weak requirement of respecting unanimity, in those (rare) situations where such unanimity exists with respect to any two alternatives.

P – Pareto Principle:

For any preference profile R in $\Re^n$ and for any two alternatives x and y in X,

$$(\forall i \in N, xP_iy) \Rightarrow xPy$$

d. The fourth property is *non-dictatorship*. It guarantees that no individual is a dictator whose preferences exclusively determine, under all circumstances, the social preferences between any two alternatives.

ND – Non-Dictatorship:

There is no individual i in N, such that, for any preference profile R in $\Re^n$ and for any two alternatives x and y in X, $xP_iy \Rightarrow xPy$.

e. The fifth and more subtle property is *independence of irrelevant alternatives*. It ensures that the social ranking of any two alternatives hinges only on the individual rankings of these two alternatives. To formally define this property, let us introduce the definition of a **restricted preference profile**. Given a preference profile R and a subset S of X, let $R|_S = (R_1|_S, \ldots, R_n|_S)$ denote the restriction of the profile R to the set S. The restricted profile $R|_S$ describes the individual preferences only regarding the alternatives included in S. The meaning of the independence property is that, if the restrictions of two different profiles R and R' to a two-element set S are identical, then the restrictions of the two social preference relations corresponding to the restricted profiles on S are also identical.

IIA – Independence of Irrelevant Alternatives:

For any two preference profiles R and R' in $\Re^n$, and for any two alternatives x and y in X,

$$R|_{(x,y)} = R'|_{(x,y)} \Rightarrow f(R)|_{(x,y)} = f(R')|_{(x,y)}$$

It should be noted that if the aggregation rule is independent of irrelevant alternatives, then the social ranking of any two alternatives hinges only on information on the ordinal individual preferences regarding those alternatives. This means that IIA implies that social preferences should disregard information on the preference intensity of the individuals regarding those alternatives, as well as evaluations or comparisons of those alternatives relative to other alternatives.

Arrow's impossibility theorem gives a breakthrough result, and undoubtedly has made a major contribution to the development of the theory of social choice. The theorem can be stated in one of the following three equivalent versions.

Theorem 4.1 – Arrow Impossibility Theorem

(Version 1)

There exists no aggregation rule that satisfies the properties U, T, P, ND and IIA.

(Version 2)

There exists no social welfare function that satisfies the properties U, P, ND and IIA.

(Version 3)

If an aggregation rule satisfies the properties U, T, P and IIA, then it is dictatorial.

The proof of the theorem in the special case of two individuals, three alternatives, and strict individual preference orderings clarifies the idea of the proof in the general case and, in particular, the role of the different properties in contributing to the impossibility of their mutual existence. The proof appears in Austen-Smith and Banks (1998), pages 31–34, example 2.4. The proof was first proposed by Feldman (1984). The general proof of the theorem that is presented below is a simple version of the proof proposed in Sen (1970). This proof is based on the corrected version of Arrow's original proof that appears in the second edition of his book, *Social Choice and Individual Values*, published in 1963. The proof consists of the proof of the following two claims.

First claim: If a certain individual is almost decisive between two alternatives, then he is decisive between every two alternatives in X and this means that the individual is a dictator (note that being "almost decisive" is weaker than being decisive).

Second claim: There exists an individual who is almost decisive between two alternatives in X.

The first claim means that if the five properties stated in the theorem are satisfied, then individual decisiveness in the weak sense is an "all or nothing" feature. Weak decisiveness of an individual is equivalent to decisiveness between **any** two alternatives. In other words, the assignment to an individual of the status of almost decisiveness between two alternatives becomes strengthened and contagious, turning to decisiveness between **any** two alternatives. The meaning of the second claim is that the five properties of the aggregation rule ensure that there exists an individual who has the privilege of (weak) decisiveness between some two alternatives.

Proof: Let us prove the third version of theorem 4.1, assuming that the individual preference relations are strict orderings (this assumption simplifies the first part of the proof). Suppose then that the aggregation rule satisfies properties U, T, P and IIA.

(1) **Definition:** A set of individuals $D, D \subset N$, is called an **almost decisive set between alternative x and alternative y** if the aggregation rule satisfies the following requirement. Given a preference profile where all members of D prefer x to y and all individuals not in D prefer y to x, the social preference is "x is preferred to y". A set of individuals D is called **decisive between alternative x and alternative y** if the aggregation rule satisfies the following requirement. Given a preference profile where all members of D prefer x to y, the social preference is "x is preferred to y".

(2) Suppose that a set of alternatives D is almost decisive between x and y.

(3) Suppose that the members of the set D prefer x to y and y to z (xP_DyP_Dz) and all the remaining individuals who are members of the set $N \setminus D$ prefer y to z and y to x $(yP_{N \setminus D}z, \ yP_{N \setminus D}x)$. Note that at this stage the assumption makes use of property U and the assumption that X includes at least three alternatives.

(4) Since D is an almost decisive set, the social preference is xPy.

(5) Since the aggregation rule satisfies property P, yPz.

(6) Since the aggregation rule satisfies property T, the previous two steps imply that xPz.

(7) Note that the members of the almost decisive set D prefer x to z, but no assumption has been made on the preferences of the remaining individuals regarding alternatives x and z. Since the aggregation rule satisfies property IIA, the social preference between these two alternatives is independent of the preferences of the individuals who are members of the set $N \setminus D$. In other words, xPz is a consequence of the assumption (xP_Dz), independent of the preference of the members of $N \backslash D$ regarding alternatives x to z. This implies that the set D is decisive between x and z. By repetition of steps (2)–(6), it can be shown that the set D is decisive between every two alternatives in X.

The claim that we have proven is valid also in the case where the set D includes a single member. We have therefore proven the first claim: if a certain individual is almost decisive between two alternatives, then he is decisive between every two alternatives in X and this means that he is a dictator. To complete the proof, let us prove the second claim, namely that there exists an individual who is almost decisive between two alternatives in X.

(8) Since the aggregation rule satisfies property P, the set of all individuals N is decisive and, therefore, also almost decisive between every two alternatives.

(9) Denote by λ the size of the smallest set which is almost decisive between any two alternatives in X. With no loss of generality, let L denote the minimal almost decisive set and let x and y be the two alternatives between which L is almost decisive.

(10) If $\lambda = 1$, then the second claim has been proven.

(11) Otherwise, suppose that $\lambda > 1$. The proof of the second claim is completed by showing that this assumption results in a contradiction. To obtain the contradiction, consider some preference profile R that satisfies:

$$for\ i \in L, \qquad xP_iyP_iz$$
$$\forall j \in L - \{i\}, \quad zP_jxP_jy$$
$$\forall k \notin L, \qquad yP_kzP_kx$$

Note that the assumption that there exists such a profile R utilizes property U and the assumption that X includes at least three alternatives.

(12) Since L is almost decisive between x and y, xPy.

(13) Since L is a minimal almost decisive set, zPy is impossible (the possibility zPy is inconsistent with the minimality of L, because it implies that the set $L - \{i\}$, that includes $\lambda - 1$ members, is almost decisive between z and y, which contradicts the minimality of L). Hence, by the assumption that the social preference relation is complete, we obtain that yRz.

(14) Since the aggregation rule satisfies property T, the two preceding steps imply that xPz.

(15) Note that only individual i prefers x to z. Furthermore, since the aggregation rule satisfies property IIA, the social preference between these two alternatives is independent of the ranking of alternative y, and in particular, it is independent of the assumption made in step (11) on the profile R. Hence, individual i is almost decisive between x and z, which contradicts the assumption $\lambda > 1$. By the first claim, this individual is a dictator.

Q.E.D.

Let us define the **Pareto extension** aggregation rule, f^P, and its corresponding social preference relation, R^P, as follows: For any x and y in X,

$$xR^Py \Leftrightarrow not[(R(y, x, R) = N \& P(y, x; R) \neq 0)]$$

It can be verified that the Pareto extension rule, like the simple majority rule, satisfies the properties U, P, ND and IIA.

The following example shows that the simple majority rule is not transitive. This example is called Condorcet's voting paradox or simply the voting paradox.

Example 4.3

Let $N = \{1, 2, 3, \}$ $X = \{x, y, z\}$ and $\mathbf{R} = \{R_1, R_2, R_3\}$ where

$$R_1 : xR_1yR_1z$$
$$R_2 : yR_2zR_2x$$
$$R_3 : zR_3xR_3y$$

In this case $|R\{x, y; \mathbf{R}\}| = 2$, $|R\{y, z; \mathbf{R}\}| = 2$, $|R\{z, x; \mathbf{R}\}| = 2$, and therefore, $xR^{maj}y$, $yR^{maj}z$ and $zR^{maj}x$. That is, the relation R^{maj} is not transitive. ∎

Given a preference profile $\mathbf{R}$, alternative x is called an unequivocal **Condorcet winner** in the set S, $S \subseteq X$, if $xP^{maj}y$ for every y in S. Note that, by definition, this alternative is unique. Since the relation R^{maj} is cyclical, the existence of a Condorcet's winner is not guaranteed. Consequently, the rational social choice function corresponding to R^{maj}, $C(S) = M(R^{maj}, S)$, is undefined. If the social choice function ensures the selection of every Condorcet's winner, it satisfies **Condorcet's criterion**, and we say that such a function is **Condorcet-consistent**.

The Borda aggregation rule satisfies properties U, T, P and ND. The following example proves that this aggregation rule does not satisfy IIA.

Example 4.4

Suppose that $\mathbf{P}$ is the preference profile of example 4.1 and $\mathbf{P'}$ is the preference profile of example 4.2. The restrictions of the profiles $\mathbf{P}$ and $\mathbf{P'}$ to the set $\{w, x\}$ are identical. But, given the two profiles $\mathbf{P}$ and $\mathbf{P'}$, the social relative rankings of these two alternatives by the Borda aggregation rule are different. $wf^B(\mathbf{P})x$, however, $xf^B(\mathbf{P'})w$. This means that the Borda aggregation rule does not satisfy IIA. ∎

The relation R^B obtained by the Borda aggregation rule is an ordering on X. Hence, the rational social choice function corresponding to it, $C(S) = M(R^B, S)$, is well defined. Since the relation R^B, which is defined on X, violates IIA, this function is different from the social choice function $C^B(P, S)$. This latter rule, the Borda rule, is defined as follows:[1]

$$\forall S \in \chi, \, \boldsymbol{P} \in \mathfrak{R}^n,$$

$$C^B(\boldsymbol{P}, S) = \left\{ x \in S : \forall y \in S, \sum_N r_i(x, S) \leq \sum_N r_i(y, S) \right\}$$

where $r_i(x, S)$ is the relative ranking of x in $P_i \mid_S$, that is, in the restriction of individual i's preference relation to S.

The Borda rule can be viewed as a **scoring rule** (point voting system): Every individual assigns a score of $m = |S| - 1$ to his best alternative in the set S, a score of $m - 1$ to his second-best alternative, and so on. The worst alternative is assigned a score of zero. The Borda rule chooses an alternative with the largest total score. Note that the plurality rule introduced in the preceding chapter can also be considered as a scoring rule. In this case, every individual assigns a score of one to his best alternative and a score of zero to all other alternatives. The Borda rule and the plurality rule do not satisfy Condorcet's criterion. The following example illustrates this with respect to the Borda rule.

Example 4.5

Suppose that $N = \{1, 2, 3, 4, 5, 6, 7\}$, $X = \{x, y, z\}$ and the preference profile consists of the following orderings:

Three individuals prefer z to x and x to y. Two individuals prefer x to y and y to z. The sixth individual prefers x to z and z to y. The seventh individual prefers y to z and z to x. This preference profile is presented in the following table.

---

[1] Note that when $S = X$, the two functions make the same choice, but when $S \subset X$, the two functions may choose different alternatives.

1	1	2	3
Ind.	Ind.	Ind.	Ind.
y	x	x	z
z	z	y	x
x	y	z	y

Under this preference profile, alternative z is a Condorcet's winner. However, the alternative selected by the Borda rule is x (verify). ∎

Arrow's impossibility theorem implies that there is no positive answer to the normative question: "What is the appropriate social preference relation?", assuming that the "appropriate" social preference relation has to satisfy properties U, T, P, ND and IIA. The theorem also implies that there is no positive answer to the positive question: "Is it possible to study social decisions on the premise that such decisions, as in the context of individual decision making, can be rationalized by a plausible preference relation, where plausibility means that the social preference relation satisfies properties U, T, P, ND and IIA?" In other words, since a plausible social preference relation does not exist, no social choice function can be rationalized by such a plausible relation. The study of social choice cannot therefore be based on the fertile methodology that utilizes the rationality principle, which is so common in economics.

Attempts to cope with Arrow's theorem have taken different forms. Many scholars have examined how the existence of a plausible aggregation rule can be guaranteed by weakening one of the desirable properties and, in particular, by weakening properties U, T and IIA. Very useful surveys of these attempts can be found in Sen's book (1970) and in his comprehensive survey articles, Sen (1977a) and Sen (1986). See also Fishburn (1973), Kelly (1988), Moulin (1981) and Mueller (2003).

Many attempts have been made to ensure the existence of an appropriate aggregation rule and, in particular, the simple majority rule, by imposing restrictions on the permissible individual preferences; that is, by weakening property U. Such restrictions cannot be justified empirically, nor by arguing that the actual report of individual preferences can be restricted to certain "non-problematic" patterns when preferences are aggregated (when the aggregation rule is applied practically). Different restrictions, such as single peakedness,[2] were stated as requirements of similarity or proximity between individual preferences. Although the definitions of such similarity took different forms, it turned out that the requirements are extremely restrictive because they are almost always equivalent to the requirement of identical individual preferences.

Scholars who gave up property T examined aggregation rules that are commonly used, focusing on the conditions that ensure that these rules satisfy acyclicity, the significance of which has been clarified in the previous chapter, and on other properties that will be dealt with in Chapter 7. These conditions were stated in terms of restrictions on the number of alternatives and the number of individuals. A very useful survey of this literature appears in Chapter 3 of Austen-Smith and Banks (1998).

The property that has raised most criticism is IIA, independence of irrelevant alternatives. The criticism of this property was based on the argument that preference aggregation cannot solely rely on information about the ordinal preferences of the individuals, which is common in neo-classical utility theory, since such information implies total disregard of the individuals' preference intensity.

The pioneering paper of Harsanyi (1955) proposed generalizing the set of alternatives X to a space of lotteries on X and, correspondingly, generalizing the individual preference relations. Such a generalization allows the requirement of standard properties that ensure the existence of the expected utility hypothesis (a standard assumption in decision making under uncertainty). These requirements relate both to the extended individual preferences and to the extended social preference relation, and they guarantee that the utilities representing individual preferences and social preferences are cardinal utilities. The additional property proposed by Harsanyi in the context of his

---

[2]   The definition of single peakedness is presented in Chapter 9.

extended set of alternatives, the unanimity or Pareto property, makes possible the axiomatization of the utilitarian social welfare function. In this case, the utility representing the social preference relation is the weighted sum of the utilities of the individuals, utilities that are defined on the space of lotteries on X. Harsanyi's possibility theorem somewhat lessens the severity of the implications of Arrow's impossibility theorem by illustrating how giving up IIA can result in axiomatization of a commonly used aggregation rule. Additional possible examples are the axiomatizations of alternative scoring rules, such as the plurality rule and the Borda rule, which are studied in the next two chapters.

Without the requirement of IIA, aggregation of individual preferences is possible by rules that use information on individual preference intensity and on interpersonal comparisons of utility. Such aggregation rules can be most useful in a broader normative analysis, beyond the scope of the analysis in the present book. For example, it is possible to characterize axiomatically the maximin rule, which is a social welfare function implied by the justice principles of John Rawls (1971). Such axiomatization was proposed, for example, by Hammond (1976). Another important example is the axiomatization of the multiplicative social welfare function proposed by John Nash (1950). These functions are of much significance in public economics, for instance, in the study of distributive justice and bargaining theory.[3]

Finally, it should be noted that there are studies which did not discard any property that appears in Arrow's impossibility theorem, but attempted to evaluate the rigor of the theorem by computing the probability that the desirable properties are inconsistent, assuming that the preference profile of society is chosen randomly. The findings of this research direction clarified that the rigor of Arrow's theorem cannot be diminished because, in practice, the probability that the desirable properties are inconsistent is far from being negligible.

---

[3] A comprehensive survey of the relevant literature appears in Sen (1977a), (1977b), (1986) and in Yaari (1981).

4.3 THE PARETIAN LIBERAL PARADOX

Dispensing with the independence of irrelevant alternatives property does not necessarily guarantee axiomatization of an aggregation rule. This is demonstrated by the Paretian liberal paradox.

Suppose that the preference relation of every individual is a strict ordering. A typical preference profile is denoted by P. Let $\Pi(X)$ be the set of all two-element subsets of X, $\Pi(X) = \{S \in \chi : |S| = 2\}$. A **right-system** is defined as an assignment of n non-identical sets that belong to $\Pi(X)$ to the individuals in N. $RS = \{S_1, \ldots, S_n\}$ is thus a right-system if $S_i \in \Pi(X)$ for every $i \in N$ and $S_i \neq S_j$ for every $i, j \in N, i \neq j$. An individual i is called decisive with respect to $\{x, y\}$ that belongs to $\Pi(X)$, if $xP_iy \Rightarrow xPy$ and $yP_ix \Rightarrow yPx$. A right-system is effective if every individual is decisive with respect to the two alternatives assigned to him. Let us introduce another desirable property of an aggregation rule, the property of Weak Liberalism (WL).

WL – Weak Liberalism

There exists a right-system $RS = \{S_1, \ldots, S_n\}$, such that every individual i in N is decisive with respect to S_i.

Theorem 4.2 – The Paretian Liberal Paradox: No acyclical aggregation rule satisfies properties U, P and WL.

Proof: Let us prove the theorem assuming that there exist two individuals. In this case $RS = \{S_1, S_2\}$, $S_1 \neq S_2$. The proof of the general case is analogous. Suppose then that an acyclical aggregation rule satisfies the properties U, P and WL.

Possibility 1: $S_1 \cap S_2 = \phi$

With no loss of generality, assume that $S_1 = \{x, y\}$, $S_2 = \{z, w\}$, $wP_1xP_1yP_1z$ and $yP_2zP_2wP_2x$. Property WL implies that $xPy \,\&\, zPw$. By property P, $wPx \,\&\, yPz$. Hence, the aggregation rule is cyclical, which contradicts the assumption that it is acyclical. We have thus proved that an acyclical aggregation rule cannot satisfy properties U, P and WL.

Possibility 2: $S_1 \cap S_2 = \phi$

With no loss of generality, assume that $S_1 = \{x, y\}$, $S_2 = \{y, w\}$, wP_1xP_1y and yP_2wP_2x. By property WL, $xPy \& yPw$. By property P, wPx. The aggregation rule is therefore cyclical, which contradicts the assumption that it is acyclical. We have thus proved that an acyclical aggregation rule cannot satisfy properties U, P and WL. **Q.E.D.**

There have been various responses to Sen's theorem. Most effort has been devoted to the attempt to enable the existence of an aggregation rule that satisfies property U and a version of weak liberalism which is different from WL. The objection to property WL was based on the recognition that under certain circumstances, it is not justified to impose the realization of his decisiveness right on an individual. Blau (1975) proposed defining such exceptional circumstances in terms of the individuals' preference profile. Gibbard (1974) suggested conditioning the realization of an individual's right of decisiveness on his consent. Harel and Nitzan (1987) proposed conditioning the implementation of the individual rights on their prior voluntary utilization of exchange in their decisiveness rights. A most useful survey of the response to the Paretian-liberal paradox up till 1984 appears in Wriglesworth (1985).

4.4 EXERCISES

Chapter 3 and 3* in Sen (1970) and the two first sections in Chapter 2 in Austen-Smith and Banks (1998) present the basic social choice model and Arrow's impossibility theorem. Chapters 6 and 6* in Sen (1970) are devoted to Sen's impossibility theorem. This chapter and the following questions summarize and clarify the basic social choice model and these two impossibility theorems.

4.1 The social choice model

Question 4.1

a. What is the set of alternatives in the standard model of exchange economy in price theory?

b. What is the preference profile in this case?

c. Suggest three plausible aggregation rules in this context (hint: make use of concepts such as efficiency, individually rational, the core or equality).

Answer

a. In an exchange economy, the set of alternatives is the set of all possible allocations in a competitive environment with no production.

b. The preference profile includes the preference relations of the consumers.

c. Here are three possible aggregation rules.

Possibility 1

Any two efficient allocations are socially equivalent, any two inefficient allocations are equivalent, and any efficient allocation is preferred to any inefficient allocation. This social preference relation is an ordering.

Possibility 2

Any two allocations in the core (allocations that are both efficient and individually rational) are socially equivalent. Any two allocations that do not belong to the core are equivalent, and any allocation in the core is socially preferred to an allocation that does not belong to the core. This social preference relation is an ordering.

Possibility 3

The egalitarian allocation is the socially best allocation and any two other alternatives are equivalent. This social preference relation is an ordering.

Question 4.2

a. What is the number of possible orderings when X includes three alternatives?

b. What is the possible number of strict orderings in this case?

c. What is the number of possible strict orderings when X includes m alternatives?

Answer

a. 13

b. 6

c. $m!$

Question 4.3

a. What is the number of possible preference profiles when X includes two alternatives and the set N includes four individuals?

b. What is the number of possible preference profiles when X includes two alternatives and the set N includes n individuals?

c. What is the number of possible preference profiles when X includes three alternatives and the set N includes three individuals?

Answer

a. 3^4

b. 3^n

c. 13^3

Question 4.4

Denote by m the number of alternatives in X and by $r_i(x)$ the relative ranking of a typical alternative x in the strict preference ordering of individual i. Suppose that individual i assigns a score of $s_i(x)$ to alternative x, $s_i(x) = [m - r_i(x)]$.[4]

a. Define the Borda social preference relation that determines the social ranking of every alternative by the total score assigned to it by all individuals.

b. Verify that, by the definition of the previous section, the four alternatives w, x, y, z in example 4.1 are ordered as follows:
$y \, R^B \, z \, R^B \, w \, R^B \, x.$

---

[4] By definition of $s_i(x)$, individual i assigns to his best alternative (the alternative ranked first) a score of $m - 1$, because in this case $r_i(x) = 1$ and so $s_i(x) = m - 1$. In a similar way, he assigns to his second-best alternative a score of $m - 2$, and so on. The worst alternative gets a score of zero.

Answer

a. The Borda social preference relation R^B can be defined as follows:

$$\forall x, y \in X, \, xR^B y \Leftrightarrow \sum_N s_i(x) \geq \sum_N s_i(y) \Leftrightarrow$$
$$\Leftrightarrow \sum_N r_i(x) \leq \sum_N r_i(y)$$

b. $\sum_N s_i(w) = 4$, $\sum_N s_i(x) = 3$, $\sum_N s_i(y) = 6$ and $\sum_N s_i(z) = 5$. Hence, by the social preference relation based on the Borda scores, $y \, R^B \, z \, R^B \, w \, R^B \, x$.

4.2 Arrow impossibility theorem

Question 4.5

Prove that the Pareto extension rule, the rule f^P, satisfies the properties P, ND and IIA.

Answer

Property P follows directly from the definition of f^P.

To prove property ND, suppose that there is a dictator i and there exist two alternatives x and y such that $xP_i y$, but for every individual j, $j \neq i$, $yP_j x$. Since i is a dictator, xPy. However, by the definition of f^P, yRx. We thus obtain a contradiction, which completes the proof. That is, the contradiction means that the negation assumption, namely that there exists a dictator i, is impossible; that is, f^P must satisfy property ND.

The rule f^P is defined in terms of conditions on the sets $R(x, y; R)$ and $P(x, y; R)$ that take into account only the individual preferences with respect to x and y. This ensures that IIA is satisfied.

Question 4.6

Define the constant aggregation rule f^c and its corresponding social preference relation, R^c, as follows: There exists a binary relation T, $T \in \Re$, such that for every $\boldsymbol{R}$ in $\Re^n$, $R^c = f^c(\boldsymbol{R}) = T$. Which of the five properties are satisfied by this rule?

Answer

The rule f^c satisfies the properties U, T, ND and IIA.

Question 4.7

Prove that the simple majority rule f^{maj} satisfies IIA and that the Borda aggregation rule f^B satisfies T.

Answer

The simple majority rule is defined in terms of conditions on the sets $R(x, y; \mathbf{R})$ that take into account only individual preferences on x and y. This ensures that it satisfies IIA.

By the Borda aggregation rule, the relationship between any two alternatives is determined by the comparison between their aggregate scores (see Question 4.4). Since the relation "greater than" is transitive, clearly the Borda rule satisfies T.

Question 4.8

a. Is a preference aggregation rule necessarily a social welfare function?
b. Is a social welfare function an aggregation rule?
c. What is the difference between a preference aggregation rule and a social choice function?

Answer

a. Since a social preference relation is not necessarily transitive, an aggregation rule is not necessarily a social welfare function.
b. Yes.
c. The range of an aggregation rule is the set B of reflexive and complete relations. The range of a social choice function is the set χ of all nonempty subsets of alternatives in X.

Question 4.9

Prove that the rational choice function corresponding to the ordering R^B, which is defined on X, differs from the Borda rule. That is, $C(S) = M(R^B, S) \neq C^B(\mathbf{R}, S)$.

Answer

When $S = X$ the two functions select the same alternatives. But, when $S \subset X$, the two functions may select different alternatives, as illustrated by the following example.

Let $X = \{x, y, z\}$, $S = \{x, z\}$, $N = \{1, 2, 3, 4, 5\}$ and $\boldsymbol{P} = (P_1, P_2, P_3, P_4, P_5)$, where

$$P_1 : xP_1yP_1z$$
$$P_2 : xP_2yP_2z$$
$$P_3 : yP_3zP_3x$$
$$P_4 : yP_4zP_4x$$
$$P_5 : zP_5xP_5y$$

In this example

$$P^B : yP^BxP^Bz$$

And, therefore, by definition, $C(S) = M(R^B, S) = \{x\}$. However, $C^B(\boldsymbol{P}, S) = \{z\}$.

Question 4.10

Explain why the Borda rule and the plurality rule (see 3.2) can be viewed as scoring rules.

Answer

By the Borda social preference relation, the social ranking of the alternatives in X is determined by the total score assigned to them by all the individuals. The score assigned by an individual to the different alternatives is determined by their ranking in his preference relation. Similarly, it is possible to determine the social ranking of the alternatives in any subset S of X. It can be verified that the Borda rule C^B $(\boldsymbol{R}, S)$ selects from S an alternative that receives the largest score.

Suppose that every individual assigns a score of one to his best alternative. In this case, the plurality rule chooses an alternative that receives the maximal score. Hence, the plurality rule can be viewed as a scoring rule. Clearly, the Borda rule is different from the plurality rule.

Question 4.11

Does the plurality rule satisfy Condorcet's property?

Answer

No, as implied by the following example. Suppose that $X = \{x, y, z\}$ and the transitive preferences of 101 individuals are as follows:

50 individuals prefer x to y and y to z.
50 individuals prefer z to y and y to x.
One individual prefers y to z and z to x.

In this case, alternative y is a Condorcet's winner, but the alternatives chosen by the plurality rule are x and z. That is, the plurality rule does not satisfy Condorcet's property.

Question 4.12

The runoff plurality has (usually) at most two rounds. A candidate is chosen in the first round, if he is supported by more than 50% of the votes. If there is no such candidate in the first round, a second round is held and the individuals choose between the two candidates who received the largest support in the first round. The candidate who receives more votes in the second round is the chosen one. Suppose that there are three candidates.

a. Is the plurality runoff a resolute choice function?
b. Is a candidate who is chosen by the plurality rule necessarily chosen by the runoff plurality?
c. Does the runoff plurality satisfy Condorcet's property?

Answer

a. The runoff plurality is not a well-defined choice function, because it disregards the possibility that in the first round more than two candidates receive equal support. Clearly, the likelihood of this event is negligible, but a formal definition has to take it into consideration.
b. No. In the example presented in Question 4.11, candidate x who is chosen by the plurality rule differs from candidate z who is chosen by the plurality runoff.

c. No. In the example of Question 4.11, candidate y who is a Condorcet's winner is different from candidate z who is chosen by the plurality runoff.

Question 4.13

Does Arrow's theorem provide theoretical justification for ruling out the possible existence of a democratic aggregation rule?

Answer

No. Arrow's theorem does not rule out the possible existence of a democratic aggregation rule that satisfies properties U, P, ND and IIA but violates transitivity T. The theorem does not exclude the possible existence of a democratic aggregation rule that satisfies properties U, T, P and ND but violates IIA.

4.5 SUMMARY

- In the context of social preference and choice the three basic notions are the **set of alternatives** X, the **preference profile** $R = (R_1, \ldots, R_n)$ defined on this set and the aggregation rule f.
- An **aggregation rule** f specifies, for any given profile of preference orderings, a complete and reflexive social preference relation, $f : \Re^n \to B$.
- $R = f(R)$ is the **social preference relation**, "socially preferred or indifferent to".
- We have discussed three aggregation rules: the **simple majority rule** f^{maj}, the **Borda aggregation rule** f^B and the **Pareto extension rule** f^P. The three corresponding social preference relations are defined below.
- Given the preference profile R, $\forall x, y \in X$, $xR^{maj}y \Leftrightarrow |R(x, y, R)| \geq n/2|$
- Given the preference profile P, $\forall x, y \in X$, $xR^B y \Leftrightarrow \sum_N r_i(x) \leq \sum_N r_i(y)$, where $r_i(x)$ is the relative ranking of alternative x in individual i's strict preference relation on X.
- Given the preference profile R, $\forall x, y \in X$, $xR^P y \Leftrightarrow not[(R(y, x, R) = N \& P(y, x; R) \neq 0)]$
- Given a preference profile R, alternative x is called an unequivocal **Condorcet winner** in the set S, $S \subseteq X$, if $xP^{maj}y$ for every y in S.

- The **Borda rule** and the **plurality rule** are scoring rules that select an alternative from S, that is assigned the largest total score. Under the plurality rule, every individual assigns a score of one to his most preferred alternative and no score to the other alternatives. Under the Borda rule, every individual assigns a score of $m = |S| - 1$ to his best alternative in the set S, a score of $m - 1$ to his second-best alternative and so on. The worst alternative is assigned a score of zero.
- We have introduced six properties of preference aggregation rules:
- **U – Unrestricted Domain:** The domain of the aggregation rule f includes all possible preference profiles. In other words, the domain of f is $\Re^n$, f : $\Re^n \to B$.
- **T – Transitivity:** Any preference relation in the range of the aggregation rule is an ordering. That is, for any preference profile R in $\Re^n$, $R = f(R)$ is transitive. Such an aggregation rule is called a **social welfare function**.
- **P – Pareto:** For any preference profile R in $\Re^n$ and any two alternatives x and y in X, $(\forall i \in N, x P_i y) \Rightarrow x P y$.
- **ND – Non-Dictatorship:** There is no individual i in N, such that, for any preference profile R in $\Re^n$ *and any two alternatives x and y in X*, $x P_i y \Rightarrow x P y$.
- **IIA – Independence of Irrelevant Alternatives:** For any two preference profiles R and R' in $\Re^n$ and any two alternatives x and y in X,
  $R|_{\{x,y\}} = R'|_{\{x,y\}} \Rightarrow f(R)|_{\{x,y\}} = f(R')|_{\{x,y\}}$.
  That is, if the restrictions of two different profiles R and R' to a two-element set S are identical, then the restrictions of the two social preference relations corresponding to the restricted profiles on S are also identical.
- **WL – Weak Liberalism:** There exists a right-system $RS = \{S_1, \dots, S_n\}$, such that every individual i in N is decisive with respect to S_i.
  The two main results of this chapter are:
- **Theorem 4.1 – Arrow Impossibility Theorem: There exists no aggregation rule that satisfies the properties U, T, P, ND and IIA.**
- **Theorem 4.2 – The Paretian-Liberal Paradox: No acyclical aggregation rule satisfies properties U, P and WL.**

5 The desirable decision rule: axiomatization

Consensus on the desirable properties of the social preference relation may result in axiomatization, namely the identification of the unique social preference relation that satisfies some desirable properties. Such a situation means that the search for a social preference relation has succeeded; not only does there exist a social preference relation that satisfies *all* the agreed-upon desirable properties, but no other relation satisfies these properties. In this chapter we present two examples of this type of solution to the social choice problem: axiomatization of the simple majority rule in the dichotomous case where the set of alternatives includes just two elements, and axiomatization of the Borda rule.

5.1 DICHOTOMOUS CHOICE AND THE SIMPLE MAJORITY RULE

In this section, we assume that there are just two alternatives, $X = \{a, b\}$. In this simple case of dichotomous choice, the individuals relate to two alternatives, a and b, and for every individual i, aP_ib, bP_ia or aI_ib. Let us denote by D_i the variable indicating the preference of individual i.

$$D_i = 1 \Leftrightarrow aP_ib$$
$$D_i = -1 \Leftrightarrow bP_ia$$
$$D_i = 0 \Leftrightarrow aIb_i$$

The n-tuple $\mathbf{D} = (D_1, D_2, \ldots, D_n)$ represents a typical preference profile $\mathbf{R} = (R_1, R_2, \ldots, R_n)$. Similar to the individual preference, there are three possibilities for the social preference: aPb, bPa or aIb. The variable D represents the social preference relation.

$$D = 1 \Leftrightarrow aPb$$
$$D = -1 \Leftrightarrow bPa$$
$$D = 0 \Leftrightarrow aIb$$

Recall that an aggregation rule f specifies a social preference relation D for any preference profile $\mathbf{D} = (D_1, D_2, \ldots, D_n)$, $D = f(\mathbf{D})$ (we assume that the rule is well defined for any preference profile). Let us denote by $N(1)$, $N(-1)$ and $N(0)$ the number of elements in the profile $\mathbf{D}$ that are equal, respectively, to 1, -1 and 0. In the dichotomous setting of this chapter, the simple majority rule is defined as follows:

$$f^{maj}(D_1, \ldots, D_n) = D = \begin{matrix} 1 \\ 0 \\ -1 \end{matrix} \Leftrightarrow N(1) - N(-1) \begin{matrix} > \\ = \\ < \end{matrix} 0$$

Or, alternatively,

$$f^{maj}(D_1, \ldots, D_n) = D = \begin{matrix} 1 \\ 0 \\ -1 \end{matrix} \Leftrightarrow \sum_N D_i \begin{matrix} > \\ = \\ < \end{matrix} 0$$

Presented below are three additional desirable properties of aggregation rules. These properties are stated in the context of dichotomous choice. The first property is anonymity (A). It ensures that the social preference is independent of the individual labeling; in particular, the social preference relation is unchanged, if the preferences of one individual change to those of another individual and vice versa. In general, a permutation of the components of a preference profile does not affect the social preference relation. The anonymity property implies that the value of the variable D depends only on the values of the profile components, the D_i's, and not on their particular association with the individuals whose preferences are aggregated. Hence, the value of the variable D hinges only on the sum $\sum_N D_i$.

A – Anonymity

The function f is symmetric in its n variables. That is, if $\mathbf{D}'$ is obtained from $\mathbf{D}$ by reallocating the elements of $\mathbf{D}$ among the n individuals, then $f(\mathbf{D}) = F(\mathbf{D}')$.

The second property is neutrality (N). It guarantees that the social preference is independent of the labeling of the alternatives. A change in the labeling of the two alternatives, which results in a reversal of their preferences, reverses the social preference between the alternatives.

N – Neutrality

For any profile $\mathbf{D} = (D_1, \ldots, D_n)$,

$$f(-D_1, \ldots, -D_n) = -f(D_1, \ldots, D_n).$$

The third property is called positive responsiveness (PR). It ensures that there is a direct positive relationship between the social status of an alternative and its status according to the individual preferences. More precisely, additional individual support for a socially preferred (indifferent) alternative preserves (strengthens) its social status.

PR – Positive Responsiveness

Suppose that D is equal to 0 or 1. Then increased support for alternative a by some single individual (the variable representing that individual's preferences changes from -1 to 0 or 1, or from 0 to 1, and there is no change in the preferences of the other individuals) changes D to 1.

The axiomatization of the simple majority rule proposed by May (1952) is considered as the pioneering characterization theorem in social choice theory.

Theorem 5.1 (May (1952)): An aggregation rule is the simple majority rule f^{maj} if and only if it is anonymous, neutral and positively responsive. In other words, the simple majority rule is the only aggregation rule that satisfies properties A, N and PR.

Proof: (Necessity) It can be readily verified that the simple majority rule satisfies the properties A, N and PR.

(Sufficiency) Notice that property A implies that the outcome of the aggregation rule depends only on the values of the profile components, the D_i's, and not on their location in the profile $\mathbf{D}$. The aggregation rule therefore depends only on $N(1)$, $N(-1)$ and $N(0)$.

Lemma 5.1

(*) $N(1) = N(-1) \Rightarrow D = 0$

Proof: Suppose that (*) does not hold and that $D = f(\mathbf{D}) = 1$. The neutrality property N implies that if $\mathbf{D}' = -\mathbf{D}$, then $D' = f(\mathbf{D}') = -1$. But, by assumption, $N(1) = N(-1)$, and therefore the values of $N(1)$, $N(-1)$ and $N(0)$ in the profile $\mathbf{D}$ and the profile $\mathbf{D}'$ are the same. Consequently, $D' = f(\mathbf{D}') = f(\mathbf{D}) = 1$. We have thus obtained a contradiction; the aggregation function is not single-valued. This implies that the assumption $D = f(\mathbf{D}) = 1$ cannot hold. In a similar way we can prove that one cannot assume that $D = -1$. We have therefore proved that $D = 0$.

Lemma 5.2

$N(1) = N(-1) \Rightarrow D = 1$

Proof: The proof follows directly from Lemma 5.1 and the positive responsiveness property PR.

By induction, using Lemma 5.2 and the PR property, it follows that for every m, $0 < m < n - N(-1)$,

$N(1) = N(-1) + m \Rightarrow D = 1$

and, therefore,

(**) $N(1) > N(-1) \Rightarrow D = 1$

Using (**) and the neutrality property N, we obtain that

(***) $N(1) < N(-1) \Rightarrow D = -1$

(*), (**) and (***) imply that the aggregation rule is necessarily the simple majority rule f^{maj}. **Q.E.D.**

Let us conclude this section with two remarks. First, in the original statement of May's theorem there appear four properties. The missing fourth property is the requirement that the aggregation rule is well defined and single-valued for any preference profile. This property is not mentioned in Theorem 5.1, because it is implicitly required by the assumptions on the aggregation rule that are presented in the previous chapter and at the beginning of this chapter. Second, the properties A, N and PR are independent in the sense that the existence of any two of them does not ensure that the remaining third property is satisfied. Such independence guarantees that the list of properties used by May in the axiomatization of the simple majority rule is irreducible.

5.2 THE BORDA RULE

Once again let us assume that X is a finite set of alternatives that has at least three elements and that the individual preference relations are strong orderings. In this setting, we will illustrate the unique characterization or axiomatization of a social choice function $C(\mathbf{P}, S)$. Recall that such a function assigns to any set of alternatives S in χ and any preference profile $\mathbf{P}$, a non-empty subset of alternatives in S. Since May's axiomatization, many results have been published in the literature characterizing different social choice functions. Sometimes, alternative axiomatizations have been proposed for the same function. The axiomatization attempts have focused on one particular family of social choice functions, namely, scoring (positional) rules. A scoring rule is defined as follows.

Assuming that there are k elements in S, let $\{S_1, S_2, \ldots, S_k\}$ be a monotone sequence of real numbers (the scores or points), $S_1 \leq S_2 \leq \ldots \leq S_k$, such that $S_1 < S_k$. Each of the n individuals (voters) ranks the alternatives, assigning S_1 points to the one ranked last, S_2 points to the one ranked next to the last, and so on. The best alternative is assigned S_k points. A *scoring rule* selects an alternative with a maximal total score. Notice that a scoring rule may choose more than one alternative. The plurality and the Borda rules introduced in the previous chapter are two such well-known scoring rules.

The *plurality rule* $C^{PL}(\mathbf{P}, S)$ is defined by the scores

$$(S_1, S_2, \ldots, S_{k-1}, S_k) = (0, 0, \ldots, 0, 1)$$

Under this rule, the alternative ranked first by the largest number of voters is elected. The *Borda rule* $C^B(\mathbf{P}, S)$ is defined by the scores

$$(S_1, S_2, \ldots, S_{k-1}, S_k) = (0, 1, \ldots, k-2, k-1)$$

Under the Borda rule, each individual reports his preferences by ranking the k alternatives from top to bottom (ties are not allowed), assigning no points to the alternative ranked last, one point to the one ranked next to the last, and so on, up to $k-1$ points for the most preferred alternative. A chosen alternative, which is called a Borda winner, receives the highest total score.

The plurality rule is simple to apply because its operation requires minimal partial information on the individual preferences. Every voter has to report only his most preferred alternative. In contrast, the use of the Borda rule requires considerably more information on the preferences of the individuals.

The plurality rule does not allow the individual to express his preference intensity, because all scores must be allocated to a single alternative. The Borda rule also limits score allocation to a fixed pattern; however, it allows the individual to express his preferences in a more complete form.

The plurality rule and the Borda rule do not satisfy the Condorcet criterion. That is, there exist preference profiles such that there exists a Condorcet winner, yet it is not chosen by these scoring rules. Clearly, such violation of the Condorcet criterion does not rule out the possibility of selection of a Condorcet winner by these rules when such a winner exists. One issue that was raised in the literature is which of these two common scoring rules is more vulnerable to violations of the Condorcet property. It turns out that the plurality rule is the more vulnerable rule. For example, when a group of 25 individuals faces 3 alternatives, the plurality rule violates the Condorcet criterion in about 21% of the possible profiles, whereas the Borda rule violates this criterion only in 9% of the profiles. When the set of alternatives includes 5 alternatives, the frequency of violation of the Condorcet criterion by the plurality rule is about 38%, provided that all profiles are equally probable, while the violation likelihood under the Borda rule is about 14%.

Not only is the plurality rule not Condorcet-consistent; under certain profiles it may choose a "Condorcet loser," an alternative that is beaten by simple majority by all other alternatives. Such a situation is not possible under the Borda rule. That is, the Borda winner cannot be a Condorcet loser.

Finally, it should be noted that the alternative chosen by the Borda rule attains the lowest average ranking of the individuals (recall that a reduction in the ranking of an alternative implies that it becomes more preferred). Alternatively, it can be shown that this alternative has the largest number of supporters in binary comparisons relative to the other alternatives.

To present the axiomatization of the Borda rule proposed by Young (1974), let us introduce the following four properties of a social choice function. The first property, neutrality (N), is similar to the neutrality property of aggregation rules introduced in the preceding section. It ensures invariance of the social choice to the labeling of the alternatives. Let σ be a permutation on X. Given a profile $\mathbf{P}$, define $\sigma(\mathbf{P})$ as the profile satisfying: $x P_i y$ in $\mathbf{P}$ if and only if $\sigma(x) P_i \sigma(y)$ in the profile $\sigma(\mathbf{P})$.

N – Neutrality

$$\forall \mathbf{P} \in \mathfrak{R}^n, S \in \chi, x \in C(\mathbf{P}, S) \Leftrightarrow \sigma(x) \in C(\sigma(\mathbf{P}), (\sigma(S))$$

The second property, cancellation (CA), ensures that the social choice is independent of the identity or the labeling of the individuals. This is reflected by the requirement that the preference of alternative x over alternative y by some individual is cancelled out by the preference of alternative y over alternative x by any other individual. Consequently if, for any two alternatives, the number of individuals who prefer the former alternative to the latter is equal to the number of individuals who prefer the latter alternative to the former, then all the alternatives are chosen by the social choice function.

CA – Cancellation

$$\forall x, y \in X, |P(x, y, P)| = |P(y, x, P)| \Rightarrow \forall S \subseteq X, C(\mathbf{P}, S) = S$$

The third property, faithfulness (F), guarantees loyalty to the individual in the sense that if he is the only member of society, then his most preferred alternative is the social choice.

F – Faithfulness

$$N = \{1\} \Rightarrow C(P_1, S) = \{z : z \in S \& \forall y \in S, zP_1y\}$$

The fourth property, consistency (C), ensures that agreement in two separate groups regarding the chosen alternative in each of these groups is preserved when the two groups are combined. More precisely, suppose that two groups of individuals, N_1 and N_2, face the same set of alternatives S, and that the intersection of their choice sets is not empty. That is, given the preference profiles of these two groups, P^1 and P^2, $C(P^1, S) \cap C(P^1, S) \neq \phi$. The consistency property makes sure that the choice set corresponding to the preference profile $\mathbf{P}^1 + \mathbf{P}^2$ of the union of the two groups, $N_1 \cup N_2$, is contained in the intersection of the choice sets of the two groups.

C – Consistency

$$C(\mathbf{P}^1, S) \cap C(\mathbf{P}^1, S) \neq \phi \Rightarrow C(\mathbf{P}^1 + \mathbf{P}^2, S) \subseteq C(\mathbf{P}^1, S) \cap C(\mathbf{P}^2, S)$$

There exist several characterizations of the Borda rule, e.g. Nitzan and Rubinstein (1981). The first characterization was proposed by Young (1974).

Theorem 5.2 (Young (1974)): A social choice function is the Borda rule if, and only if, it satisfies properties N, CA, F and C. In other words, the Borda rule is the only social choice function that satisfies neutrality, cancellation, faithfulness and consistency.

A comprehensive survey of the axiomatization attempts of scoring rules can be found in Chebotarev and Shamis (1998). The plurality rule is axiomatized in Richelson (1978). Axiomatization of the inverse plurality rule or the negative plurality rule, which will be discussed in Chapter 8, is presented in Baharad and Nitzan (2005b).

5.3 EXERCISES

The proof of Theorem 5.1 is based on May (1952). Theorem 5.2 is stated without its proof: see Young (1974).

5.1 Dichotomous choice and the simple majority rule

Question 5.1

Prove that anonymity, neutrality and positive responsiveness are independent properties of an aggregation rule.

Answer

To prove independence among the three properties, we present below three examples of aggregation rules that satisfy two of the properties, but not the third.

Example 1: The simple majority rule + chairman (individual 1) with a double vote.

$$D = \begin{matrix} 1 \\ 0 \\ -1 \end{matrix} \Leftrightarrow D_1 + N(1) - N(-1) \begin{matrix} > \\ = \\ < \end{matrix} 0$$

This rule is neutral and positively responsive, but not anonymous.

Example 2: The 2/3 qualified majority rule.

$$D = \begin{matrix} 1 \\ 0 \\ -1 \end{matrix} \Leftrightarrow N(1) - 2N(-1) \begin{matrix} > \\ = \\ < \end{matrix} 0$$

This rule is anonymous and positively responsive, but not neutral.

Example 3: The jury rule.

$$D = \begin{matrix} 1 \\ 0 \\ -1 \end{matrix} \Leftrightarrow \begin{matrix} N(1) = n \\ N(1) \neq n, N(1) \neq 0 \\ N(-1) = n \end{matrix}$$

This rule is anonymous and neutral, but not positively responsive.

Question 5.2

The corporate law requires a majority of 75% of the participants in the general meeting of the company shareholders for making a "special" decision. Such a decision can be approved or rejected. Assume that each participant has a single share.

a. Define the above dichotomous decision rule.
b. Is this rule neutral?
c. Is this rule anonymous?
d. How would your answer to the preceding questions change if one participant has a special share that assigns him a double vote relative to the other shareholders?

Answer

a. Let a and b denote, respectively, the approval and rejection of the special decision. The decision rule is:

$$D = \begin{matrix} 1 \\ 0 \\ -1 \end{matrix} \Leftrightarrow N(1) - 3N(-1) \begin{matrix} > \\ = 0 \\ < \end{matrix}$$

b. No. The rule is biased in favor of the status quo, namely in favor of rejection of the special decision.
c. Yes.
d. Assuming that individual 1 owns the special share, the rule changes to:

$$D = \begin{matrix} 1 \\ 0 \\ -1 \end{matrix} \Leftrightarrow D_1 + N(1) - 3N(-1) \begin{matrix} > \\ = 0 \\ < \end{matrix}$$

This rule does not satisfy the neutrality and the anonymity properties.

Question 5.3

The Great Sanhedrin (the supreme court and legislative body of ancient Israel) could convict a defendant by majority vote with one exception. If all members of the court supported conviction, then the defendant was acquitted.

a. Is this rule neutral?
b. Does the rule satisfy the Pareto property?
c. Is the rule positively responsive?
d. Can you rationalize the rule?

Answer
a. No.
b. No.
c. No.
d. The application of simple majority rule might be justified if the judges' decisions are assumed to be independent. A possible justification of the exception in case of unanimous decision is the fear that such unanimity is due to dependence among the judges' views. The likelihood of independent unanimity is very small and therefore its existence might be conceived as a proof of dependency that gives reason for the abandoning of the simple majority rule.

Question 5.4
Are the following statements true? Discuss briefly.

a. An aggregation rule that does not satisfy the anonymity property is undesirable.
b. An aggregation rule that does not satisfy the neutrality property is not plausible.

Answer
a. Not necessarily. In certain professional decisions, non-equal treatment of individuals might be desirable because of the heterogeneity in individual skills. In such a case, the assignment of different voting rights may be socially desirable, that is, beneficial to all the individuals, including those who are assigned less power.
b. Not necessarily. When the collective decision made in an uncertain environment is irreversible, with significant long-term implications, a bias against one alternative might be warranted, if its mistaken selection involves sufficiently high costs.

5.2 The Borda rule

Question 5.5
Prove that the simple majority rule, the Borda rule and the plurality rule are identical when the individual preference relations are strict orderings and $|X| = 2$.

Answer
With no loss of generality, suppose that m individuals prefer alternative a and, therefore, $(n - m)$ individuals prefer the other alternative b. The social choice according to the plurality and the Borda rules is identical because the total score assignments of the two alternatives, a and b, according to these rules are the same; m and $(n - m)$, respectively. By definition, in this case, the simple majority and the plurality rules are identical.

Question 5.6
Suppose that $X = \{x, y, z\}$ and the social choice function based on the Condorcet criterion is defined as follows. Given a preference profile **R** and a set of alternatives S, $S \subseteq X$, the social choice is the Condorcet winner, if such a winner exists. Otherwise, all the alternatives are chosen. The preference profile of the set of individuals $N_1 = \{1, 2, 3\}$ is $\{P_1, P_2, P_3\}$,

$$P_1 : zP_1xP_1y$$
$$P_2 : xP_2yP_2z$$
$$P_3 : yP_3zP_3x$$

The preference profile of the set of individuals $N_2 = \{4, 5, 6, 7\}$ is $\{P_4, P_5, P_6, P_7\}$,

$$P_4 : zP_4xP_4y$$
$$P_5 : zP_5xP_5y$$
$$P_6 : xP_6yP_6z$$
$$P_7 : xP_7zP_7y$$

a. What is the choice of the group N_1?

b. What is the choice of the group N_2?

c. What is the choice of the group $N_1 \cup N_2$?

d. Does the choice function satisfy the consistency property C?

Answer

a. The choice of group N_1 is the set $\{x, y, z\}$.

b. The choice of group N_2 is the set $\{x, z\}$.

c. The choice of group $N_1 \cup N_2$ is the set $\{z\}$.

d. By definition, since $\{x, y, z\} \cap \{x, z\} = \{x, z\} \not\subset \{z\}$, the social choice function does not satisfy the consistency property C.

Question 5.7

Show that the plurality rule can select an alternative that is "a Condorcet loser", an alternative that is preferred by any other alternative according to the simple majority relation.

Answer

The table below presents the preference profile of 21 individuals. The preference relations are strict orderings. There exist four types of individual. The preference relation of three, five, seven and six individuals is presented in the four columns of the table.

6	7	5	3
z	y	x	x
y	w	z	y
w	z	y	z
x	x	w	w

Alternative x is chosen by the plurality rule, but it is preferred by any other alternative according to the simple majority relation. In other words, x is a Condorcet loser.

Question 5.8

In Example 4.5, we have seen that the Borda rule does not satisfy Condorcet's criterion. Question 5.7 implies that the plurality rule also violates Condorcet's criterion.

a. Is it possible that, under a given preference profile, the plurality rule and the Borda rule violate Condorcet's criterion?

b. Is it possible that, under a given preference profile, every scoring rule violates Condorcet's criterion?

Answer

a. Yes, as implied by the answer to part **b.**

b. Yes as shown by the following example.

The table below presents the preference profile of 17 individuals. The preference relations are strict orderings. There exist four types of individual. The preference relation of each type (of six, three, four and again four individuals) is presented in the four columns of the table,

4	4	3	6
y	y	z	x
z	x	x	y
x	z	y	z

Alternative x is a Condorcet winner.

Alternative y is chosen by the plurality and the Borda rules.

Every scoring rule is defined by a vector of scores (S_1, S_2, S_3) that satisfy $S_1 \leq S_2 \leq S_3$ and $S_1 < S_3$. With no loss of generality, let $S_1 = 0$, such that $0 \leq S_2 \leq S_3 > 0$. Let us prove that any scoring rule selects alternative y.

The total score assigned to alternative x is equal to $(6S_3 + 7S_2)$.

The total score assigned to alternative y is equal to $(8S_3 + 6S_2)$.

The difference between the total score assigned to y and to x is therefore equal to

$$(8S_3 - 6S_2) - (6S_3 + 7S_2) = 2S_3 - S_2 > 0$$

That is, any scoring rule violates Condorcet's criterion because it selects alternative y, which is not the Condorcet winner.

Question 5.9

The Copeland rule is defined as follows. Any alternative x is assigned a value $c(x)$, the Copeland value. This value is equal to the difference between the number of alternatives that are inferior to x according to the simple majority relation, and the number of alternatives that are preferred to x according to the simple majority preference relation. The Copeland rule selects the alternative with the largest Copeland value. Prove that the Copeland rule satisfies Condorcet's criterion.

Answer

Suppose that $|S| = k$. If a certain alternative is a Condorcet winner, then the Copeland value assigned to it is $k-1$. This value is maximal and therefore this alternative is the only one selected by the Copeland rule. This means that the Copeland rule satisfies Condorcet's criterion.

5.4 SUMMARY

The two main results of this chapter are:

- **Theorem 5.1** (May (1952)):
- When the set of alternatives includes two elements, an aggregation rule is the simple majority rule f^{maj} if, and only if, it is anonymous, neutral and positively responsive.
- **Anonymity** ensures that the social choice is invariant to the labeling of the individuals.
- **Neutrality** ensures that social preference is independent of the titles of the alternatives.
- **Positive responsiveness** ensures that additional individual support for a socially preferred (indifferent) alternative preserves (strengthens) its social status.
- **Theorem 5.2** (Young (1974)):
  A social choice function is the Borda rule if, and only if, it satisfies the properties: neutrality, cancellation, faithfulness and consistency.

- **Neutrality** ensures invariance of the social choice to the labeling of the alternatives.
- **Cancellation** ensures that the social choice is independent of the labeling of the individuals in the following sense: the preference of alternative x over alternative y by some individual is cancelled out by the preference of alternative y over alternative x by any other individual. Consequently if, for any two alternatives, the number of individuals who prefer the former alternative to the latter is equal to the number of individuals who prefer the latter alternative to the former, then all the alternatives are chosen by the social choice function.
- **Faithfulness** guarantees loyalty to the individual in the sense that if he is the only member of society, then his most preferred alternative is the social choice.
- **Consistency** ensures that agreement in two separate groups regarding the chosen alternative in each of these groups is preserved when the two groups are combined.
- The plurality and the Borda rules are the two most common scoring rules. The comparison that we made between these two rules was based on the simplicity of their operation, the restrictions they impose on the ability of the individuals to express their preference intensity, the frequency with which they violate Condorcet's criterion, their potential to select a Condorct loser, the average ranking of the alternative they select and, finally, the number of supporters of the alternative they select in binary confrontations relative to the other alternatives.

6 Rule selection based on compromise with the unanimity criterion

Consensus on desirable properties of the social preference relation may lead to a "dead end," when the expected resolution of the social choice problem is the axiomatization of the social preference relation. This is one of the lessons of Arrow's impossibility theorem presented in Chapter 4. Nevertheless, agreement on the desirable properties can result in axiomatization, that is, in a unique characterization of the social preference relation or of the social choice rule, as we have seen in the previous chapter. But there is a third possibility. Agreement on desirable properties may lead to the identification of many social preference relations or many social choice rules that satisfy the desirable properties. The meaning of such a situation is that the search for the appropriate social preference relation or social choice function has resulted in "excessive success," which implies that the search has not ended. In other words, such success enables the selection of a desirable rule, but there is still an indeterminacy problem that raises the question: What is the most desirable rule, the rule that should be selected out of the rules satisfying the desirable properties? In this chapter we propose the metric approach of compromising with the unanimity criterion to resolve this problem.

6.1 THE UNANIMITY CRITERION

Naturally, identification of many social choice functions is expected when agreement on the desirable properties is limited, that is, when there are just a few agreed-upon desirable properties and, in particular, when the individuals agree on just one such property. It seems that the

This chapter draws on and adapts material from Farkas and Nitzan (1979).

unanimity property, which ensures the selection of a unanimously most preferred alternative, is likely to be considered as a desirable property. Let us call this property the unanimity criterion and define it as follows.

Suppose that the individual preference relations are strict orderings on the set of alternatives X. Denote by $U(x, S)$ the set of profiles where alternative x is most preferred in the set S, which is a subset of X, from the point of view of every individual.[1] A social choice function $C(\mathbf{P}, S)$ satisfies the unanimity criterion if

$$\mathbf{P} \in U(x, S) \Rightarrow C(\mathbf{P}, S) = \{x\}$$

Notice that the unanimity criterion is distinguishing, but not exhaustive. Since

$$U(x, S) \cap U(y, S) \neq \phi \Rightarrow x = y,$$

the distinguishing power of the criterion is reflected by the fact that, in preference profiles where a unanimously preferred alternative exists, the social choice is resolute. The main drawback of the unanimity criterion is its limited incidence. The criterion is not exhaustive, because the requirement it implies relates only to profiles that belong to the relatively small subset $U(S)$ of profiles that are restricted to S,

$$U(S) = \bigcup_{x \in S} U(x, S) \subset \Re^n$$

Since in most profiles unanimity regarding the most preferred alternative does not exist, $\mathbf{P}|_S \notin U(S)$, the unanimity criterion does not lead to a unique social choice function. There exists therefore a problem of indeterminacy. The multiplicity of social choice functions that satisfy the unanimity criterion raises the question of whether there exists one that compromises with the criterion in the sense that it is "closer" than all the other functions to implementing the criterion. To clarify the meaning of "being closer to implementing a criterion,"

---

[1]   In every profile in $U(x, S)$, for every individual i, x is the maximal alternative in $P_i|_S$ – the restriction of the preference relation P_i to S.

let us introduce two notions of distance: the distance between preference profiles, and the distance between a profile and a set of profiles.

6.2 DISTANCE BETWEEN PREFERENCES

A metric δ on the set of preference profiles is a function that specifies
for any two profiles a non-negative real number and satisfies three
conditions: The distance between two profiles is zero if, and only if,
the profiles are identical; the distance between the profile **P** and the
profile **Q** is equal to the distance between **Q** and **P**; The sum of the
distances between **P** and **Q** and between **Q** and **R** is greater than or
equal to the distance between **P** and **R**. The function $\delta : \mathbf{P}^n \times \mathbf{P}^n \to R_+$
is a metric, then, if and only if it satisfies the following conditions:

1) **Normalization**

$$\forall\, \mathbf{P}, \mathbf{Q} \in \mathbf{P}^n, \ \delta(\mathbf{P}, \mathbf{Q}) = 0 \leftrightarrow \mathbf{P} = \mathbf{Q} \qquad :$$

2) **Symmetry**

$$\forall\, \mathbf{P}, \mathbf{Q} \in \mathbf{P}^n, \ \delta(\mathbf{P}, \mathbf{Q}) = \delta(\mathbf{Q}, \mathbf{P})$$

3) **Triangle inequality**

$$\forall\, \mathbf{P}, \mathbf{Q}, \mathbf{R} \in \mathbf{P}^n, \ \delta(\mathbf{P}, \mathbf{Q}) + \delta(\mathbf{Q}, \mathbf{R}) \geq \delta(\mathbf{P}, \mathbf{Q}) \qquad :$$

As we shall see below, in every metric compromise the metric δ has
a crucial role in the selection of the social choice rule. The next
question therefore is: What is the appropriate metric for evaluating the
proximity between preference profiles? The answer to this question
can be axiomatic, that is, the identification of a reasonable metric
can be based on the specification of desirable properties the metric
should satisfy.[2] In an extreme case, the axiomatic approach results in
the characterization of a unique metric. Such an axiomatization of a
unique reasonable metric, the inversion metric, has been proposed by

---

[2]   See Lehrer and Nitzan (1985).

Kemeny and Snell (1962).[3] In the current chapter we use two metrics: the inversion metric and the extreme top metric.

The **inversion metric** $\delta_1(\mathbf{P}, \mathbf{Q})$ is defined as the minimal number of interchanges between neighboring alternatives in the individual preference relations that is required to transform the profile $\mathbf{P}$ to $\mathbf{Q}$.

The **top metric** $\delta_2(\mathbf{P}, \mathbf{Q})$ is defined as the minimal number of interchanges between two alternatives (not necessarily neighboring alternatives) in the individual preference relations that is required to transform the most preferred alternatives in the profile $\mathbf{P}$ to those in $\mathbf{Q}$.

Given the metric δ, the distance d between a profile $\mathbf{P}$ and a set of profiles V is defined as follows:

$$d(\mathbf{P}, V) = \min_{Q \in V} \delta(\mathbf{P}, \mathbf{Q})$$

Let us denote by d_1 and d_2 the distance functions corresponding to the inversion metric δ_1 and the top metric δ_2.

Example 6.1
Suppose that the set of alternatives is $X = \{x, y, z, w\}$ and two preference relations are defined on it, P and Q,

$$P : xPyPzPw$$
$$Q : xQwQyQz$$

To transform the relation P to the relation Q, at least two interchanges of neighboring alternatives, an interchange between z and w and an interchange between w and y, are required. By the inversion metric δ_1, the distance between the profile $\mathbf{P} = (P)$ and the profile $\mathbf{Q} = (Q)$ is therefore equal to 2. To transform the best alternative in the relation P to the most preferred alternative in the relation Q, no interchanges are required; in both of the relations the most preferred alternative is

---

[3]   A survey of the metric approach in the context of social choice appears in Barthelemy and Monjardet (1981). See also Campbell and Nitzan (1986) and Baigent (1987).

x. By the top metric δ_2, the distance between the profile $\mathbf{P} = (P)$ and the profile $\mathbf{Q} = (Q)$ is therefore equal to 0. ∎

Example 6.2

Suppose that $N = \{1, 2, 3\}$, $\mathbf{P} = \{P_1, P_2, P_3\}$ and $\mathbf{Q} = \{Q_1, Q_2, Q_3\}$,

$$P_1 : xP_1yP_1z$$
$$P_2 : xP_2yPz_1$$
$$P_3 : xP_3yP_3z$$
$$Q_1 : xQ_1yQ_1z$$
$$Q_2 : yQ_2zQ_2x$$
$$Q_3 : zQ_3xQ_3y$$

In this case, by the inversion metric, the distance between the profile $\mathbf{P}$ and the profile $\mathbf{Q}$ is equal to $\delta_1(\mathbf{P}, \mathbf{Q}) = 4$.

By the top metric, the distance between the profile $\mathbf{P}$ and the profile $\mathbf{Q}$ is equal to $\delta_2(\mathbf{P}, \mathbf{Q}) = 2$.

By both metrics, the distance between the profile $\mathbf{P}$ and the set of profiles $U(x, X) = U(x)$ is equal to 0. By the inversion metric, the distance between the profile $\mathbf{Q}$ and the set of profiles $U(x)$ is equal to $d_1(\mathbf{Q}, U(x)) = 3$, however, by the top metric, the distance between the profile $\mathbf{Q}$ and the set of profiles $U(x)$ is equal to $d_2(\mathbf{Q}, U(x)) = 2$. ∎

6.3 THE METRIC COMPROMISE WITH THE UNANIMITY CRITERION

Given the metric δ on the set of possible profiles, it is natural to define a social choice function applying a social preference relation which is a compromise among the individual preference relations.[4] The metric δ enables measurement of the proximity between profiles and, in particular, of the proximity between individual preference relations that are in fact profiles that include a single preference relation. Every preference profile $\mathbf{P} = (P_1, \ldots, P_n)$ can therefore be initially assigned a

---

[4] This approach was proposed by Kemeny (1959).

social preference relation P^c, a compromise preference relation that on average is the closest, according to the metric δ, to the preference relations of the individuals (the P_i's). In a second stage, it is possible to assign to any subset S, $S \subseteq X$, the most preferred alternatives according to the restriction of the compromise relation P^c on S. In other words, the proposed social choice function is the rational choice function that corresponds to the compromise preference relation P^c, $C(\mathbf{P}, S) = M(P^c, S)$[5]. This direct compromise approach has several disadvantages. In particular, the social preference relation P^c is not necessarily unique and, consequently, the proposed social choice function is not necessarily resolute.

In this chapter, we try to complement the axiomatic approach discussed in the two preceding chapters. Therefore, we are not pursuing further the direct compromise approach among the individual preference relations, but focus on metric compromise with the unanimity criterion. The idea stimulating this alternative compromise approach was proposed in 1876 by Charles Dodgson, the author of *Alice in Wonderland*, better known under his pseudonym, Lewis Carroll. In his essay, Dodgson studied alternative voting methods and discussed the drawbacks of their outcome in situations where a Condorcet winner does not exist. Dodgson's argument was clarified by applying the following example.

Example 6.3

Suppose that the set of alternatives is $X = \{a, b, c, d\}$ and that the preferences of thirteen individuals are presented in the following table (originally, the alternatives are referred to as candidates and the individuals as voters). In this case the social preference based on the simple majority rule is cyclical

$$a R^{maj} b R^{maj} c R^{maj} d R^{maj} a;$$

---

[5] Recall that $M(P^c, S) = \{x \varepsilon S \in S : \forall y \varepsilon S, x P^c y\}$

that is, there is no Condorcet winner. Dodgson criticizes the application of the plurality rule, claiming that in the preference profile of this example, each of the candidates a, c and d requires four changes of candidates in order to win (that is, to become a Condorcet winner), while b needs just a single change. See, for instance, the change between the two candidates marked by * in the preference relation of voter 8. Still, and this is what bothers Dodgson, under the plurality rule candidate a wins the election.

a	a	a	a	b	b	b	c	c	c	d	d	d
b	b	b	b	d	d	d	d	a	a	b	b	b
c	c	c	c	c	c	c	a^*	b	b	c	c	c
d	d	d	d	a	a	a	b^*	d	d	a	a	a

From this argument, it is possible to infer that, in Dodgson's view, the social choice rule should implement the simple majority rule in the following way. If there exists an alternative that is a Condorcet winner, then the rule should select it. If a Condorcet winner does not exist, then the rule should select an alternative that requires the minimal number of changes in the individual preference relations in order to become a Condorcet winner. In addition, the above example and the applied argument that relates to it seem to imply that Dodgson defines changes in the individual preference relations as interchanges between neighboring alternatives in the individual preference relations. The social choice rule apparently proposed by Dodgson, as implied by his example and supporting arguments, can thus be defined as follows. If there exists a Condorcet winning alternative under the preference profile **P**, the rule selects that winner. If not, the rule selects an alternative whose distance (based on the inversion metric) from the set of profiles under which that alternative is a Condorcet winner to the profile P is smaller than the distance between P to the set of profiles under which any other alternative is a Condorcet winner. It seems then that the proposed social choice function compromises in a metric sense with Condorcet's criterion. Inspired by Dodgson's idea, we now propose the social choice function that compromises in a metric sense with the unanimity criterion, a criterion that is apparently easy to support because of its very limited and unquestionable incidence. In our case, the metric can be the inversion metric or any other metric.

A social choice rule $C(\mathbf{P}, S)$ compromises with the unanimity criterion according to the metric δ if, for every subset S of the set of alternatives X and for every preference profile $\mathbf{P}$ defined on X,

$$C(\mathbf{P}, S) = \{x \in S : \forall y \in S,\ d(\mathbf{P}|_s, U(x, S)) \leq d(\mathbf{P}|_s, U(y, S))\}$$

In such a case, we say that the social choice rule $C(\mathbf{P}, S)$ has a rationalization of compromising with the unanimity criterion according to the metric δ.

6.3.1 The example of the Borda rule

The characterization of the Borda rule as a social choice rule that compromises with the unanimity criterion according to the inversion metric has been proposed by Farkas and Nitzan (1979).

Theorem 6.1: For every $S \subseteq X$ and $\mathbf{P} \in \mathbf{P}^n$,

$$C^B(\mathbf{P}, S) = \{x \in S : \forall y \in S,\ d_1(\mathbf{P}|_s, U(x, S)) \leq d_1(\mathbf{P}|_s, U(y, S))\}$$

Proof: Denote by $r_i(x, S)$ the relative ranking of x in $P_i|_S$. Notice that the minimal number of interchanges of neighboring alternatives that is required to transform alternative x to the best alternative in the strict preference relation of individual i is equal to $(r_i(x, S) - 1)$. Hence, $d_1(\mathbf{P}|_s, U(x)) = \sum_N [r_i(x, S) - 1]$ and therefore,

$$C(\mathbf{P}, S) = \{x \in S : \forall y \in S,\ d_1(\mathbf{P}|_s, U(x, S)) \leq d_1(\mathbf{P}|_s, U(y, S))\}$$
$$= \left\{ x \in S : \forall y \in S, \sum_N [\, r_i(x, S) - 1] \leq \sum_N [\, r_i(y, S) - 1] \right\}$$
$$= \left\{ x \in S : \forall y \in S, \sum_N r_i(x, S) \leq \sum_N r_i(y, S) \right\} = C^B(\mathbf{P}, S)$$

Q.E.D.

Notice that Theorem 6.1 can be viewed as an alternative axiomatization to the one presented in Theorem 5.2 of the previous chapter.

6.3.2 The example of the plurality rule

The characterization of the plurality rule as a social choice rule that compromises with the unanimity criterion according to the top metric is one of the examples that has been presented in Nitzan (1981).

Theorem 6.2 For every $S \subseteq X$ and $\mathbf{P} \in \mathbf{P}^n$,

$$C^{PL}(\mathbf{P}, S) = \{x \in S : \forall y \in S, \ d_2(\mathbf{P}|_s, U(x, S)) \leq d_2(\mathbf{P}|_s, U(y, S))\}$$

Proof: Denote by $t(x)$ the number of individuals who consider alternative x as the most preferred in $\mathbf{P}|_S$.

$$
\begin{aligned}
C(\mathbf{P}, S) &= \{x \in S : \forall y \in S, \ d_2(\mathbf{P}|_s, U(x, S)) \leq d_2(\mathbf{P}|_s, U(y, S))\} \\
&= \{x \in S : \forall y \in S, n - t(x) \leq n - t(y)\} \\
&= \{x \in S : \forall y \in S, t(x) \geq t(y)\} = C^{PL}(\mathbf{P}, S)
\end{aligned}
$$

Q.E.D.

6.4 EXTENSIONS

In a similar way to the characterization of the Borda rule and the plurality rule, other social choice rules can be presented as a compromise with the unanimity criterion according to metrics that are different from the inversion and the top metrics.

Agreement on desirable properties of metrics may lead to the axiomatization of a reasonable family of social choice rules; the family of rules that can be presented as compromise with the unanimity criterion according to the metrics that satisfy the desirable properties. Such a characterization of the family of scoring rules has been proposed by Lehrer and Nitzan (1985).

Another possible extension is the application of alternative, broader criteria, other than the unanimity criterion, as a compromise target for the social choice rule. The criterion proposed by Condorcet, winning by simple majority against all other alternatives, is one such criterion that extends the incidence of the unanimity criterion. Clearly, if there is a consensus that a certain alternative is the best one, then that alternative is a Condorcet winner (of course, the opposite claim is not valid). The definition of a social choice rule proposed by Dodgson is apparently based on this extension. It might be interesting to check if certain common rules can be characterized as compromise with Condorcet's criterion. If the answer to this question is positive, it might be useful to compare those social choice rules with the rules that compromise in a metric sense with the unanimity criterion.

6.5 EXERCISES

The following questions summarize, illustrate and clarify the metric compromise approach with the unanimity criterion.

6.1 The unanimity criterion

Question 6.1

What are the advantages and the main drawback of the unanimity criterion?

Answer

The unanimity criterion has two main advantages: its desirability is not questionable, and it is a distinguishing criterion. The main drawback of this criterion is its limited incidence.

Question 6.2

What is the problem with the limited incidence of the unanimity criterion?

Answer

The limited incidence of the unanimity criterion causes the indeterminacy problem. Many social choice functions satisfy the criterion and therefore the remaining question is which of them should be used by the individuals.

6.2 Distance between preferences

Question 6.3
Discuss the following claim: "There is no difference between the function δ and the function d because both of them are used to measure distance between preferences."

Answer
Indeed the two functions are used to measure distance between preferences. But δ measures distance between preference profiles, whereas d measures distance between profiles and sets of profiles.

Question 6.4
What is the range of the top metric when the number of alternatives is m and the number of individuals is n?

Answer
The range of the top metric is the natural numbers between 0 and n.

Question 6.5
a. What is the maximal distance according to the inversion metric between two strict orderings on three alternatives?
b. What is the maximal distance according to the inversion metric between two strict orderings on four alternatives?
c. What is the maximal distance according to the inversion metric between two strict orderings on m alternatives?
d. What is the range of the inversion metric when the number of alternatives is m and the number of individuals is n?

Answer
a. 3.
b. 6.
c. $m(m-1)/2$
d. The range is the natural numbers between 0 and $nm(m-1)/2$.

6.3 The metric compromise with the unanimity criterion

Question 6.6

Suppose that $X = \{x, y, a, b, c\}$, $N = \{1, 2, 3, 4, 5, 6, 7, 8, 9\}$ and the preference profile P of the nine individuals is given in the following table:

4	3	2
y	b	x
x	c	a
a	y	b
c	a	c
b	x	y

a. Which alternative is a unanimity winner?

b. Which alternative is a Condorcet winner?

c. Which alternative is selected by the plurality rule?

d. Discuss the following claim: "The social choice rule that compromises with the unanimity criterion according to the inversion metric selects, in this case, the same alternative that is chosen by the social choice rule that compromises with Condorcet's criterion according to the inversion metric."

Answer

a. A unanimity winner does not exist.

b. A Condorcet winner does not exist.

c. The plurality rule selects alternative y.

d. The claim is true.

The distance between the profile **P** and the set of profiles where x is a Condorcet winner is equal to 3 (three interchanges between x and y in three of the four preference relations in the left column of the table are required). The distance between the profile **P** and the set of profiles where y is a Condorcet winner is equal to 2 (in one of the three preference relations in the second column of the table, one interchange between y and c and one interchange between y and *b* are required). The distance between the profile **P** and the set of profiles where *a*, *b* or *c* is a Condorcet winner is larger than 2. We thus obtain that alternative *y* is selected by the social choice rule that compromises with Condorcet's criterion according to the inversion metric. The distance between the profile **P** and the set of profiles where *y* is a unanimity winner is equal to 14. This distance is smaller than the distance between **P** and the set of profiles where *x*, *a*, *b* or *c* wins unanimously. Alternative *y* is therefore chosen by the social choice rule that compromises with the unanimity criterion according to the inversion metric.

Question 6.7

Suppose that $X = \{x, y, a, b, c, d, e, f, z\}$, $N = \{1, 2, 3\}$ and $\mathbf{P} = (P_1, P_2, P_3)$ (see the table).

P_1	P_2	P_3
a	x	y
z	*d*	z
c	*b*	*b*
y	*a*	x
x	e	*c*
b	f	*a*
f	y	e
e	z	*d*
d	*c*	f

a. Discuss the following claim: "The social choice rule that compromises with the unanimity criterion according to the inversion metric chooses in this case the same alternatives that are chosen by the social choice rule that compromises with the unanimity criterion according to the top metric."

b. Discuss the following claim: "The social choice rule that compromises with the unanimity criterion according to the inversion metric chooses in this case the same alternatives that are chosen by the social choice rule that compromises with Condorcet's criterion according to the inversion metric."

Answer

a. The claim is incorrect. The social choice rule that compromises with the unanimity criterion according to the inversion metric chooses alternative x. The social choice rule that compromises with the unanimity criterion according to the top metric chooses alternatives x, y and a.

b. The claim is incorrect. The social choice rule that compromises with the unanimity criterion according to the inversion metric chooses alternative x. The social choice rule that compromises with Condorcet's criterion according to the inversion metric chooses alternative z.

Question 6.8
Is there a social choice function that compromises with the unanimity criterion according to the inversion metric and also compromises with Condorcet's criterion according to some metric (for instance, the inversion or the top metric)?

Answer
No. Such a function does not exist. The proof is based on the observation that there exists a preference profile where a Condorcet winner exists, but it is not chosen by the Borda rule (see Example 4.5). By Theorem 6.1, the alternative chosen by the Borda rule must be selected by the social choice function that compromises with the unanimity criterion according to the inversion metric. The alternative that is a Condorcet winner must be chosen by the social choice function that compromises with Condorcet's criterion according to any metric. Hence, there exists a profile where the choice functions based on the different compromises must choose different alternatives.

Question 6.9

Suppose that $X = \{x, y, a, b, c\}$, $N = \{1, 2, 3, 4, 5\}$ and $\mathbf{P} = (P_1, P_2, P_3, P_4, P_5)$,

P_1	P_2	P_3	P_4	P_5
x	y	c	x	y
y	a	x	y	b
a	c	y	b	a
b	b	a	c	x
c	x	b	a	c

a. Which alternative is chosen by a social choice function that compromises with Condorcet's criterion according to any metric?

b. Which alternative is chosen by a social choice function that compromises with the unanimity criterion according to the inversion metric?

Answer

a. Alternative x.

b. Alternative y.

Question 6.10

Discuss the following claim: "If a criterion is distinguishing, then a social choice function that compromises with it according to the inversion metric is necessarily resolute."

Answer

The claim is incorrect. The unanimity criterion is distinguishing, but the social choice function that compromises with it, the Borda rule, is not resolute.

Question 6.11

Discuss the following claim: "If two criteria are distinguishing, then necessarily one is more exhaustive than the other."

Answer

The claim is incorrect. The unanimity criterion that applies when there is a consensus about the most preferred alternative and the inverse unanimity criterion that applies when there is a consensus about the least preferred alternative (the criterion requires the selection of an alternative that is the worst according to all the individuals) are distinguishing criteria, but they are equally exhaustive; they apply with respect to the same number of preference profiles.

Question 6.12
Discuss the following claim: "A distinguishing criterion is not necessarily a maximally exhaustive criterion (the criterion applies on all possible profiles) and a maximally exhaustive criterion is not necessarily distinguishing."

Answer
The two parts of the claim are correct. The unanimity criterion and Condorcet's criterion are distinguishing, but they are not maximally exhaustive. The "two-individual oligarchy criterion" is maximally exhaustive, but it is not distinguishing. This criterion requires the selection of an alternative if it is the best alternative from the point of view of individual 1 or individual 2. This criterion is maximally exhaustive because it applies to every profile, but it is not distinguishing because it is possible that in a certain profile the best alternative from the point of view of individual 1 differs from the best alternative from the point of view of individual 2. In this case the "two-individual oligarchy criterion" requires the selection of two different alternatives.

6.6 SUMMARY

- $U(x, S)$ is the set of profiles where alternative x is most preferred in the set S, from the point of view of every individual.
- **The unanimity criterion:** $\mathbf{P} \in U(x, S) \Rightarrow C(\mathbf{P}, S) = \{x\}$. This criterion is distinguishing but not exhaustive.
- A metric between preference profiles is a function $\delta : \delta : \mathbf{P}^n \to \mathbf{R}_+$, that satisfies three properties:

1) **Normalization**

$$\forall\ P,\ Q \in P^n,\ \delta(P, Q) = 0 \leftrightarrow P = Q \qquad :$$

2) **Symmetry**

$$\forall\ P,\ Q \in P^n,\ \delta(P, Q) = \delta(Q, P)$$

3) **Triangle inequality**

$$\forall\ P,\ Q,\ R \in P^n,\ \delta(P, Q) + \delta(Q, R) \geq \delta(P, Q) \qquad :$$

- The **inversion metric** $\delta_1(P, Q)$) is defined as the minimal number of interchanges between neighboring alternatives in the individual preference relations that is required to transform the profile P to Q.
- The **top metric** $\delta_2(P, Q)$ is defined as the minimal number of interchanges between two alternatives (not necessarily neighboring alternatives) in the individual preference relations that is required to transform the most preferred alternatives in the profile P to those in Q.
- Given the metric δ, the distance d between a profile P and a set of profiles V is defined as follows:

$$d(P, V) = \min_{Q \in V} \delta(P, Q)$$

- A social choice rule $C(P, S)$ compromises with the unanimity criterion according to the metric δ if, for every subset S of the set of alternatives X and for every preference profile P defined on X,

$$C(P, S) = \{x \in S : \forall y \in S,\ d(P|_s, U(x, S)) \leq d(P|_s, U(y, S))\}$$

The two main results of this chapter are:

- **Theorem 6.1:** For every $S \subseteq X$ and $P \in P^n$,

$$C^B(P, S) = \{x \in S : \forall y \in S,\ d_1(P|_s, U(x, S)) \leq d_1(P|_s, U(y, S))\}$$

- **Theorem 6.2:** For every $S \subseteq X$ and $P \in P^n$,

$$C^{PL}(P, S) = \{x \in S : \forall y \in S,\ d_2(P|_s, U(x, S)) \leq d_2(P|_s, U(y, S))\}$$

7   Paradoxes of voting

Arrow's impossibility theorem implies that there is no way to transform the individuals' preference profile to a "reasonable," non-dictatorial social preference relation that ensures the existence of a well-defined, consistent social choice that is essentially similar to the rational choice of every individual in society. The theorem therefore raises doubts regarding the meaning and applicability of notions such as the "public interest," "national objective," "representative individual" or "reasonable man." Since there is no reasonable, non-dictatorial social preference relation that ensures the existence of a well-defined social choice rule, one may expect that the use of different collective choice rules is associated with "paradoxes," that is, with the violation of some plausible properties. This chapter is devoted to the illustration of several such paradoxes. As already noted, different individuals are usually interested in different choice rules. Consequently, a democratic system faces the basic difficulty of securing agreement on the voting rule it applies. The examples presented below point then to another difficulty; the choice rules used by political-economic systems may be deficient in the sense that under certain circumstances they result in paradoxical outcomes.

The various paradoxes will be illustrated assuming that the aggregation rule is the simple majority rule, or that the social choice rule is the plurality rule, the plurality runoff, the sequential majority rule or the Borda rule. Applying these rules we will demonstrate violation of the following properties: transitivity, Condorcet's consistency,

This chapter adapts some of the examples presented in Nurmi (1999), in particular, the examples in Tables 3-13, 5-3, 8-1, 8-2 and 8-3, and in Ordeshook (1986), in particular, the examples in Tables 2.5 and 2.6.

Pareto-consistency, consistency in contraction, consistency in expansion, independence of feasible alternatives, independence of the agenda, and monotonicity. The violation of transitivity by the simple majority rule implies that there does not exist a choice function that is rationalized by the simple majority preference relation. The violation of consistency in contraction and consistency in expansion imply that the social choice rule is not rationalizable. The violation of the other properties implies that the functioning of the choice rule is deficient, paradoxical or unreasonable, because it does not satisfy basic democratic expectations regarding the relationship between the decisions of the voters and the collective decision.

7.1 CONDORCET'S VOTING PARADOX

The following table reintroduces a preference profile of three individuals, individuals 1, 2 and 3, that gives rise to Condorcet's voting paradox, which was discussed in Chapter 4, Example 4.3.

Example 7.1

P_1	P_2	P_3
x	y	z
y	z	x
z	x	y

In this case, $xR^{maj}y$, $yR^{maj}z$ and $zR^{maj}x$. That is, the social preference relation of simple majority R^{maj} is not transitive. By Theorem 3.1, there does not exist, therefore, a choice function that is driven by the simple majority social preference relation. ∎

Cyclicity of the social preference relation R^{maj} has two embarrassing implications; it can be exploited both for manipulating the agenda and for extracting resources from the voters. Let us clarify these two disadvantages using the above preference profile, assuming that the social choice function is the sequential majority rule. This rule has two stages. In the first stage, a decision is made on the sequence of possible binary confrontations between the alternatives.

In the second stage, the winner in each binary confrontation is determined by simple majority and the sequential majority rule results in the selection of the final winner; the winner of the last binary confrontation. The sequence of binary confrontations is usually called the agenda and it is often determined by the chairman (who can be one of the voters).[1] In Example 7.1, there are three possible agendas. Since there are only three alternatives, the possible agendas differ in the two alternatives selected for the first confrontation. According to the first agenda, the first confrontation is between alternatives x and y and the winner is confronted with alternative z. In the second agenda, the first confrontation is between alternatives x and z and the winner is then confronted with alternative y. In the third agenda, the first confrontation is between alternatives y and z and the winner is then confronted with alternative x. It can be readily verified that the selected alternative under the sequential majority rule and the first agenda is alternative z; alternative x defeats y in the first confrontation. Alternative z defeats x in the second confrontation and is therefore the selected alternative. Similarly, it can be verified that the selected alternative under the second agenda is alternative y and the chosen alternative under the third agenda is alternative x. The sequential majority rule is therefore vulnerable to agenda manipulations when the simple majority social preference relation is not transitive.

To clarify why intransitivity of the simple majority relation gives rise to the possible existence of 'pumping money' from the voters that implies the existence of potential inefficiency, suppose that the sequential majority rule is based on the first agenda that results in the selection of alternative z. In this case, individual 1 and individual 2 have an incentive to invest resources (money) in altering the existing agenda. In particular, these individuals prefer the second agenda that results in the selection of alternative y, an alternative that is superior to alternative z for both of them. These individuals are thus ready

---

[1] In case of a tie between two alternatives, the agenda specifies the winner who continues to the next confrontation.

to invest resources and transfer them to the agenda setter, provided that the second agenda replaces the first agenda. But given the second agenda, again, there are two individuals who have an incentive to invest resources in modifying the agenda (verify). More resources can thus be pumped from the individuals. Due to the cyclicity of the social preference relation, there always exist incentives to change the selected alternative by investment that results in the modification of the agenda. In other words, the system is vulnerable to inefficiency – the pumping of money from some voters in return for the fulfillment of their expectations regarding the change in the selected alternative.

One may wonder whether, given a certain preference profile, the non-existence of a Condorcet's winner is equivalent to the cyclicity of the simple majority social preference relation. The answer to this question is negative. Given the preference profile, cyclicity indeed implies the non-existence of a Condorcet's winner; however, the non-existence of a Condorcet's winner under a given preference profile does not imply cyclicity, as illustrated by the following example.

Example 7.2

The following table presents the preference profile of the group $N = \{1, 2, 3, 4\}$. The strict preference relations are defined on the alternatives x, y and z.

P_1	P_2	P_3	P_4
x	y	z	z
y	x	x	y
z	z	y	x

Under this preference profile, a Condorcet's winner does not exist, but the simple majority social preference relation is acyclic (verify). ∎

A common measure of the severity of the voting paradox is the probability of its existence; that is, the probability that, under the individuals' preference profile, the simple majority social preference relation is cyclic. The following table presents the probability of the voting paradox in several cases where the number of alternatives

Table 7.1 *The probability of the voting paradox*

# of individuals # of alternatives	3	5	7	9	11	...	At the limit
3	.056	.069	.075	078.	080.	...	.088
4	.111	.139	.150	156.	.160	...	.176
5	.160	.200	.215	.230	251.	...	.251
6	.202	.255	.258	.284	.294	...	.315
7	.239	.299	.305	.342	.343	...	.369
:	:	:	:	:	:	:	:
At the limit	1	1	1	1	1	...	1

is odd, assuming that the possible preference profiles are equally probable. Under this assumption, the probability of the voting paradox is equal to the proportion of profiles that give rise to the paradox out of all the possible profiles.

Note that, given the number of alternatives, the probability of the paradox increases with the number of individuals. The last column of the table specifies the limit of this probability when the number of voters is sufficiently large (approaches infinity). Given the number of individuals, the probability of the voting paradox increases with the number of alternatives. But the rate of increase of this probability in the second case is higher than the rate of increase of this probability in the first case (compare the rate of increase of the probabilities along the columns and the rows).

When the number of alternatives is sufficiently large, the limit of the probability of the voting paradox is equal to 1.

7.2 CONDORCET'S INCONSISTENCY

The existence of a Condorcet's winner is not guaranteed, and this implies that there does not exist a social choice function that is driven by the simple majority social preference relation R^{maj}. Nevertheless, there exist social choice functions that are not driven by the simple majority preference relation, but are faithful to Condorcet's ideal regarding the desirable social choice. Such faithfulness is manifested by the following property: If a Condorcet's winner exists under a certain preference profile, then these social choice functions select this winner. As will be recalled from Chapter 4, a choice function that ensures the selection of every Condorcet's winner satisfies Condorcet's criterion, and we say that such a function is Condorcet-consistent. The sequential majority rule is a resolute social choice function that is Condorcet-consistent. On the one hand, given the agenda, this rule results by definition in an unequivocal choice, that is, the choice of a single alternative. On the other hand, if there exists a Condorcet's winning alternative, this winning alternative is the chosen one (verify). The Copeland rule is also Condorcet-consistent.[2] However, there are many rules that do not satisfy Condorcet's criterion, including rules that are based on some form of the majority principle. The following example illustrates that the plurality rule and the plurality-runoff rule do not satisfy Condorcet's criterion.

Example 7.3
The following table presents the preference profile of 101 individuals. The preference relations are strict and they are defined on three alternatives, x, y and z. There are three types of individual. The three preference relations of the individuals are presented in the columns of the table.

50	50	1
x	z	y
y	y	z
z	x	x

---

[2] The Copeland rule is defined as follows: Any alternative x is assigned a value, the **Copeland value**, $c(x)$. This value is equal to the difference between the number of alternatives that are inferior to x according to the simple majority relation and the number of alternatives that are preferred to x according to this relation. The Copeland rule selects the alternative with the maximal Copeland value. The proof that this rule is Condorcet-consistent appears in the answer to Question 5.9.

In this case, alternative y is a Condorcet's winner, but the alternatives chosen by the plurality rule and the runoff-plurality rule[3] are x and z. That is, both rules do not satisfy Condorcet's criterion. ∎

Not only can the plurality rule select an alternative that is not a Condorcet's winner, but the selected alternative can be a 'Condorcet's loser' (an alternative that is defeated by simple majority by any other alternative). Such an example appears in Question 7.7. Let us conclude this section by noting that not only the plurality rule, but all the scoring rules introduced in Chapter 5, including the Borda rule, are not Condorcet-consistent. Furthermore, it is possible that in a certain preference profile, all the scoring rules violate Condorcet's criterion (see Question 5.8).

7.3 VIOLATION OF THE PARETO CRITERION

In the example of the voting paradox presented in Section 7.1, the alternative chosen under a given agenda is defeated by some other alternative in a confrontation resolved by simple majority. Let us now present an example where the chosen alternative under the sequential majority rule is defeated by another alternative in a confrontation resolved by the unanimity rule. In other words, there exists an alternative preferred by all the individuals to the chosen alternative. In such a case we say that the sequential majority rule violates the Pareto criterion.

Example 7.4

The following table presents the preference profile of three individuals, defined on the four alternatives x, y, z and w.

---

[3] Suppose that individuals vote for their most preferred alternative. By the plurality-runoff rule, there are at most two voting rounds. An alternative is chosen by the rule if, in the first round, it receives at least 50% of the votes. If such an alternative does not exist, then a second voting round is held, and the individuals vote for one of the two alternatives that obtained the largest number of votes in the first round. The alternative that defeats the other one by simple majority is the chosen one. See Questions 4.11 and 4.12.

P_1	P_2	P_3
x	y	w
y	w	z
w	z	x
z	x	y

Suppose that by the existing agenda, the first confrontation is between alternatives y and w, the winner competes against alternative x and in the third and final stage, the winner in the second stage is confronted against alternative z. Under the sequential majority rule, the chosen alternative is z (verify). But this alternative is inferior to alternative w according to every individual, that is, the sequential majority rule violates the Pareto criterion. ∎

7.4 VIOLATION OF CONSISTENCY

The consistency property defined in Chapter 5 deals with the relationship between the choice sets of two distinct groups N_1 and N_2 and the choice set of the group N, the union of N_1 and N_2, $N = N_1 \cup N_2$, assuming that the choice is made from a set of alternatives S. The property ensures that the choice set corresponding to the preference profile of the group N is contained in the intersection of the two choice sets corresponding to the groups N_1 and N_2. This means that consensus regarding the chosen alternative when the choice is undertaken separately by each group is preserved when the groups are combined. The following example illustrates that the two-stage sequential majority rule violates the consistency property.

Example 7.5

Suppose that both of the sets N_1 and N_2 include 100 individuals. The strict preference relations of the 200 individuals are defined on the three alternatives x, y and z. The following tables present the preference profiles of group N_1 and group N_2.

	N_1	
25	40	35
z	y	x
y	z	z
x	x	y

	N_2	
5	55	40
x	y	z
z	z	y
y	x	x

In group N_1, under the two-stage sequential majority rule, alternative y is chosen in the second stage (verify). In group N_2, alternative y is chosen in the first stage (verify). But in the combined group N, alternative z is chosen in the second stage. (In the first stage, no alternative secures at least 50% of the votes and consequently a second voting round is held; the individuals confront alternatives y and z that obtained the largest number of votes in the first voting round. Alternative z wins the election because it obtains 105 votes relative to 95 votes obtained by alternative y.) The two-stage sequential majority rule thus violates the consistency property.

	N	
40	95	65
x	y	z
z	z	y
y	x	x

Additional examples of inconsistent rules appear in Questions 5.6 and 7.7. ∎

7.5 VIOLATION OF CONSISTENCY IN CONTRACTION AND IN EXPANSION

Consistency in contraction, property α, means that, if a certain alternative x is chosen from a set of alternatives T, and this set is contracted by elimination of some alternatives that are different from x, then alternative x is necessarily chosen from the contracted set. Consistency in contraction is significant because it is one of the two necessary and sufficient properties for the rationalizability of the social choice function. In Chapter 3, it is shown that the plurality rule violates this property (see Example 3.2). We show below that the Borda rule also violates property α.

Example 7.6

The preference profile of fifteen individuals, which is defined on the four alternatives x, y, z and w, is presented in the following table.

one individual	one individual	two individ.	two individ.	three individ.	three individ.	three individ.
z	z	w	z	z	y	x
y	w	x	y	w	x	y
x	y	y	w	x	z	z
w	x	z	x	y	w	w

In this case, the total score assigned by the Borda aggregation rule to the four alternatives is equal, respectively, to (see Question 4.2):

$$\sum_N s_i(x) = 23, \ \sum_N s_i(y) = 24, \ \sum_N s_i(z) = 27, \ \sum_N s_i(w) = 16$$

The selected alternative by the Borda rule is therefore z.

Suppose now that the set of alternatives is contracted to a set that includes the three alternatives x, y and z. In such a case, the total score assigned by the Borda rule to the three alternatives is equal, respectively, to:

$$\sum_N s_i(x) = 16, \ \sum_N s_i(y) = 15, \ \sum_N s_i(z) = 14$$

Contraction of the set of alternatives results in the selection, by the Borda rule, of alternative x, even though alternative z, the alternative chosen before the elimination of alternative w, belongs to the contracted set of alternatives. This means that the Borda rule violates property α. ∎

Consistency in expansion, property β, means that if alternative x is chosen from a set of alternatives S and from a set of alternatives T that contains S, then any other alternative that is chosen from S is also chosen from T. In Question 3.7, it is shown that the plurality rule violates property β, that is, it is inconsistent in expansion.

7.6 INVERTED ORDER PARADOX

Under certain aggregation rules, the elimination of an alternative can change the ranking of the remaining alternatives. Furthermore, the ranking of those alternatives can be inverted relative to their original ranking (the ranking prior to the elimination of one of the alternatives). Such a possibility is referred to as an instance of **the inverted order paradox**. The following example clarifies that the Borda aggregation rule f^B (see Chapter 4) is vulnerable to the inverted order paradox.

Example 7.7

The preference profile of seven individuals, which is defined on the four alternatives x, y, z and w, is presented in the following table.

Individual 1	Individual 2	Individual 3	Individual 4	Individual 5	Individual 6	Individual 7
x	w	y	x	w	y	x
z	x	w	z	x	w	z
y	z	x	y	z	x	y
w	y	z	w	y	z	w

In this case, the total score assigned by the Borda aggregation rule to the four alternatives is equal, respectively, to (see Question 4.2):

$$\sum_N s_i(x) = 15, \quad \sum_N s_i(y) = 9, \quad \sum_N s_i(z) = 8, \quad \sum_N s_i(w) = 10$$

Hence, $x \, R^B \, w \, R^B \, y \, R^B \, z$ (the definition of R^B appears in Section 4.1).

Suppose now that alternative x is eliminated, that is, the set of alternatives is contracted to the set that includes the three alternatives y, z and w. In such a case, the total score assigned by the Borda rule to the remaining three alternatives is equal, respectively, to:

$$\sum_{N} s_i(w) = 6, \quad \sum_{N} s_i(y) = 7, \quad \sum_{N} s_i(z) = 8$$

Hence, after the contraction of the set of alternatives, we obtain that, by the Borda aggregation rule, $z\ R^B\ y\ R^B\ w$. That is, the ranking of y, z and w has been inverted, after the elimination of alternative x, relative to their original ranking. ∎

7.7 THE WINNER-TURNS-LOSER PARADOX

Under certain aggregation rules, the elimination of an alternative can change the ranking of the remaining alternatives. Furthermore, not only can the ranking of the remaining alternatives be inverted relative to their original ranking, as demonstrated in the previous section, but the alternative chosen in the original situation can become the least preferred alternative in the new situation. Such a possibility is referred to as an instance of **the winner-turns-loser paradox**. The following example illustrates that the Borda aggregation rule is vulnerable to this paradox.

Example 7.8

The preference profile of seven individuals, which is defined on the four alternatives x, y, z and w, is presented in the following table.

Individual 1	Individual 2	Individual 3	Individual 4	Individual 5	Individual 6	Individual 7
x	y	z	x	y	z	x
y	z	w	y	z	w	y
z	w	x	z	w	x	z
w	x	y	w	x	y	w

In this case, the total score assigned by the Borda aggregation rule to the four alternatives is equal, respectively, to:

$$\sum_{N} s_i(x) = 11, \quad \sum_{N} s_i(y) = 12, \quad \sum_{N} s_i(z) = 13, \quad \sum_{N} s_i(w) = 6$$

Hence, $z\ R^B\ y\ R^B\ x\ R^B\ w$.

Suppose now that alternative w is eliminated, that is, the set of alternatives is contracted to the set that includes the three alternatives x, y and z. In such a case, the total score assigned by the Borda rule to the remaining three alternatives is equal, respectively, to:

$$\sum_N s_i(x) = 8, \quad \sum_N s_i(y) = 7, \quad \sum_N s_i(z) = 6$$

Hence, after the contraction of the set of alternatives, we obtain that, by the Borda aggregation rule, $x\ R^B\ y\ R^B\ z$. That is, after the elimination of alternative w, the ranking of the alternatives x, y and z has been inverted relative to their original ranking, and the winning alternative in the original situation z has become the least preferred one (the loser) in the new situation. ■

Note that if the Borda aggregation rule is vulnerable to the winner-turns-loser paradox under a certain preference profile, then under this profile the Borda rule violates property α, consistency under contraction.

7.8 THE NO-SHOW PARADOX

A social choice function is vulnerable to the no-show paradox, if there exists a preference profile that induces some of the individuals not to take part in the social choice. The existence of such an incentive implies that the outcome (the chosen alternative) when these individuals do not take part in the social choice is preferred from their point of view to the alternative chosen when they do take part in the social choice. The following example clarifies that the two-stage majority rule is vulnerable to the no-show paradox.

Example 7.9

The preference profile of 100 individuals who face three candidates, x, y and z, is presented in the following table.

25 voters	2 voters	47 voters	26 voters
z	y	y	x
x	z	z	y
y	x	x	z

Note that the preferences of 49 voters are identical. By the two-stage majority rule, candidate x wins the elections in the second stage securing 51% of the votes (verify).

Suppose that the 47 voters whose preferences are described in the third column of the table do not take part in the elections. In this case the candidate chosen in the second stage is z (verify). This means that the 47 voters have an incentive to abstain, because, from their point of view, candidate z who is elected without their participation is preferred to the chosen candidate x who is elected when they take part in the social choice. ■

7.9 EXERCISES
The material presented in this chapter is sufficient to tackle the following questions. A more comprehensive coverage of the topics discussed in this chapter is offered in Nurmi (1999).

7.1 Condorcet's voting paradox

Question 7.1
The following table presents the preference profile of the group $N = \{1, 2, 3, 4\}$.

P_1	P_2	P_3	P_4
x	y	z	z
y	x	x	y
z	z	y	x

Given this profile, explain why there does not exist a Condorcet's winner, while the simple majority social preference relation is acyclic.

Answer
By the simple majority relation, in this case all the alternatives are equivalent. There does not exist, therefore, an alternative that defeats any other alternative by the simple majority preference relation. Hence, by definition a Condorcet's winner does not exist and the simple majority relation is acyclic.

Question 7.2

a. What is the base relation of the sequential majority rule?

b. Is the sequential majority rule rationalizable?

Answer

a. For the confrontation between two alternatives, there exists just one possible agenda. This implies that the base relation of the sequential majority rule is the simple majority social preference relation R^{maj} (see Section 3.2).

b. By Proposition 3.1, a choice function is rationalizable if, and only if, it is rationalizable by its base relation. Since the base relation is not transitive, the sequential majority rule is not rationalizable.

7.2 Condorcet's inconsistency

Question 7.3

Given the preference profile of Example 7.4, is alternative z a Condorcet's loser?

Answer

No, because it defeats alternative z by simple majority.

Question 7.4

Discuss the following claim: "A choice function that allows expression of preference intensity among the alternatives does not satisfy Condorcet's criterion."

Answer

Question 5.6 implies that every scoring rule violates Condorcet's criterion (Condorcet's consistency). Hence, if expression of preference intensity means that the applied social choice function is a scoring rule, then the claim is true.

7.3 Violation of the Pareto criterion

Question 7.5

Discuss the following claim: "The Pareto principle presented in Section 4.2 and the Pareto criterion presented in Section 7.3 are identical."

Answer

The Pareto principle presented in Section 4.2 is a property of the aggregation rule that determines the social preference relation. The Pareto criterion presented in Section 7.3 is a property of the social choice function. The claim is not true, because the properties are of different functions. Nevertheless, there is a tight relationship between the two properties when the social choice function is driven by the social preference relation obtained by the aggregation rule (see Section 3.1). In this case, if the aggregation rule satisfies the Pareto principle, then the social choice function satisfies the Pareto criterion and, vice versa, if the social choice function driven by the social preference relation satisfies the Pareto criterion, then the aggregation rule satisfies the Pareto principle (verify).

7.4 Violation of consistency

Question 7.6

The members of the Likud party in Israel are active in one of the three party branches: the central, northern and southern branches. There are three candidates for the leadership of the party: x, y and z. In the elections held in all three branches of the party, candidate y was chosen as the preferred party leader. In each branch, the members of the national party center who are members of the branch took part in the elections. By the party rules, the leader of the party is chosen at the party center. The general director of the party is certain that candidate y is going to be chosen as the party leader by the members of the party center. What is your opinion of his prediction?

Answer

If the social choice function applied at the party center satisfies the consistency property, then candidate y will be elected to the party leader. If the choice function violates the consistency property, candidate y is not necessarily elected to the party leader. For example, suppose that the applied social choice function is the two-stage plurality runoff and that the party center N includes 200 members. 100 of these members belong to the central branch N_1. 49 of the center members belong to the northern branch N_2. The remaining 51 members belong to the southern branch N_3. The preference profile of the center members in the three branches are presented in the following three tables.

N_1

35	40	25
x	y	z
z	z	y
y	x	x

N_2

20	27	2
z	y	x
y	z	z
x	x	y

N_3

20	28	3
z	y	x
y	z	z
x	x	y

In the central branch N_1, candidate y is chosen in the second voting round, and in the other two branches, N_2 and N_3, the same candidate is elected in the first voting round. However, at the party center N, the elected candidate is z.

	N	
65	95	40
z	y	x
y	z	z
x	x	y

Question 7.7

Does the sequential majority rule satisfy the consistency property?

Answer

The sequential majority rule is inconsistent, as illustrated by the following example.

Suppose that the set of alternatives is $X = \{x, y, z\}$. The preference profile of the 28 members of the lower house N_1 and the preference profile of the 24 members of the upper house N_2 are presented in the following tables.

N_1	
12 voters	16 voters
y	z
z	y
x	x

N_2		
8 voters	8 voters	8 voters
z	y	x
x	z	y
y	x	z

According to the sequential majority rule, in the first stage the alternatives are x and y, and the winner is confronted with alternative z. By this sequential majority rule, alternative z is chosen both at the lower and the upper house. In contrast, when the elections are held at the joint meeting of the two houses, N, the chosen alternative is y rather than z. The sequential majority rule thus violates the consistency property.

$$N$$

16 voters	8 voters	20 voters	8 voters
z	z	y	x
y	x	z	y
x	y	x	z

7.5 Violation of consistency in contraction and in expansion

Question 7.8

Using the preference profile of the 200 members of the Likud party N that was presented in Question 7.6, explain why the plurality rule is inconsistent in contraction.

Answer

By the plurality rule, candidate y is chosen from the set of candidates that includes x, y and z. When candidate x is eliminated and the choice is made from the set that includes candidates y and z, the chosen candidate is z. This means that the plurality rule is inconsistent in contraction.

7.6 Inverted order paradox

Question 7.9

Construct an example of a preference profile such that the Borda rule does not satisfy consistency in contraction and the Borda aggregation rule is vulnerable to the inverted order paradox.

Answer

The following table presents a preference profile of fifteen individuals which is defined on the four alternatives x, y, z and w. This profile was introduced in Section 7.5 to illustrate the violation of consistency in contraction by the Borda rule. In this case, the total score assigned by the Borda aggregation rule to the four alternatives is equal, respectively, to:

$$\sum_N s_i(x) = 23, \quad \sum_N s_i(y) = 24, \quad \sum_N s_i(z) = 27, \quad \sum_N s_i(w) = 16$$

One voter	One voter	2 voters	2 voters	3 voters	3 voters	3 voters
z	z	w	z	z	y	x
y	w	x	y	w	x	y
x	y	y	w	x	z	z
w	x	z	x	y	w	w

Hence, by the Borda aggregation rule, $z\ R^B\ y\ R^B\ x\ R^B\ w$.

Suppose now that the set of alternatives is contracted to the set containing the three alternatives x, y and z. In this case, the total score assigned to the three alternatives is equal, respectively, to:

$$\sum_N s_i(x) = 16, \quad \sum_N s_i(y) = 15, \quad \sum_N s_i(z) = 14$$

We therefore obtain that after the elimination of alternative z, by the Borda aggregation rule, $x\ R^B\ y\ R^B\ z$. That is, the original ranking of alternatives x, y and z has been reversed. The Borda aggregation rule is thus vulnerable to the inverted order paradox.

7.7 The winner-turns-loser paradox

Question 7.10
Are the following claims true? Discuss briefly.

a. If the aggregation rule is vulnerable to the inverted order paradox, then it is vulnerable to the winner-turns-loser paradox.

b. If the aggregation rule is vulnerable to the winner-turns-loser paradox, then it is vulnerable to the inverted order paradox.

c. Given a certain preference profile, if the Borda aggregation rule is vulnerable to the winner-turns-loser paradox, then it also violates the property of consistency in contraction.

d. Given a certain preference profile, if the Borda aggregation rule violates the property of consistency in contraction, then it is vulnerable to the winner-turns-loser paradox.

e. Given a certain preference profile, if the Borda aggregation rule violates the property of consistency in contraction, then it vulnerable to the inverted order paradox.

Answer

a. Not true. Under a certain preference profile, the aggregation rule can be vulnerable to the inverted order paradox, but not vulnerable to the winner-turns-loser paradox; see Example 7.7.
b. True.
c. True.
d. Not true. The fact that the original winner is not chosen after the contraction of the set of alternatives does not imply that he turns into a loser (the most inferior alternative).
e. Not true. As claimed above, the fact that the original winner is not chosen after the contraction of the set of alternatives does not imply that he turns into a loser. Furthermore, even if the original winner turns into a loser, it is possible that the ranking of the other alternatives is not inverted relative to their original ranking.

7.8 The no-show paradox

Question 7.11

Prove that the sequential majority rule is vulnerable to the no-show paradox.

Answer

Let the set of alternatives be $X = \{x, y, z\}$. The preference profile of the five members of group N_1 is presented in the following table.

N_1		
2 voters	2 voters	One voter
y	x	z
x	z	y
z	y	x

Suppose that, by the sequential majority rule, in the first stage, a confrontation is held between alternatives x and y, and the winner confronts alternative z. By this sequential majority rule, the chosen alternative is z. Let us assume now that the two-member group N_2 is added to the group N_1. Note that the most preferred alternatives of the two members of N_2 is z.

N_2

2 voters

z

x

y

The sequential majority rule is vulnerable to the no-show paradox because the chosen alternative from the augmented set N, $N = N_1 \cup N_2$, is x. Paradoxically, the absence from the group N improves the situation of the two members of N_2, who prefer the choice of alternative z to the choice of x.

Question 7.12

Discuss the following claim: "If a social choice function is vulnerable to the no-show paradox, then it is vulnerable to inconsistency."

Answer

The claim is incorrect. Given a particular preference profile, it is possible that the social choice function is vulnerable to the no-show paradox and to inconsistency (see Question 7.11). However, under a different preference profile, the social choice function can be vulnerable to the no-show paradox, but not to inconsistency (see Example 7.9).

7.10 SUMMARY

- The social preference relation of simple majority R^{maj} is not transitive. There does not exist, therefore, a choice function that is driven by R^{maj}.

- Cyclicity of the social preference relation R^{maj} has two embarrassing implications; it can be exploited for manipulating the agenda and for extracting resources from the voters.
- A choice function that ensures the selection of every Condorcet's winning alternative satisfies **Condorcet's criterion**, and we say that such a function is Condorcet-consistent.
- All the scoring rules, and in particular the plurality and the Borda rules, are not Condorcet-consistent. The plurality runoff rule also violates Condorcet's criterion.
- A social choice function violates the **Pareto criterion** if, under some preference profile, it chooses an alternative that is inferior for all individuals to some other alternative. The sequential majority rule violates the Pareto criterion. That is, some chosen alternative under the sequential majority rule is defeated by another alternative in a confrontation resolved by the unanimity rule.
- The **consistency** property ensures that consensus regarding a chosen alternative, when the choice is undertaken separately by each group, is preserved when the groups are combined. The plurality runoff violates the consistency property.
- **Consistency in contraction** means that, if a certain alternative x is chosen from a set of alternatives T, and this set is contracted by elimination of some alternatives that are different from x, then alternative x is necessarily chosen from the contracted set. The plurality and the Borda rules violate consistency in contraction.
- **Consistency in expansion** means that, if alternative x is chosen from a set of alternatives S and from a set of alternatives T that contains S, then any other alternative that is chosen from S is also chosen from T. The plurality rule is inconsistent in expansion.
- The elimination of an alternative can invert the original ranking of the remaining alternatives. Such a possibility is referred to as an instance of **the inverted order paradox**. The Borda aggregation rule is vulnerable to the inverted order paradox.
- The elimination of an alternative that is not the chosen one can invert the original ranking of the remaining alternatives. In such a case, an

alternative that is chosen originally may become the least preferred alternative. Such a possibility is referred to as an instance of **the winner-turns-loser paradox**. The Borda aggregation rule is vulnerable to the winner-turns-loser paradox.

- A social choice function is vulnerable to the **no-show paradox**, if there exists a preference profile that induces some of the individuals not to take part in the social choice. The existence of such an incentive implies that the chosen alternative, when these individuals do not take part in the social choice, is preferred from their point of view to the alternative chosen when they do take part in the social choice. The sequential majority rule is vulnerable to the no-show paradox.

8 Majority tyranny

Social choice functions which satisfy Condorcet's criterion (see Section 4.2 and Section 7.2) are vulnerable to the problem of majority decisiveness: If a certain alternative is the most preferred alternative of more than 50% of the individuals (voters), then that alternative is always chosen by society, regardless of the preferences of the minority and, in particular, the intensity of its preferences. This problem can be resolved by increasing the required simple majority to a special or supra majority q, $q > \frac{1}{2}$, or by augmenting the simple majority rule with constitutional constraints that protect the minority. The former solution is not satisfied with Condorcet's criterion and, in attempting to protect the minority, it insists that the choice function satisfies a stricter, more demanding, criterion; the chosen alternative should secure the support of a special majority in confrontation with any other alternative. The second solution attempts to protect the minority in an extreme way by preventing the choice of certain alternatives that violate the basic rights of the minority (alternatives that are considered unlawful). While the former solution discriminates among alternatives by creating a bias in favor of one of the alternatives, usually the status quo, the latter solution discriminates against individuals by creating a bias in favor of the minority. The first objective of this chapter is to clarify how the problem of majority decisiveness can be resolved or ameliorated by using scoring rules: unbiased voting rules which allow some restricted expression of preference intensities. The second objective of the chapter is

This chapter adapts and draws on material from two papers. The first part of Chapter 8 (Sections 8.1–8.4) is based on Baharad and Nitzan (2002). The second part of Chapter 8 (Sections 8.5–8.6) is based on Baharad and Nitzan (2007b).

to identify the optimal scoring rule: the "golden voting rule" that provides the proper balance between the need to protect the minority and the need to avoid erosion of the majority principle. That is, to find the desirable balance between securing an effective implementation of the will of the majority while preventing it from being tyrannical.

The problem of majority decisiveness is related to the classical notion of majority tyranny that has attracted a lot of attention, especially since the second half of the eighteenth century. Such majority tyranny is characterized by two basic elements. First, factionalism: that is, effective implementation of goals pursued by a specific majority group; and second, "unjustness" of at least one favored alternative x imposed by that majority group. In contrast to the classical notion of majority tyranny, the point of departure of this study is the different weaker notion of *decisiveness of the majority*, any majority. This is an important property of preference aggregation rules or of voting rules, which has been extensively studied by social choice theorists (Arrow 1963; Sen 1970, see Section 4.2). Majority decisiveness is defined as the ability of any majority group to impose its will whenever its members share a common view regarding the desirable collective decision. The incidence of majority decisiveness is not restricted to "unjust" alternatives, so it is not necessarily bad or undesirable. To simplify terminology, we will refer to the weaker problem of majority decisiveness as the problem of majority tyranny.

8.1 SCORING RULES

In this chapter we assume that the set of individuals (voters) includes at least three members, $n \geq 3$, the set of alternatives (candidates) includes at least three elements, $k \geq 3$, and the individual preference relations are strict (indifference is not allowed). Recall (see Section 5.2) that a *scoring rule* is defined as follows:

Given a set of k candidates, S, let $\{S_1, S_2, \ldots, S_k\}$ be a monotone sequence of real numbers, $S_1 \leq S_2 \leq \cdots \leq S_k$ such that $S_1 < S_k$. Each of the n voters ranks the candidates, assigning S_1 points to the one ranked last, S_2 points to the one ranked next to the last, and so on. Under a *scoring rule* a candidate with a maximal total score is elected. If the sequence $\{S_1, S_2, \ldots, S_k\}$ is strictly monotone, that is, $S_1 < S_2 < \cdots < S_k$, the scoring rule is called a *strict scoring rule*.

A scoring rule is unbiased toward voters and unbiased toward alternatives. Unbiasedness toward voters (anonymity) requires invariance of the voting rule with respect to permutations of voters' preferences; if the preference relations of the voters are permuted, then the outcome of the voting rule is not affected. Unbiasedness toward alternatives (minimal neutrality) requires appropriate variance of the voting rule with respect to permutations of the alternatives; if the alternatives are permuted in the preferences of the voters, then the alternative(s) selected by the voting rule change(s) accordingly. This property ensures that the labeling of the alternatives is immaterial, all that matters is the voters' preferences.

The most common scoring rules are the plurality and the Borda rules, which were introduced in Section 5.2.

The *plurality rule* is a scoring rule defined by

$$S^{\mathrm{P}} = (S_1, S_2, \ldots, S_{k-1}, S_k) = (0, 0, \ldots, 0, 1).$$

Under this rule, the candidate who is ranked first by the largest number of voters is elected.

The *Borda rule* is a strict scoring rule defined by

$$S^{\mathrm{B}} = (S_1, S_2, \ldots, S_{k-1}, S_k) = (0, 1, \ldots, k-2, k-1)$$

Under the Borda rule, each voter reports his preferences by ranking the k candidates from top to bottom (ties are not allowed), assigning no points to the candidate being ranked last, one point to the one being ranked next to the last, and so on, up to $k - 1$ points to the most preferred candidate. A candidate with the highest total score, called a Borda winner, is elected.

Another scoring rule that will be dealt with later in this chapter is the *inverse plurality* or the *negative plurality* rule. This rule is defined by

$$S^{ip} = (S_1, S_2, \ldots, S_{k-1}, S_k) = (0, 1, \ldots, 1, 1)$$

As in the case of the plurality rule, the information required for the operation of the inverse plurality rule is modest. Every voter has to report only his worst candidate and not, as under the plurality rule, his most preferred candidate.

8.2 MAJORITY DECISIVENESS

A group T is called a decisive majority if it can impose its will (ensure the selection of a candidate in whom the group is interested), regardless of the preferences of the minority or its voting strategy. This means that decisiveness does not require information on the preferences or on the actual votes of the individuals who do not belong to the group T. The existence of decisiveness depends on the voting rule applied by the voters. When the decisive majority group is T, $|T| = \alpha n$, we say that there exists an α-majority decisiveness, or that the voting rule is vulnerable to an α-majority tyranny, $1/2 < \alpha < 1$. Henceforth, for simplicity, α is assumed to be a fraction with denominator n. The following example illustrates the possible existence of majority tyranny when the social choice function is the Borda rule.

Example 8.1

Suppose that there are three voters whose true preference relations over the four alternatives a, b, c, e are presented in the following Table 8.1.

In such a case, alternative b is selected by the Borda rule because it receives the largest number of points (seven), whereas alternative a, which is preferred by a majority of 66%, receives only six points. However, voters 1 and 2 can guarantee the selection of alternative a, even without knowing voter 3's preferences. Suppose that voters 1 and 2 report the preferences presented in Table 8.2.

In such a case, independent of voter 3's preferences, the selection of alternative a is guaranteed, since it already receives six points from

Table 8.1

Rank	Voter 1's Preferences	Voter 2's Preferences	Voter 3's Preferences	Borda's Rank
1st	a	a	b	b (seven points)
2nd	b	b	e	a (six points)
3rd	c	e	c	e (three points)
4th	e	c	a	c (two points)

Table 8.2

Rank	Voter 1's Preferences	Voter 2's Preferences	Voter 3's Preferences	Borda's Rank
1st	a	a	?	a (at least six points)
2nd	b	e	?	? (at most five points)
3rd	c	c	?	?
4th	e	b	?	?

voters 1 and 2, where every other alternative receives only two points. The maximal score that can be assigned by voter 3 to any of these alternatives is three points, which cannot change the sure selection of alternative a. In this example, therefore, the group that includes voter 1 and voter 2 is decisive. Since similar examples can be constructed for majority coalitions that consist of voters 1 and 3 or of voters 2 and 3, when $k = 4$, $n = 3$ and the social choice function is the Borda rule, there exists a 2/3-majority decisiveness. ∎

The severity of the α-majority tyranny problem depends on the size of the majority, namely, on α as well as on the extent of strategic voting manipulations performed by the members of the majority coalition. *Ceteris paribus*, the severity of the problem decreases with an increase in the majority size. A decisiveness of 90% of the voters is less of a problem than a decisiveness of 55%. A less obvious characteristic of majority decisiveness is the degree of coordinated strategic voting exercised by the members of the majority coalition. In the non-strategic voting theory, voters are assumed to sincerely reveal their (true) preferences. That is, voting manipulations of any sort are ruled out. However, in the more recent strategic-voting theory, typically, any conceivable preference manipulation is allowed, which clearly facilitates the attainment of decisiveness. Strategic voting enables the attainment of decisiveness by a smaller majority. It therefore aggravates the majority-tyranny problem. Nevertheless, effective strategic voting depends on the information available to the members of the majority group (information about the preferences of the group members) and on coordination between them. The difficulties associated with information gathering and coordination may therefore prevent effective manipulative voting.

As already noted, scoring rules are unbiased. That is, they are anonymous and neutral. Unbiasedness toward voters implies that if there is an α-majority decisiveness of some specific group, then there is an α-majority decisiveness of any group of size α. That is, due to the anonymity property, decisiveness is contagious: the incidence of effective concentration of decision-making power is not restricted to a specific majority group. Unbiasedness toward alternatives implies that if there exists an α-majority decisiveness of some group which can impose a particular ("unjust") alternative, then it can impose the selection of any alternative. That is, due to the neutrality property, decisiveness is contagious in another sense: the incidence of the effectivity of the decisive majority coalition is not restricted to a specific alternative or subset of alternatives, but is unlimited. By definition then, under the anonymous and neutral scoring rules the classical tyranny of the majority is impossible. However, the lesser problem of majority tyranny (decisiveness) may still exist.

A resolution of the problem of majority decisiveness requires that such decisiveness does not exist. That is, there exists no α-majority decisiveness, $\frac{1}{2} < \alpha < 1$. Let us turn to the resolution of the problem assuming, first, that the majority-coalition members report their sincere preferences and then, that they act strategically when coordinating the reporting of their preferences.

8.3 RESOLUTION OF THE PROBLEM OF MAJORITY TYRANNY UNDER SINCERE VOTING

Theorem 8.1: Under sincere voting, a scoring rule defined by $\{S_1, S_2, \ldots, S_k\}$ is immune to an α-majority tyranny, $\frac{1}{2} < \alpha < 1$, if and only if,

$$\alpha(S_k - S_{k-1}) < (1 - \alpha)(S_k - S_1) \tag{1}$$

Proof: Suppose that αn members of an $\alpha-$ *majority* coalition, $\frac{1}{2} < \alpha < 1$, share the same preference regarding the best (most preferred) alternative a and regarding the second-best alternative b. Also, suppose that for the $(1 - \alpha)n$ minority voters the best alternative is b, and the least preferred alternative is a. Notice that if the majority consensus alternative a is selected under this most unfavorable profile, namely, under a profile where the majority consensus a gets minimal support from the minority and the challenger b receives maximal support from the members of both the majority and minority coalitions, then the majority consensus a is selected under any other profile, so, by definition, the majority is tyrant. Hence, an α-majority decisiveness does not exist, if under the assumed most unfavorable profile the total score of alternative a is less than the total score of b. That is, the condition ensuring immunity to decisiveness of an α-majority is:

$$\alpha n S_k + (1 - \alpha) n S_1 < \alpha n S_{k-1} + (1 - \alpha) n S_k$$

which is equivalent to (1). The proof is therefore complete. **Q.E.D.**

If the scoring rule is immune to tyranny of any α-majority, $\frac{1}{2} < \alpha < 1$, then we say that it is immune to majority tyranny or that the problem of majority decisiveness is resolved. In such a case, the rule must therefore be immune to majority decisiveness for $\alpha = \frac{n-1}{n}$. Immunity to majority decisiveness does not imply that every voter is a vetoer, but that every voter has a veto power under at least one preference profile. Theorem 1 has the following direct consequences (see Problems 8.3–8.7):

Conclusion 1. A scoring rule is immune to majority tyranny if, and only if,

$$(n-1)(S_k - S_{k-1}) < (S_k - S_1) \tag{2}$$

Conclusion 2. The plurality rule is vulnerable to majority tyranny.

Conclusion 3. The Borda rule is vulnerable to majority tyranny if, and only if, $n > k$.

Conclusion 4. The Borda rule is immune to an α-majority tyranny if $\alpha < \frac{k-1}{k}$. An alternative form of the condition ensuring the immunity of the Borda rule to an α-majority tyranny is $k > \frac{1}{(1-\alpha)}$. That is, a sufficient increase in the number of alternatives is an effective means of preventing the tyranny of an α-majority.

Conclusion 5. The inverse plurality rule is immune to majority tyranny.

8.4 RESOLUTION OF THE PROBLEM OF MAJORITY TYRANNY UNDER INSINCERE VOTING

Theorem 8.2: Let $\alpha\, n = m(k - 1)$ for some integer m. Under coordinated strategic voting a scoring rule defined by $\{S_1, S_2, \ldots, S_k\}$ is immune to an α-majority tyranny, $\frac{1}{2} < \alpha < 1$, if

$$\alpha > \frac{S_k - S_1}{2S_k - S_1 - \overline{S}}, \quad \text{where } \overline{S} = \frac{1}{k-1} \sum_{j=1}^{k-1} S_j. \tag{3}$$

Proof: Suppose that all αn members of an α-majority coalition, $\frac{1}{2} < \alpha < 1$, share the same preference regarding the best alternative a. To impose the selection of its consensus alternative a, that is, to be decisive, the α-majority coalition must prevent the selection of *any* alternative other than candidate a at *all* possible preference profiles. An effective strategy for attaining this goal must have two components. First, such a strategy requires that every member of the majority coalition sincerely reports the majority consensus a as his most preferred candidate. Second, such a strategy requires the minimization of the maximal total score assigned by the majority coalition to one of the remaining $k-1$ alternative candidates, that is, to the "coalition's reported second best" candidate. This means that the majority-coalition members need to coordinate their reported preferences in order to avoid overloading of scores as much as possible. That is, they have to equally spread the coalition's assigned scores over the remaining $k-1$ candidates, subject to the constraint of the scores $\{S_1, S_2, \ldots, S_{k-1}\}$ that must be assigned to these candidates. Under these constraints, even if the coalition members share the same preference relation (not only the same best alternative), where the score assigned by the coalition to its true second-best alternative under sincere voting is the maximal possible score $(\alpha n S_{k-1})$, the α-majority coalition can ensure that the average score $\overline{S}$ assigned by its members to the coalition's reported second-best candidate is only equal to $\frac{1}{k-1} \sum\limits_{j=1}^{k-1} S_j$. Since, by assumption, $\alpha n = m(k-1)$ for some integer m, this average score is achieved when the coalition members' reported preferences are cyclical over the $k-1$ alternatives that are ranked as second, third, and so on up to the $k-1$ position (the scores assigned to these alternatives range from S_1 to S_{k-1}). Such a strategy is effective, that is, the α-majority coalition is tyrant, if the lowest possible total score assigned to candidate a under any preference profile, $\alpha n S_k + (1 - \alpha)n S_1$, is greater than the highest possible total score that can be assigned to any other alternative under any preference profile, $\alpha n \overline{S} + (1 - \alpha)n S_k$. That is, a sufficient condition for an α-majority decisiveness is

$$\alpha n S_k + (1 - \alpha)n S_1 > \alpha n \overline{S} + (1 - \alpha)n S_k$$

which is equivalent to the requirement that $\alpha > \frac{S_k - S_1}{2S_k - S_1 - \overline{S}}$.   **Q.E.D.**

When the majority group voters coordinate their actions and vote strategically, the following conclusions are obtained from Theorem 2 (see Questions 8.9, 8.10 and 8.13).

Conclusion 1. The plurality rule is vulnerable to majority tyranny.

Conclusion 2. The Borda rule is vulnerable to α-majority tyranny, $\alpha = \frac{2k-2}{3k-2}$. Hence, when the number of candidates is sufficiently large, the Borda rule is vulnerable to a 2/3-majority tyranny.

Conclusion 3. If $k \geq n$, then there always exists a scoring rule that is immune to majority tyranny. In particular, the inverse plurality rule is such an immune voting rule.

This means that when the number of candidates is larger than or equal to the number of voters, even when the majority-group members coordinate their actions and vote strategically, majority tyranny can be avoided by using the inverse plurality rule.

Scoring rules are defined by an inflexible system of scores. The two results we have presented imply that protection against majority tyranny can be used as a possible justification for the rigidity of the scores system. In other words, the restricted voters' ability to express their preferences, a restriction which takes the form of a rigid scores system, accounts for the ability of a scoring rule to provide protection against majority tyranny.

8.5 EROSION IN THE MAJORITY PRINCIPLE VS. MAJORITY TYRANNY

On the one hand, the vulnerability of a scoring rule to an α^*-majority tyranny of any majority that is equal to or is larger than the fraction α^* of the number of the voters, entails a certain restriction on the ability of the minority to effectively express its preference intensity. On the other hand, the ability of a scoring rule to prevent the tyranny of a majority smaller than α^* can be interpreted as erosion in the majority principle, because any such majority is not decisive, that is, to some extent (in certain voting profiles) it loses its ability to determine the outcome of the social choice. The tyranny implied by majority decisiveness and the erosion in the majority status are two possible worrying aspects associated with the implementation of the majority principle by using scoring rules which are characterized by different degrees α^* of majority decisiveness. Focusing on the first problematic aspect enables the evaluation of alternative scoring rules on the basis of their degree of immunity to majority tyranny represented by α^*. When the second aspect is also taken into account, the question is: Which scoring rule attains the golden compromise between effective implementation of the will of the majority and prevention of majority tyranny? This rule properly balances the need to allow the minority to express the intensity of its preferences, such that majority tyranny is prevented, and the need to prevent erosion in the majority principle. The answer to the question, that is, the identity of the golden voting rule, hinges, first, on the "costs" of majority tyranny and of the erosion in the majority principle and, second, on the assessment of these costs by the agent who tries to identify the optimal scoring rule. In the next section, we present a possible answer to the question of the appropriate voting rule, the use of which provides a (partial) answer both to the problem of majority tyranny and to the problem of the erosion in the majority principle.

8.6 THE GOLDEN SCORING RULE

To measure the costs of majority decisiveness, we make the standard assumption that all possible preference profiles are equally likely (the so called impartial culture assumption). The first type of costs of majority decisiveness corresponding to some α^+ is measured by $C^1(\alpha^+)$ – the proportion of preference profiles in which an α-majority tyranny, $\alpha \geq \alpha^+$, is realized. The second type of costs of majority decisiveness corresponding to some α^+ is measured by $C^2(\alpha^+)$ – the proportion of preference profiles in which the α-majority principle, $\alpha < \alpha^+$, is eroded. Under the impartial culture assumption,[1] $C^1(\alpha^+)$ is thus the probability that an α^+-majority group, $\alpha \geq \alpha^+$, shares the same view regarding the most preferred alternative. $C^2(\alpha^+)$ is the probability that an α-majority group, $\alpha < \alpha^+$, and the corresponding $(1 - \alpha)$-minority

---

[1] For the sake of simplicity we have based the formal analysis on the commonly used impartial culture assumption. Our results are robust, however, because they are valid under many alternative preference cultures.

group unanimously prefer two different alternatives, and the majority cannot guarantee the selection of its most favorable alternative. In the Appendix we show that:

$$C^1(\alpha^+) = k \sum_{i=\alpha^+ n}^{n-1} \left(\frac{1}{k}\right)^i \cdot \left(\frac{k-1}{k}\right)^{n-i} \cdot \binom{n}{i} \tag{4}$$

and

$$C^2(\alpha^+) = \sum_{i=\lfloor 0.5n+1 \rfloor}^{\alpha^+ n-1} \left(\frac{1}{k}\right)^i \cdot \left(\frac{1}{k}\right)^{n-i} \cdot \binom{n}{i} \cdot \left(\frac{k!}{(k-2)!}\right) \tag{5}$$

where $\lfloor t \rfloor$ is the largest integer that is equal to or smaller than t and $\lceil t \rceil$ is the smallest integer that is equal to or larger than t.

The two types of probabilistic costs $C^1(\cdot)$ and $C^2(\cdot)$, mentioned above, depend on the particular α^+ corresponding to a scoring rule, on the number of alternatives k, and on the number of voters n. The normative constitutional motive to identify the golden voting rule takes into account the two types of costs of implementing the majority principle. That is, it can be based on some function that is positively related to the costs $C^1(\cdot)$ and $C^2(\cdot)$. A natural such function is the weighted sum $\beta C^1(\cdot) + (1 - \beta) C^2(\cdot)$, where β and $(1 - \beta)$ are the weights assigned to the two types of costs. The golden voting rule is a scoring rule that minimizes this weighted sum. Given the weight β assigned to $C^1(\alpha^+)$, the number of alternatives k, and the number of voters n, the golden voting rule is a scoring rule that results in a minimal degree of decisiveness α^+ that solves the following problem:

$$\underset{\alpha^+}{Min} \; \beta \cdot C^1(\alpha^+) + (1 - \beta) \cdot C^2(\alpha^+) \tag{6}$$

or

$$\underset{\alpha^+}{Min} \beta \cdot k \sum_{i=\alpha^+ n}^{n-1} \left(\frac{1}{k}\right)^i \cdot \left(\frac{k-1}{k}\right)^{n-i} \cdot \binom{n}{i} \tag{7}$$

$$+ (1 - \beta) \cdot \sum_{i=\lfloor 0.5n+1 \rfloor}^{\alpha^+ n-1} \left(\frac{1}{k}\right)^i \cdot \left(\frac{1}{k}\right)^{n-i} \cdot \binom{n}{i} \cdot \left(\frac{k!}{(k-2)!}\right)$$

Let $\Delta C^i_-(\alpha) = C^i(\alpha) - C^i\left(\alpha - \frac{1}{n}\right)$ and $\Delta C^i_+(\alpha) = C^i\left(\alpha + \frac{1}{n}\right) - C^i(\alpha)$, for $i = 1, 2$.

The necessary and sufficient conditions for an interior solution α^* of the above problem are:

$$\beta \Delta C^1_-(\alpha^*) + (1 - \beta)\Delta C^2_-(\alpha^*) \leq 0 \quad \text{and}$$

$$\beta \Delta C^2_+(\alpha^*) + (1 - \beta)\Delta C^2_+(\alpha^*) \geq 0 \tag{8}$$

or, at α^*,

$$\frac{\Delta C^2_-}{\Delta C^2_- - \Delta C^1_-} \leq \beta \leq \frac{\Delta C^2_+}{\Delta C^2_+ - \Delta C^1_+} \tag{9}$$

By (4) and (5), the necessary and sufficient conditions are:

$$\frac{1}{1 + (k - 1)^{(1-\alpha^*)n}} \leq \beta \leq \frac{1}{1 + (k - 1)^{(1-\alpha^*)n-1}} \tag{10}$$

Let $f(t)$ be the maximal fraction with a denominator n that is smaller than or equal to $\left(t + \frac{1}{n}\right)$. Notice that an $f(\alpha^*)$-majority coalition can impose the selection of its unanimously favored alternative in the strict sense, that is, the $(1 - f(\alpha^*))$-minority group cannot also secure the selection of some other alternative. When the majority group members coordinate their votes, Theorem 8.2 implies that:

Claim 8.1

(i) The minimal degree of majority tyranny corresponding to the plurality rule defined by S^p is

$$\alpha^+(S^p) = \alpha^p = f(1/2).$$

(ii) The minimal degree of majority tyranny corresponding to the inverse plurality rule defined by S^{ip} is

$$\alpha^+(S^{ip}) = \alpha^{ip} = f\left(\frac{k-1}{k}\right)$$

Notice that when α^* is a corner solution, only one of the inequalities in (10) holds. In particular, when $\alpha^* = f(1/2)$, the necessary and sufficient condition is:

$$\beta \leq \frac{1}{1 + (k - 1)^{(1-\alpha^*)n-1}} \tag{11}$$

When $\alpha^* = f\left(\frac{k-1}{k}\right)$, the necessary and sufficient condition is:

$$\beta \geq \frac{1}{1 + (k - 1)^{(1-\alpha^*)n}} \tag{12}$$

Theorem 8.3

(i) When $n \leq k$, the inverse plurality rule is the golden voting rule if $\frac{1}{2} \leq \beta \leq 1$.

(ii) When $n > k$ and n is sufficiently large, the inverse plurality rule is the golden voting rule for every $\beta, \delta \leq \beta \leq 1, \delta \to 0$.

(iii) Independent of n and k, if $\beta = 0$, the plurality rule is the golden voting rule.

Proof

(i) By substituting α^{ip} into (12), we obtain that the golden voting rule is the inverse plurality rule if the weight β assigned to the cost of majority tyranny satisfies:

$$\frac{1}{1 + (k-1)^{\lfloor \frac{n}{k} \rfloor}} \leq \beta^{ip} \leq 1 \tag{13}$$

since $n \leq k$, $\left\lfloor \frac{n}{k} \right\rfloor = 0$ and, in turn, $\frac{1}{2} \leq \beta \leq 1$.

(ii) By substituting α^{ip} into (12), we obtain that the golden voting rule is the inverse plurality rule if the weight β assigned to the cost of majority tyranny satisfies inequality (13).

Since $n > k > 2$, $\lim_{n \to \infty} \frac{1}{1+(k-1)^{\lfloor \frac{n}{k} \rfloor}} \to 0$. That is, α^{ip} satisfies (12) and therefore it is the solution of problem (6) for almost every positive β.

(iii) By substituting α^p into (11), we obtain that the golden voting rule is the plurality rule if the weight β assigned to the cost of majority tyranny satisfies:

$$0 \leq \beta^p \leq \frac{1}{1 + (k - 1)^{\lceil \frac{n}{2} \rceil - 1}}. \tag{14}$$

Obviously, $\beta = 0$ satisfies this condition. **Q.E.D.**

By part (iii) of the theorem, when majority tyranny is not considered as a problem, $\beta = 0$, the plurality rule is always the golden rule. Simply, when $\beta = 0$, the objective function in (6) reduces to $C^2(\cdot)$. In such a case the costs are minimized and are equal to zero when $\alpha^* = \alpha^p = f(\frac{1}{2})$, that is, when the scoring rule is the plurality rule.

By part (ii) of the theorem, in a typical voting context where n is sufficiently large, the inverse plurality rule is the golden voting rule if majority tyranny is considered even as a slight problem (β is positive). This result is due to the existence of a very large gap between $C^1(\cdot)$ and $C^2(\cdot)$ when n is large. In such a case, even a very small β, the weight assigned to $C^1(\cdot)$, is sufficient to make $\beta \cdot C^1(\alpha^+)$ the dominant term in (6). The minimization of the weighted sum in (6) therefore requires the minimization of $\beta \cdot C^1(\alpha^+)$, and, in turn, of $C^1(\cdot)$, which is attained by α^{ip}. In other words, the inverse plurality rule is the golden rule.

By part (i) of the theorem, when the number of alternatives exceeds the number of voters, the inverse plurality rule is the golden rule whenever the weight assigned to the cost of majority tyranny is equal to or larger than the weight assigned to the cost of the erosion in the majority principle. The intuition behind this result is the following. In such a case, even a majority of $n - 1$ voters cannot guarantee the selection of its most favored alternative, because there exists at least one alternative the score of which is equal to the score of the majority's preferred alternative, or to that score minus one. The single-voter minority can thus assign zero points to this alternative, which prevents the possibility of it being the unique selection. Obviously, under the inverse plurality rule then, when $k \geq n$, the cost of majority tyranny is minimal. Since for given n and k, $C^1(\cdot) > C^2(\cdot)$, $\frac{1}{2} \leq \beta \leq 1$ implies that the sum of the weighted costs is minimal.

8.7 APPENDIX
The decisiveness of a certain majority group is realized when all its members prefer the same candidate. The probability that such a majority group of size i chooses, unanimously, the same candidate is $k\left(\frac{1}{k}\right)^i$. The probability that the corresponding minority group of size

$n - i$ chooses any other candidate than the one chosen by the majority is $\left(\frac{k-1}{k}\right)^{n-i}$. Since the scoring rule is anonymous, multiplying the product of the above probabilities by $\binom{n}{i}$ yields the probability that the decisiveness of some i-majority group is realized. Summing this term over all possible such i-majority groups yields

$$C^1(\alpha^+) = k \sum_{i=\alpha^+ n}^{n-1} \left(\frac{1}{k}\right)^i \cdot \left(\frac{k-1}{k}\right)^{n-i} \cdot \binom{n}{i} \tag{4}$$

Notice that when α^+ is equal to 1, the cost associated with majority tyranny is 0. In such a case no terms are summed up in (4).

Similarly, letting i denote the size of non-decisive majorities, i ranging from $\lfloor 0.5n + 1 \rfloor$ to $\alpha^+ n - 1$, $\left(\frac{1}{k}\right)^i$ and $\left(\frac{1}{k}\right)^{n-i}$ are, respectively, the probabilities that a majority of size i and a minority of size $n - i$ choose, unanimously, two different alternatives. The number of possible partitions of the voters to groups of size i and $n - i$ is $\binom{n}{i}$. The number of pairs of different alternatives unanimously chosen by the majority and minority groups is $\left(\frac{k!}{(k-2)!}\right)$. Hence the probability of erosion of the majority principle is

$$C^2(\alpha^+) = \sum_{i=\lfloor 0.5n+1 \rfloor}^{\alpha^+ n - 1} \left(\frac{1}{k}\right)^i \cdot \left(\frac{1}{k}\right)^{n-i} \cdot \binom{n}{i} \cdot \left(\frac{k!}{(k-2)!}\right) \tag{5}$$

Notice than when α^+ is equal to $\lfloor 0.5n + 1 \rfloor$, the cost associated with erosion in the majority status is 0. In such a case no terms are summed up in (5).

8.8 EXERCISES
The purpose of the following exercises is to clarify concepts and apply the three main results.

8.1 Scoring rules

Question 8.1
1. Does a scoring rule necessarily enable expression of preferences intensity?

2. In what sense does a scoring rule enable expression of preferences intensity?

3. In what sense does a scoring rule enable limited expression of preferences intensity?

Answer

1. No. The plurality rule and the inverse plurality rule are dichotomous rules that enable each individual to provide information on his most preferred or his least preferred alternative, but they do not enable any distinction between the remaining alternatives.

2. When the scoring rule is defined by different scores, the rule takes into account the ranking of all the alternatives. In this case the difference in the relative ranking of any two alternatives is represented by the difference in their scores. This difference can be used as an index of preference intensity of one alternative relative to the other. For example, when the scoring rule is the Borda rule, if the difference between the relative rankings of two alternatives is some constant, then the difference in the scores assigned to these alternatives is also a constant. In particular, the score difference between any two neighboring alternatives in a ranking is a constant equal to 1.

3. A scoring rule enables a limited expression of preferences intensity because the system of scores is arbitrary, imposed and uniform. The arbitrariness, imposition and uniformity are due to the fact that the scores system is not determined by the individuals and it does not allow variability in the preference intensity of one alternative in comparison to another alternative, as long as the alternatives are of equal relative ranking, but are ranked by different individuals.

8.2 Majority decisiveness

Question 8.2

Suppose that the social choice function is the Borda rule, $k = 5$, $n = 4$ and voting is sincere. Is a three-member majority coalition tyrannical (decisive)?

Answer

No. In this case $S_k - S_{k-1} = 1$ and $S_k - S_1 = 4$. Substituting these values in (1) we obtain that, for $k = 5$ and $n = 4$, the Borda rule is immune to α-majority tyranny if, and only if, $\alpha < (1 - \alpha)4$ or $\alpha < 0.8$. Therefore, in this case the Borda rule is immune to an 0.75-majority tyranny. That is, a three-member majority coalition is not decisive.

8.3 Resolution of the problem of majority tyranny under sincere voting

Answer the following four questions assuming that voting is sincere.

Question 8.3

Prove that a scoring rule is immune to majority tyranny if, and only if,

$$(n - 1)(S_k - S_{k-1}) < (S_k - S_1) \qquad (2)$$

Answer

The proof is directly obtained by substituting $\alpha = \frac{n-1}{n}$ in (1).

Question 8.4

Prove that the plurality rule is vulnerable to majority tyranny.

Answer

Under the plurality rule, $S_{k-1} = S_1 = 0$ and $S_k = 1$. Inequality (2) can therefore be written as: $n-1<1$. Independent of the values of n and k, this inequality is not satisfied. Hence, by Theorem 8.1, when the voting is sincere, the plurality rule is vulnerable to α-majority tyranny for any α, $1/2 < \alpha < 1$. In other words, the plurality rule is vulnerable to majority tyranny.

Question 8.5

Prove that the Borda rule is immune to majority tyranny if, and only if, $n < k$.

Answer

Under the Borda rule, $S_1 = 0$, $S_{k-1} = k - 2$ and $S_k = k - 1$. Inequality (2) directly yields the inequality: $n < k$.

Question 8.6

Prove that the Borda rule is immune to an α-majority tyranny if, and only if, $\alpha < \frac{k-1}{k}$.

Answer

Under the Borda rule, $S_1 = 0$, $S_{k-1} = k - 2$ and $S_k = k - 1$. By substituting these values in (1) we get the inequality: $\alpha < \frac{k-1}{k}$.

Question 8.7

Prove that the inverse plurality rule is immune to majority tyranny.

Answer

Under the inverse plurality rule, $S_1 = 0$ and $S_{k-1} = S_k = 1$. Substituting these values in (2) we get: $0 < 1$. That is, this inequality is satisfied independent of the values of n and k. This means that when the voting is sincere, the inverse plurality rule is immune to α-majority tyranny for any α, $1/2 < \alpha < 1$. In other words, the inverse plurality rule is immune to majority tyranny.

8.4 Resolution of the problem of majority tyranny under insincere voting

Question 8.8

Suppose that the preferences of three voters on the four alternatives a, b, c, d are presented in Table 8.3 below. In this case, if voting is sincere the chosen alternative by the Borda rule is alternative b (it receives the largest number of points – seven).

1. Is the Borda rule vulnerable to majority tyranny?
2. What coordinated voting strategy of voters 1 and 2 ensures that their most preferred alternative a is selected, independent of the vote of voter 3?

Table 8.3

Rank	Voter 1's Preferences	Voter 2's Preferences	Voter 3's Preferences	Borda's Rank
1st	a	a	b	b (7 points)
2nd	b	b	c	a (6 points)
3rd	c	c	d	c (4 points)
4th	d	d	a	d (1 point)

Answer

1. Yes. When $k = 4$ and the social choice function is the Borda rule, $S_1 = 0$, $S_2 = 1$, $S_3 = 2$, $S_4 = 3$. Therefore, $\alpha = 2/3 > \frac{3-0}{6-0-1} = \frac{3}{5} = \frac{S_k - S_1}{2S_k - S_1 - \bar{S}}$. That is, by Theorem 8.2, any majority coalition of two voters $(\alpha = 2/3)$ is decisive. In other words, the Borda rule is vulnerable to majority tyranny.

2. Voter 1 reports that his preferences are: $a \succ c \succ d \succ b$. Voter 2 reports that his preferences are: $a \succ b \succ d \succ c$. By this strategy, every alternative other than a receives an equal number of points (2 points) from voters 1 and 2. This coordinated voting strategy ensures that alternative a is selected, independent of the vote of voter 3 (verify).

Question 8.9

Prove that under insincere voting the plurality rule is vulnerable to majority tyranny.

Answer

In Question 8.4, we proved that the plurality rule is vulnerable to majority tyranny under sincere voting. Clearly, it is also vulnerable to majority tyranny under insincere coordinated voting. When the social choice function is the plurality rule, $S_k = 1$, $\bar{S} = 0$, $S_1 = 0$, and, therefore, inequality (3) is satisfied for every α, $1/2 < \alpha < 1$.

Question 8.10

Prove that under insincere voting the Borda rule is vulnerable to an α-majority tyranny, $\alpha = \dfrac{2k-2}{3k-2}$.

Answer

Under the Borda scoring rule, $S_1 = 0$, $S_k = k - 1$ and

$$\bar{S} = \frac{1}{k-1} \sum_{j=1}^{k-1} S_j = \frac{1}{k-1}(0 + 1 + \cdots + (k-2)) = \frac{1}{(k-1)} \frac{(k-2)(k-1)}{2}$$

Therefore, by Theorem 8.2, the Borda rule is vulnerable to an α-majority tyranny provided that

$$\alpha > \frac{S_k - S_1}{2S_k - S_1 - \bar{S}} = \frac{(k-1)}{2(k-1) - \frac{(k-2)(k-1)}{2(k-1)}} = \frac{2(k-1)}{4(k-1) - (k-2)} = \frac{2k-2}{3k-2},$$

Question 8.11

Suppose that the number of alternatives is even. Let the dichotomous scoring rule "Borda equivalent" be defined by the scores:. $\{S_1, S_2, \ldots, S_k\} = \{0, 0, \ldots, 0, 0, 1, 1, \ldots, 1, 1\}$.

1. In what sense is this rule dichotomous?
2. What is the advantage of the "Borda equivalent" rule relative to the Borda rule?
3. Are the two rules identical?
4. In what sense are the two scoring rules equivalent?

Answer

1. This rule is dichotomous because every alternative is assigned one point or no points. This means that by this scoring rule, according to every individual the alternatives are partitioned into two sets of equal size – the set of preferred alternatives (the relative ranking of these alternatives is smaller than or equal to k/2), and the remaining inferior alternatives (the relative ranking of these alternatives is larger than k/2).

2. Operatively, the "Borda equivalent" rule is simpler because each individual is required to reveal less information; under the Borda rule

Table 8.4

Voter 1	Voter 2	Voter 3
a	b	d
c	c	a
b	d	b
d	a	c

the required information is the complete ranking of the alternatives, whereas under the "Borda equivalent" rule the required information is only the k/2 (most) preferred alternatives.

3. No. Suppose that the preference profile of three voters on the four alternatives a, b, c, d is presented in Table 8.4.

By the Borda rule, the chosen alternatives are a and b, which receive five points (verify). By the "Borda equivalent" rule, the chosen alternatives are a and c, which receive two points (verify). This example is sufficient to prove that the two scoring rules are not identical.

4. The "Borda equivalent" rule, like the Borda rule, is vulnerable to α-majority tyranny, $\alpha = \frac{2k-2}{3k-2}$. Under the "Borda equivalent" rule, $S_1 = 0$, $S_k = 1$ and $\bar{S} = \frac{1}{(k-1)}\left(\frac{k}{2} - 1\right) = \frac{(k-2)}{2(k-1)}$. Hence, as under the Borda rule (see previous question), $\frac{S_k - S_1}{2S_k - S_1 - \bar{S}} = \frac{1}{2 - \frac{(k-2)}{2(k-1)}} = \frac{2(k-1)}{4(k-1) - (k-2)} = \frac{2k-2}{3k-2}$.

Question 8.12

Discuss the following claim: "It is reasonable to assume that majority tyranny is less severe in elections with a relatively large number of voters."

Answer

The assertion is plausible: Theorem 8.1 and Theorem 8.2 imply that majority tyranny is more severe when voting is insincere (coordinated). It is reasonable to assume that voting coordination is more unlikely in elections with a large number of voters. In such elections, therefore, majority tyranny is less severe.

Question 8.13

Prove that when $k \geq n$, even when voting is insincere, the inverse plurality rule is immune to majority tyranny.

Answer

Under the inverse plurality rule, $S_1 = 0$, $S_k = 1$ and $\bar{S} = \frac{k-2}{k-1}$. Therefore, by Theorem 8.2, the inverse plurality rule is vulnerable to α-*majority* tyranny provided that $\alpha > \frac{S_k - S_1}{2S_k - S_1 - \bar{S}} = \frac{1}{2 - \frac{k-2}{k-1}} = \frac{1}{\frac{2(k-1)-(k-2)}{(k-1)}} = \frac{k-1}{k}$. Since, by assumption, $k \geq n$, this inequality is not satisfied even when $\alpha = \frac{n-1}{n}$. This means that the inverse plurality rule is immune to majority tyranny.

Question 8.14

The unrestricted point voting scheme assigns to every voter an equal initial endowment of points. The rule enables unlimited flexibility in allocating points to the alternatives/candidates. Discuss the following claim: "The unrestricted point voting scheme is superior to any other (rigid) scoring rule because, in addition to providing protection against majority tyranny, it gives the voters an opportunity for maximal expression of preference intensity."

Answer

The assertion is incorrect, because the unrestricted point voting scheme does not provide protection against majority tyranny. Under this rule, a majority (any majority) coalition can secure the choice of an alternative preferred by the coalition by assigning all the endowed points to that alternative. The effectiveness of such point concentration guarantees decisiveness of even a simple-majority coalition. One can claim, therefore, that the unrestricted point voting scheme is equivalent to the plurality rule; they are both vulnerable to majority tyranny.

8.5 Erosion in the majority principle vs. majority tyranny

Question 8.15

Explain why the unrestricted point voting scheme and approval voting are:

1. Different rules.
2. Equivalent in terms of protection against majority tyranny.
3. Equivalent in terms of protection against erosion in the majority principle.

Answer

1. Approval voting is a flexible, dichotomous scoring rule. The unrestricted point voting scheme is more flexible but not dichotomous. The extra flexibility enabled by this latter rule may result in a chosen alternative that differs from the alternative chosen by approval voting, as illustrated by the following example. Table 8.5 presents the preferences of three voters on the three alternatives a, b and c and their point allocation under approval voting. According to this allocation the chosen alternative is a.

   Table 8.6 presents the point allocation of these voters under the unrestricted point voting scheme, assuming that every voter is assigned 10 points. According to this allocation the chosen alternative is b.

2. The two rules are vulnerable to majority tyranny, whether voting is sincere or insincere. Under the unrestricted point voting scheme, the voters in any majority coalition can secure the selection of a preferred alternative by assigning all the endowed points to that alternative. Under approval voting, the voters in any majority coalition can secure the selection of a preferred alternative by supporting only that alternative (in this situation the majority coalition actually applies the plurality rule).

3. Under sincere voting, the two rules enable erosion in the majority principle. Consider a preference profile where a is the best alternative and c is the worst alternative for $(n-1)$ individuals. Not only is c the least preferred alternative, but it is "considerably inferior" relative to all

Table 8.5

Voter 3		Voter 2		Voter 1	
c	1	a	1	a	1
b	0	b	0	b	1
a	0	c	0	c	0

Table 8.6

Voter 3		Voter 2		Voter 1	
c	5	a	5	a	5
b	3	b	4	b	4
a	2	c	1	c	1

other alternatives. Consequently, these voters assign an equal number of points to all the alternatives but a. The remaining voter prefers b "considerably" relative to the other alternatives and therefore he assigns points only to b. In such a case, even though a is the best alternative for $(n - 1)$ voters, the chosen alternative is b. The erosion in the majority principle is thus maximal; the most preferred alternative of a single voter is chosen both under the unrestricted point voting scheme and under approval voting.

Question 8.16

Rank the following three scoring rules: plurality rule, Borda rule and inverse plurality rule by their degree of immunity to majority tyranny.

Answer

By Theorems 8.1 and 8.2, the most immune rule to majority tyranny is the inverse plurality rule; next comes the Borda rule, and then the plurality rule. This order is valid both under sincere voting (see Conclusions 2, 3, 4 and 5 of Theorem 8.1) and insincere voting (see Conclusions 1, 2, and 3 of Theorem 8.2).

8.6 The Golden Scoring Rule

Question 8.17

Discuss the following claim: "The golden voting rule can be different from the plurality rule and the Borda rule. However, in any case the Borda rule is always preferred to the plurality rule."

Answer

Theorem 8.3 implies that the initial clause of the claim is true. The second clause is false. Given the weight β of the cost of majority tyranny, the comparison between the two rules is based on the comparison between the value of the objective function (see Problem (6)) corresponding to the minimal degree of decisiveness of the Borda rule, $\alpha^B = \frac{2k-2}{3k-2}$, and the value of the objective function corresponding to the minimal degree of decisiveness of the plurality rule, $\alpha^P = f(1/2)$. When the number of alternatives and the number of voters are relatively small and the weight β is sufficiently large, the plurality rule can be superior to the Borda rule (verify).

8.9 SUMMARY

- A group T is called a *decisive majority* if it can impose its will (ensure the selection of a candidate the group is interested in), regardless of the preferences of the minority or its voting strategy. This means that decisiveness does not require information on the preferences or on the actual votes of the individuals who do not belong to the group T.

- The existence of majority tyranny hinges on the rule applied by the voters. When the decisive majority group is T, $|T| = \alpha n$, we say that there exists an α-*majority decisiveness*, or that the voting rule is vulnerable to an α-majority tyranny, $1/2 < \alpha < 1$ (α is a fraction with a denominator equal to n).

- A resolution of the problem of majority tyranny requires that such decisiveness does not exist. That is, there exists no α-*majority* decisiveness, $1/2 < \alpha < 1$. The possibility of such resolution has been examined under the assumptions of sincere and insincere voting.

- **Theorem 8.1:** Under sincere voting, a scoring rule defined by $\{S_1, S_2, \ldots, S_k\}$ is immune to an α-majority tyranny, $\frac{1}{2} < \alpha < 1$, if and only if,

$$\alpha \left(S_k - S_{k-1}\right) < \left(1 - \alpha\right)\left(S_k - S_1\right)$$

- Under sincere voting, the following conclusions are obtained from Theorem 8.1:

  Conclusion 1. A scoring rule is immune to majority tyranny if, and only if,

  $$\left(n - 1\right)\left(S_k - S_{k-1}\right) < \left(S_k - S_1\right)$$

  Conclusion 2. The plurality rule is vulnerable to majority tyranny.
  Conclusion 3. The Borda rule is vulnerable to majority tyranny if, and only if, $n > k$.
  Conclusion 4. The Borda rule is immune to an α-majority tyranny if $\alpha < \frac{k-1}{k}$.
  Conclusion 5. The inverse plurality rule is immune to majority tyranny.

- **Theorem 8.2:** Let $\alpha n = m(k - 1)$ for some integer m. Under coordinated strategic voting, a scoring rule defined by $\{S_1, S_2, \ldots, S_k\}$ is immune to an α-majority tyranny, $\frac{1}{2} < \alpha < 1$, if

$$\alpha > \frac{S_k - S_1}{2S_k - S_1 - \bar{S}}, \quad \text{where } \bar{S} = \frac{1}{k-1}\sum_{j=1}^{k-1} S_j.$$

- Under insincere voting, the following conclusions are obtained from Theorem 8.2:

  Conclusion 1. The plurality rule is vulnerable to majority tyranny.
  Conclusion 2. The Borda rule is vulnerable to α-majority tyranny, $\alpha = \frac{2k-2}{3k-2}$. Hence, when the number of candidates is sufficiently large, the Borda rule is vulnerable to a 2/3-majority tyranny.

Conclusion 3. If $k \geq n$, then there always exists a scoring rule that is immune to majority tyranny. In particular, the inverse plurality rule is such an immune voting rule.

This means that when the number of candidates is larger than or equal to the number of voters, even when the majority-group members coordinate their actions and vote strategically, majority tyranny can be avoided by using the inverse plurality rule.

- The tyranny implied by majority decisiveness and the erosion in the majority status are two possible worrying aspects that are associated with the implementation of the majority principle by using scoring rules that are characterized by different degrees α^* of minimal majority decisiveness. When these two aspects are taken into account, the question is: Which scoring rule attains the golden compromise between effective implementation of the will of the majority and prevention of majority tyranny by allowing the minority to express the intensity of its preferences? The last part of the chapter provides the answer to this question. We identify the golden voting rule assuming:

1. All preference profiles are equally likely.
2. The first type of costs of majority decisiveness, $C^1(\alpha^+)$, corresponding to a scoring rule characterized by a minimal degree of decisiveness α^+, is measured by the proportion of preference profiles in which an α-majority tyranny, $\alpha \geq \alpha^+$, is realized.
3. The second type of costs of majority decisiveness, $C^2(\alpha^+)$, corresponding to a scoring rule characterized by a minimal degree of decisiveness α^+, is measured by the proportion of preference profiles in which the α-majority principle, $\alpha < \alpha^+$, is eroded.
4. The choice of the golden voting rule is based on the assumption that the weight assigned to the cost of majority tyranny is β and the weight assigned to the cost of erosion in the majority principle is $(1 - \beta)$.

- The golden voting rule is a scoring rule characterized by a minimal degree of decisiveness α^+ that minimizes the weighted cost of the two types of costs corresponding to α^+. In other words, the golden voting rule is characterized by a degree of decisiveness α^+ that solves the following problem:

$$\underset{\alpha^+}{Min}\ \beta \cdot C^1(\alpha^+) + (1 - \beta) \cdot C^2(\alpha^+)$$

- **Theorem 8.3**

  (i) When $n \le k$, the inverse plurality rule is the golden voting rule if $\frac{1}{2} \le \beta \le 1$.

  (ii) When $n > k$ and n is sufficiently large, the inverse plurality rule is the golden voting rule for every β, $\delta \le \beta \le 1$, $\delta \to 0$.

  (iii) Independent of n and k, if $\beta = 0$, the plurality rule is the golden voting rule.

9 The problem of inefficient provision of public goods

In earlier chapters, the social choice was conceived as mechanical: the social decision rule transforms individual choices into a social choice, assuming that individuals are naïve; their behavior conforms to their (true) preference relations, but is not based on strategic considerations. In such a case, the rule aggregating preferences does not necessarily satisfy the Pareto principle. That is, the social preference relation violates the unanimity property (see Theorem 4.1 and Theorem 4.2) or, alternately, the social decision rule does not satisfy the Pareto criterion, as demonstrated in Example 7.4 with respect to the sequential majority rule. In this chapter, we no longer ignore strategic considerations, that is, the possibility that individuals are aware of the relationship between their behavior and the social choice, and take into account the expected actions (voting, decisions) of the other individuals. The discussion will focus on the problem of inefficiency in the economic context of public-good provision. This problem is usually dealt with in public-economics discussions that attempt to justify government intervention on the basis of the market failure argument. We first clarify the fundamental reason for the inefficiency of the social decision rule and, in particular, the inefficiency of the simple majority rule, in the absence of strategic considerations. Allowing strategic behavior, we will then show that it is possible that all individuals choose their optimal strategy and yet the social choice is inefficient. In such a case, we say that a "social dilemma" exists. The use of the word "dilemma" is intended to convey the paradoxical sense that this possibility arouses. We will present this inefficiency problem of collective action, assuming that individuals behave strategically and that the social decision rule is a market-like decentralized rule, which is based on voluntary provision of the public good (every individual makes a decision on the quantity of the public good s/he wants to purchase or on whether s/he wants to take part in the provision of the public good).

9.1 THE COLLECTIVE DECISION RULE AND INEFFICIENT PROVISION OF A PUBLIC GOOD

In an economic/social context, collective decisions are often made on the provision and funding of public goods. Such goods are characterized by two basic features: first, once provided (produced), it is impossible to prevent their consumption, at least to some extent, by all members of society, the consumers. This characteristic is called "*non-excludability.*" Second, the provision of a certain quantity of a public good enables concurrent consumption, at least to some extent, by all consumers. In other words, in contrast to a private good, the consumption of a public good by one individual does not preclude its consumption (at least partial consumption) by any other individual. For this reason, this feature is called "*non-rivalry.*" Education services, health services, public parks, museums, transportation infrastructure, a lighthouse or national defense are examples of public goods. When the good is perfectly non-excludable and perfectly non-rival, it is called a *pure public good*. It is difficult to find examples of such goods. National defense is the common example of a pure public good.

The condition for efficient provision of a pure public good (henceforth, we assume that only two goods exist: a private good and a pure public good) is the equality between the marginal social cost of the public good in terms of the private good and the sum of the subjective marginal rates of substitution of all consumers between the two goods. When the collective decision regarding the quantity of the public good is made by resorting to standard collective decision rules, there is no reason to expect that this equality will be satisfied. The fundamental reason is that the preferences and, in turn, the decisions of every individual who takes part in the collective decision only partly depend on the funding of the provision of the public good and on the individual's marginal rate of substitution between the two goods. The social decision rule takes into account the individual decisions, but may take into consideration the decisions of some, not all, of the individuals. Even if the rule takes into account the decisions of all individuals, there is no reason to expect that its outcome, namely, the collective decision on the quantity of the public good, will satisfy the equality that is a necessary condition for efficiency. In other words, there is no reason to expect that the allocation of resources will be efficient, because individual decisions are based on individual incentives and not on the aggregate social interest, and because although the collective decision rule reflects the individual incentives, there is no guarantee that it can secure the required necessary condition for the attainment of an efficient social decision regarding the quantity of the provided public good. In fact, the social decision rule usually does not succeed in ensuring the existence of the necessary condition for efficiency. This assertion is clarified below, assuming that the social choice function is the simple majority rule, the Borda rule or the dictator rule.

9.2 VOTING

Denote by n the number of individual consumers and suppose that two goods exist: a pure public good and a private good. Let G denote the quantity of the public good and let x_i be the quantity of the private good consumed by individual i. Individual i's utility is denoted by $U^i(G, x_i)$ and his income is M_i (the quantity of the private good at his disposal), $i = 1, \ldots, n$. We assume that the marginal cost of the public good in terms of the private good is fixed and equal to 1 and that the burden of the funding of the public good is equally shared by all consumers. That is, from the point of view of every consumer, the unit cost of the public good is equal to $1/n$ and therefore his cost share when G units of the public good are provided is G/n. We also let the individual preferences satisfy the standard axioms of consumer theory and, in particular, the (strict) convexity axiom. Under these assumptions, every consumer has a unique optimal bundle of

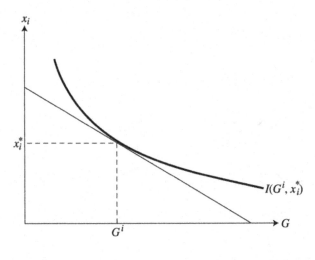

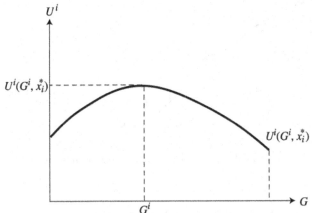

FIGURE 9.1 The optimal quantity of the public good for individual i

commodities. This means that every consumer has a unique, most preferred quantity of the public good. Let G^i denote the most preferred quantity of consumer i. The utility of consumer i from the bundle that includes the quantity G of the public good is therefore given by $U^i\left(G, M_i - \dfrac{G}{n}\right)$.

The budget constraint of a typical consumer i, his optimal bundle (G^i, x_i^*) and the indifference curve of this bundle, $I(G^i, x_i^*)$, are presented in the upper part of Figure 9.1. The lower part of the figure

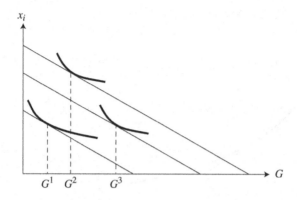

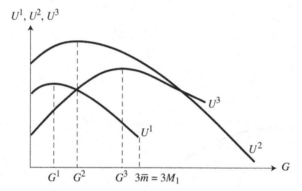

FIGURE 9.2 The optimal quantity of the public good for individuals 1, 2 and 3

presents the consumer's utility corresponding to different quantities of the public good, assuming that his bundle satisfies the budget constraint: $x_i + \dfrac{G}{n} = M_i$. The strict convexity of the consumer's preference relation implies that the curve depicting his utility is single-peaked (verify).

The upper part of Figure 9.2 presents the budget lines, optimal bundles and indifference curves of three consumers. The lower part of the figure shows the corresponding three single-peaked utilities of these consumers. Suppose now that the social choice rule determines the provided quantity of the public good. The set of alternatives in this case is thus one-dimensional. In addition, assume that the provided quantity of the public good is feasible for all consumers. That is, every consumer is able to cover his cost share of the public-good provision. This means that for every consumer i, the following inequalities hold: $0 \leq \frac{G}{n} \leq M_i$. In other words, the set of alternatives X is $X = \{G : 0 \leq \frac{G}{n} \leq \overline{m} = \min(M_1, M_2, \ldots, M_n)\}$. This set is thus represented by the interval $[0, n\overline{m}]$ on the horizontal axis in Figure 9.2. Given the consumers' preferences, the choice rule determines a particular quantity G of the public good that is feasible for every consumer.

9.2.1 The simple majority rule

Let us examine the chosen quantity of the public good when the collective decision is made by applying the simple majority rule; the chosen quantity is the Condorcet winner, namely, the quantity that defeats any other alternative by a simple majority (see Chapter 7). When there are three consumers whose preferences are depicted in Figure 9.2, the quantity G^2 is the collective choice (verify). In general, by the median voter theorem, since the voters' preferences are single-peaked, the chosen alternative is the median of the distribution of the most preferred quantities of voters $G^1, G^2, \ldots, G^n$. With no loss of generality, suppose that $G^1 \leq G^2 \leq \ldots \leq G^n$. If n is odd, the median of this distribution is the quantity $G^m = G^{\frac{n+1}{2}}$ and this quantity is a Condorcet winner. Consumer m is referred to as the median voter (the definition of the single-peakedness property and the median-voter theorem are presented in Appendix 9.1). The question we are concerned with is whether G^m is efficient. In other words, is the allocation of resources $((G^m, M_1 - \frac{G^m}{n}), (G^m, M_2 - \frac{G^m}{n}), \ldots, (G^m, M_n - \frac{G^m}{n}))$ efficient?

Since G^m is the optimal quantity for the median voter, individual m, and since we assume that $G^m < nM_m$, the necessary condition for optimality is satisfied, namely, the subjective marginal rate of substitution of individual m between the public and the private goods is equal to the ratio of their prices.

$$MRS_m \left(G^m, M_m - \frac{G^m}{n} \right) = \frac{1}{n} \qquad (1)$$

In contrast, the necessary condition for an efficient quantity of the public good G^e, $G^e < n\overline{m}$ ($\overline{m} = \min\{M_1, M_2, \ldots, M\}$), is the equality between the sum of subjective marginal rates of substitution of all individuals and the rate of product transformation between the public and the private goods:

$$\sum_{i=1}^{n} MRS_i \left(G^e, M_i - \frac{G^e}{n} \right) = 1 \qquad (2)$$

The condition that characterizes the efficient quantity of the public good is different from the condition that characterizes the optimal quantity of the public good for the median voter. In general, therefore, $G^m \neq G^e$. That is, one cannot expect that the quantity chosen by the simple majority rule will be efficient. In addition, one cannot assume that the chosen quantity is larger or smaller than the efficient quantity. The quantity chosen by the simple majority rule (the most preferred quantity according to the median voter) is characterized by equality (1) that determines G^m and by the property that half of the voters prefer (in the weak sense) a larger quantity and half of the voters prefer a smaller quantity. The condition that characterizes voting equilibrium under simple majority disregards questions like "by how much are the quantities preferred by the other voters (other than the median voter) larger or smaller than G^m?" or "to what extent do these voters prefer quantities that differ from G^m?". The disregard of this information, information that is taken into account in equality (2) that characterizes G^e, explains the difference between G^e and G^m. Note that conditions (1) and (2) are satisfied at the same quantity of the public good if

$$MRS_m \left(G^m, M_m - \frac{G^m}{n} \right) = \left(\sum_{i=1}^{n} MRS_i \left(G^m, M_i - \frac{G^m}{n} \right) \right) \Big/ n$$

Hence, if the subjective marginal rate of substitution of the median voter at his optimal bundle is equal to the average subjective marginal rate of substitution of the consumers/voters, then the quantity of the public good chosen by the simple majority rule is efficient, $G^e = G^m$.

Example 9.1

Let us examine the relationship between the efficient quantity of the public good and the quantity obtained in the voting equilibrium under the simple majority rule, assuming that the utility function of individual i is quasi-linear:

$$U^i(G, x_i) = b_i \ln G + x_i$$

By condition (1), the voting equilibrium quantity under the simple majority rule, G^m, must satisfy the equality:

$$\frac{b_m}{G^m} = \frac{1}{n}$$

where b_m is a parameter that characterizes the preferences of the median voter m.

Therefore,

$$G^m = nb_m$$

By condition (2), the efficient quantity of the public good, G^e, must satisfy the equation:

$$\frac{\sum_{i=1}^{n} b_i}{G^e} = 1$$

Therefore,

$$G^e = \sum_{i=1}^{n} b_i$$

We have thus obtained that

$$G^e > G^m \Leftrightarrow \frac{\sum_{i=1}^{n} b_i}{n} > b_m$$

That is, the efficient quantity of the public good is larger than the voting equilibrium quantity under the simple majority rule if the average value of the parameters b_i is larger than the parameter b_m that characterizes the preferences of the median voter m. ∎

9.2.2 The dictatorial rule

When the collective choice is determined by a dictatorial rule, that is, the collective decision is made by a certain individual d, the chosen quantity is usually different from the efficient one. The reason is similar to that clarified in the preceding section; the condition that characterizes the optimal bundle of the dictator is different from the necessary condition for an efficient quantity of the public good.

9.2.3 The Borda rule

Suppose that the set of alternatives includes the optimal quantities of the voters, that is, $X = \{G^1, G^2, \ldots, G^n\}$. The quantity chosen by the Borda rule, G^B, takes into account the relative ranking of all the alternatives by all voters (see Chapter 4 and Chapter 5). Recall that the alternative chosen by the Borda rule has the highest average ranking of all the individuals. This feature differs from the condition that characterizes an efficient quantity of the public good, (2), and therefore there is no reason to expect that $G^B = G^e$.

9.2.4 The unanimity rule

Suppose that the collective choice is determined by the unanimity rule; the chosen quantity is supported by all voters. This means that the chosen quantity is optimal from the viewpoint of every individual. Obviously, such a quantity is a Condorcet winner and, in fact, it defeats any alternative quantity by any majority. The obvious problem in using the unanimity rule is that such a quantity usually does not exist in an economy where prices of goods are fixed and individuals differ in tastes or income. In particular, such a unanimously supported quantity does not exist when the individuals differ and the price of the public good is equal to $1/n$, as we have assumed. In contrast, such an optimal quantity does exist when the individuals differ and there are differential prices of the public good. If these differential prices are Lindahl (1919) prices or taxes, then not only does a quantity exist that is chosen unanimously, but this quantity is efficient. The attainment of efficiency by Lindahl prices is based on the principle that each individual i pays a price p_i that is equal to his subjective marginal rate of substitution, MRS_i, in the efficient quantity of the public good, G^*, and the corresponding quantity of the private good $M_i - p_i G^*$. That is, $(p_i = MRS_i(G^*, M_i - p_i G^*)$. Lindahl prices thus guarantee unanimity with respect to the desirable quantity of the public good G^*.

9.3 VOLUNTARY PROVISION OF THE PUBLIC GOOD

Suppose that the collective choice on the provided quantity of the public good is made in a market-like decentralized way; every individual i makes a voluntary decision on his bundle (g_i, x_i), given his income M_i, the prices of the public and the private goods p_G and p_X, and his utility function $U^i(G, x_i)$. Notice that individual i decides to purchase the quantity g_i of the public good; however, the actual quantity that he consumes, the aggregate quantity voluntarily provided by all the consumers, hinges on the quantities chosen by other individuals, since, by assumption, the public good is a pure public good, $G = \sum_{i=1}^{n} g_i$. For simplicity, let us suppose that the equilibrium prices are $p_G = p_X = 1$ and that the individuals' utility functions are quasi-linear, that is, $U^i(G, x_i) = f_i(G) + x_i$, where $f'(G) > 0$ and $f''(G) < 0$. Given the (competitive) equilibrium prices of the two goods, individual i chooses the optimal quantity g_i^*. This quantity is the solution of the problem:

$$\underset{g_i \geq 0}{Max} \ f_i\left(g_i + \sum_{k \neq i} g_k^*\right) + (M_i - g_i). \tag{3}$$

By definition, $(g_1^*, \ldots, g_n^*)$ is a Nash equilibrium in a game where the players are the n consumers, the strategy set of consumer i is the set $S_i = \{g_i : 0 \leq g_i \leq M_i\}$, and the payoff function of consumer i is

$$U^i(g_1, \ldots, g_n) = \ f_i\left(g_i + \sum_{k \neq i} g_k^*\right) + (M_i - g_i).$$

g_i^* must therefore satisfy the necessary and sufficient condition for a solution of the above problem (the Kuhn–Tucker conditions for a solution of the consumer's problem):

$$f_i'\left(g_i^* + \sum_{k \neq i} g_k^*\right) \leq 1 \tag{4}$$

and

$$g_i^* > 0 \Rightarrow \left(f_i'\left(g_i^* + \sum_{k \neq i} g_k^*\right) = 1\right) \tag{5}$$

In a Nash equilibrium $(g_1^*, \ldots, g_n^*)$ then, for every individual i,

$$f_i'(G^*) \leq 1 \tag{6}$$

and

$$g_i^* > 0 \Rightarrow f_i'(G^*) = 1 \tag{7}$$

Therefore, when $n > 1$ and $G^e > 0$,

$$\sum_{i=1}^{n} MRS_i(G^*, M_i - g_i^*) = \sum_{i=1}^{n} f_i'(G^*) > 1 \tag{8}$$

This means that the necessary condition for an efficient provision of the public good is not satisfied (see equation (2), Furthermore, the public good is under-provided, that is, $G^* < G^e$.

In Figure 9.3 the efficient quantity of the public good G^e is obtained at the intersection between the curve describing the (vertical) sum of the individuals' subjective marginal rates of substitution with the horizontal line that indicates the price of the public good (by assumption, the marginal cost of providing the public good is fixed and equal to 1). The equilibrium quantity of the public good G^e is obtained at a point where the sum of the marginal rates of substitution is larger than the marginal cost of the public good. The problem of inefficiency of the public good is often called the "free-rider problem"; every individual has an insufficient incentive to purchase the

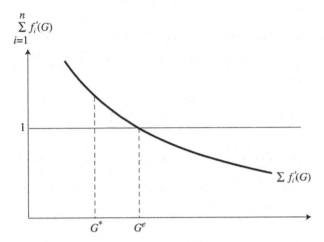

FIGURE 9.3 The efficient and equilibrium quantities of the public good

public good because he enjoys the aggregate quantities of the public good purchased by the other individuals.

We have presented the problem of inefficient voluntary provision of a public good under simple assumptions on the number of private goods, the prices of the goods, the strategies of the individuals and their utility functions, disregarding the technology (production function) of the public good. In the public-economics literature, the problem of inefficient voluntary provision of a public good is analyzed using different alternative models. See for example, the books by Cornes and Sandler (1986) and Olson (1965) or the papers by Bergstrom, Blume and Varian (1986), Chamberlin (1974) and Gradstein and Nitzan (1990). In the exercises, there are questions that clarify why the inefficiency problem is also relevant when individual utility functions are not quasi-linear or when the strategy set of every individual is binary (the individual decides whether or not to take part in the provision of the public good). There are also questions that clarify why the free-rider problem is more severe when the marginal utilities of individuals differ, the price of the public good rises, the number of consumers increases, or when the relative significance of the private good in the utility functions of the individuals is increased.

9.4 APPENDIX

By assumption, the set of alternatives is one-dimensional and the most preferred quantity of the public good for individual i is G^i, that is,

$$G^i = \arg\max v^i(G : n, M_i) = U^i\left(G, M_i - \frac{G}{n}\right)$$

The preferences of individual i with respect to the public good are single-peaked if:

$$\left(G'' \geq G' \geq G^i \text{ or } G'' \leq G' \leq G^i\right) \Rightarrow v(G'') \leq v(G')$$

The median voter theorem: If the individuals' preferences with respect to the public good are single-peaked, then there exists a quantity of the public good that is a Condorcet winner. This quantity is G^m, the most preferred quantity for the median voter.

Proof: Suppose that the quantity G^m is compared with an alternative quantity G'' where $G'' < G^m$. Since individuals' preferences are single-peaked, by definition, every individual i whose most preferred quantity, G^i, satisfies the inequality $G^m \leq G^i$, prefers G^m to G'' and therefore votes for G^m. This means, since G^m is the median of the distribution of the most preferred quantities of the individuals, that a majority votes for G^m. Similarly, a majority votes for G^m when $G'' > G^m$. The quantity G^m therefore defeats any alternative quantity by a simple majority. That is, G^m is a Condorcet winner.   **Q.E.D.**

9.5 EXERCISES

In this chapter, we dealt briefly with the topic of public goods. The student can find a more complete treatment of the subject in a standard course on public economics.

The paper by Gradstein and Nitzan (1990) comprehensively examines the issue of binary voluntary provision of a public good; every individual makes a decision on whether or not to take part in the provision of the public good. Question 8 is based on the model presented in this paper.

9.1 The collective decision rule and inefficient provision of a public good

Question 9.1

1. What is an impure public good?
2. "A fishing lake is not a pure public good, but it is an extreme one." Discuss.
3. "An internet service is not a pure public good, but it is an extreme one." Discuss.
4. Explain why it is difficult to find an example of a pure public good.

Answer

1. An impure public good is characterized by a certain (incomplete) degree of non-excludability and by some (incomplete) degree of non-rivalry.
2. Entry to the fishing lake may not be restricted, that is, this good can be characterized by an extreme degree of non-excludability. Nevertheless, it is not characterized by the second property of non-rivalry. A fishing lake is therefore an extreme public good in terms of the first property. Such a good is called a "commons good."
3. The use of the internet service by some consumer does not lessen the ability of any other consumer to use it. That is, an internet service is characterized by an extreme degree of non-rivalry. However, it is not characterized by the second property of non-excludability. The internet service is therefore an extreme public good in terms of the second property. Such a good is called a "club good."
4. It is difficult to find an example of a pure public good because almost every good is characterized by some degree of excludability and some degree of rivalry. This is true even when the good is national defense, the standard example of a pure public good. The reason is that usually the government can restrict the population in the nation (e.g., through

migration laws) and the quality and quantity of national defense are affected by the population size: the number of consumers.

9.2 Voting

Question 9.2

Suppose that the provided quantity of the public good is determined by the simple majority rule: the chosen quantity defeats any alternative feasible quantity by a simple majority. Suppose that there is a single public good that is financed by imposing an equal tax on the consumption of the public good.

1. "The simple majority rule is not a social choice function." Discuss.
2. "The median voter is a dictator." Discuss.
3. "The collective decision is inefficient: The provided quantity of the public good is necessarily lower than the efficient quantity." Discuss.
4. "The income distribution of the voting population has no effect on the provided quantity of the public good." Discuss.
5. "The provided quantity of the public good is independent of the funding form of the public good." Discuss.

Answer

1. True. The reason is that a Condorcet winning quantity (a quantity that beats any alternative feasible quantity by a simple majority) does not necessarily exist, see Chapter 7.1.

2. False. Since the special decisive status of the median voter depends on his preferences as well as on the preferences of the other voters, he is not a dictator. Put differently, the identity of the median voter is not fixed; it is determined by the characteristics of the income distribution and the nature of the preferences of all voters.

3. Usually the collective decision is indeed inefficient. But the provided quantity of the public good is not necessarily smaller than the efficient quantity. If the following inequality is satisfied:

$$MRS_m\left(G^m, M_m - \frac{G^m}{n}\right) > \left(\sum_{i=1}^{n} MRS_i\left(G^m, M_i - \frac{G^m}{n}\right)\right) \bigg/ n$$

where G^m is the chosen quantity, the optimal quantity from the median voter's point of view, then the chosen quantity under the simple majority rule G^m is larger than the efficient quantity G^* (verify).

4. False. The income distribution affects the identity of the median voter and, in turn, the decision on the provided quantity of the public good.

5. False. The form of the funding of the public good, that is, the taxes imposed on the voters, affect the identity of the median voter and, in turn, the chosen quantity of the public good.

Question 9.3

"The quantity of the public good can be determined by voting based on the unanimity rule. This rule can ensure the selection of an efficient quantity of the public good. Furthermore, an efficient quantity can be reached only by using the unanimity rule." Discuss the two parts of the claim.

Answer

The first part of the claim is true. The unanimity rule can ensure the selection of an efficient quantity of the public good. In particular, the Lindahl (1919) mechanism, which is based on the attainment of unanimous agreement regarding the preferred quantity, can ensure efficiency. Specifically, this mechanism is based on a differential price system where every individual pays a price p_i which is equal to his subjective marginal rate of substitution MRS_i at the efficient quantity G^* of the public good and the corresponding quantity of the private good $M_i - p_i G^*$. That is, $p_i = MRS_i (G^*, M_i - p_i G^*)$. Such a system of Lindahl prices or taxes ensures unanimity with respect to the preferred quantity of the public good. This preferred quantity is G^*.

The second part of the claim is false. An efficient quantity of the public good does not require the unanimity rule. In particular, an efficient quantity can be chosen by alternative rules, such as the simple majority rule, as we have seen in section 9.2.1.

Question 9.4

Suppose that the choice of the provided quantity of a public good is based on the simple majority rule: the chosen quantity defeats any alternative feasible quantity by a simple majority. Suppose that there is a single public good that is financed by imposing an equal tax on the consumption of the public good. Discuss the following assertion: "Under these assumptions, the chosen quantity of the public good is unaltered when the consumers act strategically; their voting is not necessarily naïve (directly consistent with their sincere preferences)."

Answer

The assertion is correct because, under the above assumptions, every voter has an incentive to vote according to his true preferences. Hence, the chosen quantity of the public good is unaltered when the consumers are allowed to act strategically.

Question 9.5

Suppose that there are two goods; a private good X and a public good G, and that the prices of these goods, p_G and p_X, are equal to 1. Suppose that the choice of the provided quantity of the public good is based on the simple majority rule: the chosen quantity defeats any alternative feasible quantity by a simple majority, and that the funding of the public good is based on a proportional income tax. The imposition of such a tax implies that the ratio between the tax paid by an individual and his income is equal to t. The tax rate t is uniform and the budget of the government is balanced. That is, $t \cdot M_1 + t \cdot M_2 + \ldots + t \cdot M_n = p_G \cdot G$, where M_i, $i = 1, 2, \ldots, n$, is the income of individual i. Finally, assume that individuals share identical tastes, the public good is neutral and the income distribution is asymmetric, such that there are few individuals whose income is larger than the average income and many individuals whose income is smaller than the average income. Prove that under these assumptions, the provided quantity of the public good is larger than the efficient quantity.

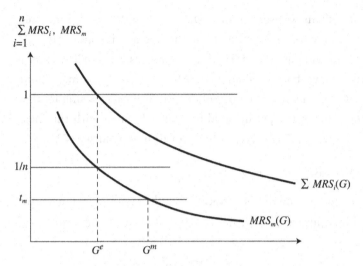

FIGURE 9.4 Diagrammatic exposition of the answer of Question 9.5 (over-provision of the public good)

Answer

Since the public good is financed by a proportional income tax,

$$tn\bar{M} = G$$

where $\bar{M}$ is the average income (the total income is equal to $n\bar{M}$). Hence,

$$t = \frac{G}{n\bar{M}}$$

When the provided quantity of the public good is G, the total tax paid by individual i is therefore equal to T_i,

$$\frac{GM_i}{n\bar{M}} = T_i$$

Therefore, from the point of view of individual i, the price of one unit of the provided quantity of the public good is equal to

$$t_i = \frac{\mathrm{d}T_i}{\mathrm{d}G} = \frac{M_i}{\bar{M}}\frac{1}{n}$$

Due to the assumed asymmetry of the income distribution (there are few individuals whose income is larger than the average income and many individuals whose income is smaller than the average income), the median income is smaller than the average income, $M_m < \bar{M}$. Since the individuals share identical preferences, the median voter is the individual with the median income (verify). Hence, from the point of view of individual m, the price of the public good t_m is smaller than $1/n$ – the price of the public good for the individual with the mean income $\bar{M}$ (verify). Therefore, in the equilibrium quantity G^m,

$$MRS_m(G^m, M_m - t_m G^m) = t_m < \frac{1}{n}$$

By this inequality and the assumption that the public good is a neutral good (which implies that $n\, MRS_m = \sum_{i=1}^{n} MRS_i$) we obtain that

$$n\, MRS_m(G^m, M_m - t_m G^m) = \sum_{i=1}^{n} MRS_i(G^m, M_i - t_m G^m) < 1$$

By the convexity of the individual preference relation, the function $\sum_{i=1}^{n} MRS_i(G^m, M_i - t_m G^m)$ is monotone-decreasing in G^m and therefore the equality that characterizes the efficient quantity of the public good

$$\sum_{i=1}^{n} MRS_i(G^e, M_i - t_i G^e) = 1$$

is satisfied in a quantity that is smaller than G^m. We have thus proved that $G^m > G^e$, that is, the public good is over-provided.

9.3 Voluntary (private) provision of a public good

Question 9.6

Using the model presented in section 9.3 of voluntary private provision of the public good, prove that if $n > 1$ and $G^e > 0$, then the public good is under-provided, that is, $G^* < G^e$.

Answer

In a Nash equilibrium $(g_1^*, \ldots, g_n^*)$, for every individual i,

$$f_i'(G^*) \leq 1 \tag{6}$$

and

$$g_i^* > 0 \Rightarrow f_i'(G^*) = 1 \tag{7}$$

Let us distinguish between two possibilities:

Possibility 1: $G^* = 0$. In this case, clearly, $G^* < G^e$.

Possibility 2: $G^* > 0$. In this case, since by assumption, $n > 1$ and $f'(G) > 0$, we obtain that $\sum\limits_{i=1}^{n} f_i'(G^*) > 1$. Since by assumption, $f''(G) < 0$, the function $\sum\limits_{i=1}^{n} f_i'(G)$ is monotone-decreasing in G. Therefore, the solution of the equation $\sum\limits_{i=1}^{n} f_i'(G^e) = 1$, which is the necessary condition for efficiency, must be obtained in a quantity that is larger than G^*. That is, $G^* < G^e$.

Question 9.7

"Within the model presented in section 9.3 of voluntary provision of the public good, if there is heterogeneity in the marginal utilities of individuals from the public good, such that for any quantity $G \geq 0$, $f_1' < f_2' < \ldots < f_n'$, and if, in equilibrium, $G^* > 0$, then the free-rider problem is particularly severe; one individual provides the public good and all the remaining individuals free ride on him." Discuss.

Answer

The claim is true. If for any quantity $G \geq 0$, $f_1' < f_2' < \ldots < f_n'$, then the condition that characterizes Nash equilibrium $(g_1^*, \ldots, g_n^*)$:

$$f_i'(G^*) \leq 1 \tag{6}$$

and

$$g_i^* > 0 \Rightarrow f_i'(G^*) = 1 \tag{7}$$

can be satisfied only in the following way:
Condition (7) is satisfied for individual $i = n$: for any individual i, $i \neq n$, $g_i^* = 0$, and condition (6) is satisfied as a strict inequality, $f_i'(G^*) < 1$. This implies that only one individual, the individual with

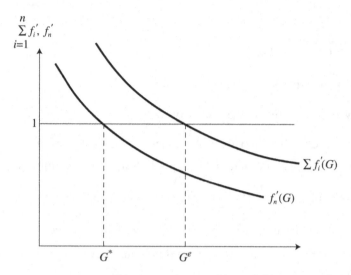

FIGURE 9.5 Diagrammatic exposition of the answer of Question 9.7 (under-provision of the public good)

the largest marginal utility from the public good, provides the public good and all the remaining individuals are free riders. In Figure 9.5, the efficient quantity of the public good, G^e, is obtained at the intersection between the curve that presents the sum of the individual subjective marginal rates of substitution and the horizontal line that represents the price of the public good (the marginal cost of providing the public good is fixed and equal to 1). The equilibrium quantity of the public good, G^*, is obtained at the intersection between the curve that describes the subjective marginal rate of substitution of individual n and the horizontal line that represents the price of the public good.

Question 9.8

Two individuals $(n = 2)$ can voluntarily take part in the provision of a public good.

The production function of the public good is:

$$f(m) = \begin{cases} 0 & m = 0 \\ \delta & m = 1 \\ 1 & m = 2 \end{cases}$$

where m is the number of individuals who take part in the provision of the public good, $m \leq 2$. Suppose that the individual cost of participation is c, $0 < c < 1$. The production function satisfies the "law of diminishing marginal productivity" and therefore $0.5 < \delta < 1$. The utility function of individual i, $i = 1,2$, is:

$$h_i(s_1, s_2) = \begin{cases} f(m) - c & s_i = 1 \\ f(m) & s_i = 0 \end{cases}$$

$s_i = 1$ means that individual i decides to participate in the provision of the public good. $s_i = 0$ means that individual i decides "not to participate." Notice that $m = s_1 + s_2$.

1. Construct the payoff matrix of the game.
2. What is the pure strategy Nash equilibrium?
3. What is an efficient outcome in this game?
4. Is the Nash equilibrium necessarily efficient?
5. Prove that the Nash equilibrium is efficient, if the cost of participation c is smaller than the marginal product of the first participant, δ.

Answer

The payoff matrix of the game is:

$$s_2 =$$

	1	0
$s_1 = $ 1	$(1 - c), (1 - c)$	$(\delta - c), \delta$
0	$\delta, (\delta - c)$	$\delta, (\delta - c)$

2. There are three possibilities:

Possibility 1: $(1 - c) \geq \delta > (\delta - c) > 0$.
In this case, there is a unique Nash equilibrium, $(s_1^*, s_2^*) = (1, 1)$. This equilibrium is also a dominant-strategy equilibrium and the equilibrium outcome is $((1 - c), (1 - c))$.

Possibility 2: $\delta \geq (1 - c) > 0 > (\delta - c)$.

In this case, there is a unique Nash equilibrium, $(s_1^*, s_2^*) = (0, 0)$. This equilibrium is also a dominant-strategy equilibrium and the equilibrium outcome is $(0, 0)$. This case gives rise to a "prisoner dilemma."

Possibility 3: $\delta \geq (1 - c) > (\delta - c) > 0$.
In this case, there are two Nash equilibria: $(s_1^*, s_2^*) = (1, 0)$ and $(s_1^*, s_2^*) = (0, 1)$. The corresponding equilibrium outcomes are $(\delta, \delta - c)$ and $(\delta - c, \delta)$.

3. An outcome (x, y) is efficient if no alternative outcome (x', y') exists, such that $x' \geq x$, $y' \geq y$ and at least one of these inequalities is a strict inequality.
4. No. In the case of possibility 2, the Nash equilibrium outcome is inefficient.
5. $c < \delta$ is consistent with possibility 1 and possibility 3. In both cases, the Nash equilibrium outcome is efficient (verify).

Question 9.9

Suppose that there are two goods: a private good X and a pure public good G, and that the prices of these goods, p_G and p_X, are equal to 1. The n consumers are identical in their preferences and in their income M. The utility function that represents the preferences of individual i is $U^i(G, x_i) = G^\beta x_i^\alpha$, where $0 < \alpha, \beta < 1$.

1. What is the quantity of the public good, G^*, in the Nash equilibrium $(g_1^*, \ldots, g_n^*)$ of the game where individuals voluntarily determine their purchase of the public good?
2. What is the efficient quantity G^e of the public good?
3. What is the free-riding problem or the prisoner dilemma in this case?
4. Let the severity of the free-riding problem be represented by the ratio between G^e and G^*. Prove that the severity of the free-riding problem is positively related to the number of consumers n.
5. Prove that the severity of the free-riding problem is positively related to α/β.

Answer

1. In a Nash equilibrium, every individual chooses g_i^* that solves the following problem:

$$\underset{g_i \geq 0}{Max}\, U^i\left(g_i + \sum_{k \neq i} g_k^*\right),\ M - g_i) = \left(g_i + \sum_{k \neq i} g_k\right)^\beta (M - g_i)^\alpha$$

$g_i^*, g_i^* > 0$, satisfies the first-order condition:

$$\beta G^{*\beta - 1}(M - g_i^*)^\alpha - \alpha(G^*)^\beta(M - g_i^*)^{\alpha - 1} = 0$$

or,

$$\beta(ng_i^*)^{\beta - 1}(M - g_i^*)^\alpha - \alpha(ng_i^*)^\beta(M - g_i^*)^{\alpha - 1} = 0$$

which gives:

$$g_i^* = -\frac{\alpha}{\alpha + \beta}(n - 1)g_i^* + \frac{\beta}{\alpha + \beta}M$$

Hence,

$$g_i^* = \frac{\beta}{n\alpha + \beta}\,M$$

In equilibrium, the provided quantity of the public good is therefore equal to:

$$G^* = ng_i^* = \frac{n\beta}{n\alpha + \beta}\,M$$

2. In the efficient quantity of the public good, the following equality is satisfied:

$$\sum_{i=1}^n MRS_i\left(G, M - \frac{G}{n}\right) = 1$$

That is,

$$n\frac{\beta(M - g_i)^\alpha G^{\beta - 1}}{\alpha(M - g_i)^{\alpha - 1}G^\beta} = 1$$

Therefore,

$$g_i = \frac{\beta}{\alpha + \beta}M$$

and

$$G^e = \frac{n\beta}{\alpha + \beta} M$$

3. The free-riding problem takes the following form:

$$G^e = \frac{n\beta}{\alpha + \beta} M > G^* = \frac{n\beta}{n\alpha + \beta} M$$

4. $\dfrac{G^e}{G^*} = \dfrac{n\alpha + \beta}{\alpha + \beta}$. This ratio is monotone-increasing in n, that is, the severity of the free-riding problem is positively related to the number of consumers n.

5. It can be easily verified that $\dfrac{G^e}{G^*} = \dfrac{n\alpha + \beta}{\alpha + \beta}$ is monotone-increasing in α/β. That is, the severity of the free-riding problem is positively related to α/β.

Question 9.10

Mention some possible reasons for the increased severity of the free-riding problem.

Answer

1. The existence of variability in the marginal utilities of the consumers from the public good: see Question 9.7.
2. An increased cost of participation in the provision of the public good: see Question 9.8, part 5.
3. An increase in the number of individuals: see Question 9.9, part 4.
4. An increase in the relative significance of the private good in the utility functions of the individuals: see Question 9.9, part 5.

Question 9.11

Suppose that there are two goods: a private good X and a pure public good G, and that the prices of these goods are equal to 1. The n consumers share the same preferences; however, they can differ in their income, M_i. The utility function that represents the preferences of individual i is $U^i(G, x_i) = x_i G + x_i$.

1. Suppose that two individuals $(n = 2)$ who differ in their income, $M_1 = 8$ and $M_2 = 10$, make a voluntary decision on the amount they purchase

from the public good. What is the quantity of the public good G^* in a Nash equilibrium (g_1^*, g_2^*) where $g_1^* > 0$ and $g_2^* > 0$? Is this equilibrium efficient?

2. Suppose that n individuals who share the same preferences and the same income M make a voluntary decision on the amount they purchase from the public good.

   a. What is the quantity of the public good G^* in a Nash equilibrium $(g_1^*, \ldots, g_n^*)$, where, for every i, $g_i^* > 0$?

   b. What is the efficient quantity G^e of the public good?

   c. What is the effect of an increase in the number of individuals on the difference between G^e and G^*?

   d. What is the value of $\lim_{n \to \infty} (G^e - G^*)$?

Answer

1. The utility (payoff) functions of the two individuals are:

$$U^1(G, x_1) = x_1 G + x_1 \text{ and } U^2(G, x_2) = x_2 G + x_2$$

or

$$U^1(g_1) = (M_1 - g_1)(g_1 + g_2) + (M_1 - g_1)$$

and

$$U^2(g_2) = (M_2 - g_2)(g_1 + g_2) + (M_2 - g_2)$$

In a Nash equilibrium (g_1^*, g_2^*), every individual (player) decided to purchase a quantity of the public good that maximizes his utility function, given the quantity purchased by the other individual (player). Solving the system of equalities that characterizes an interior equilibrium ($g_1^* > 0$ and $g_2^* > 0$), we obtain (verify) that $(g_1^*, g_2^*) = (5/3, 11/3)$. This equilibrium is inefficient because there exists an alternative pair of strategies (g_1, g_2) that gives a higher utility to every individual relative to his utility in equilibrium. In equilibrium, the utility of both individuals is equal to 40.11. However, when $(g_1, g_2) = (3, 5)$, the utility of every individual increases to 45 (verify).

2 a. The system of equalities that characterizes an interior Nash equilibrium $(g_1^*, \ldots, g_n^*)$, where for every i, $g_i^* > 0$ is (verify):

$$g_1^* = \frac{1}{2}(M - 1 - (g_2^* + g_3^* + \ldots + g_n^*))$$

$$g_2^* = \frac{1}{2}(M - 1 - (g_1^* + g_3^* + \ldots + g_n^*))$$

$$g_n^* = \frac{1}{2}(M - 1 - (g_1^* + g_2^* + \ldots + g_{n-1}^*))$$

Summing up all the equations (note that on the right side, every term g_i^* will appear $(n - 1)$ times), we obtain the equality:

$$\sum_{i=1}^{n} g_i^* = \frac{1}{2}\left(n(M - 1) - (n - 1)\sum_{i=1}^{n} g_i^*\right)$$

or rearranging terms:

$$(n + 1)\sum_{i=1}^{n} g_i^* = n(M - 1)$$

That is,

$$\sum_{i=1}^{n} g_i^* = G^* = \frac{n}{(n + 1)}(M - 1)$$

or

$$g_i^* = \frac{1}{(n + 1)}(M - 1)$$

2b. The efficient quantity of the public good G^e is characterized by the equality:

$$\sum_{i=1}^{n} MRS_i\left(G, M - \frac{G}{n}\right) = 1$$

That is,

$$\sum_{i=1}^{n} \frac{M - g_i}{G + 1} = 1$$

or

$$\sum_{i=1}^{n} M - \sum_{i=1}^{n} g_i = G + 1$$

or

$$nM - 1 = 2G$$

Hence,

$$G^e = \frac{nM - 1}{2}$$

2c. $\quad \dfrac{\partial(G^e - G^*)}{\partial n} = \dfrac{M}{2} - \dfrac{(M - 1)}{(n + 1)^2} > 0$

2d. Verify that $\lim\limits_{n \to \infty} (G^e - G^*) = \infty$.

9.6 SUMMARY

- In an economic/social context, collective decisions are often made on the provision and funding of public goods.
- A public good is characterized by two basic features: first, once provided, it is impossible to prevent its consumption, at least to some extent, by all the consumers. This characteristic is called "*non-excludability.*" Second, the provision of a certain quantity of a public good enables concurrent consumption, at least to some extent, by all the consumers. This feature is called "*non-rivalry.*"
- Assuming that there are two goods, a private good and a pure public good, the condition for the efficient provision of the public good is the equality between the marginal social cost of the public good in terms of the private good and the sum of the subjective marginal rates of substitution of all the consumers between the two goods.
- When the quantity of the public good is chosen by the simple majority rule (the chosen quantity defeats any alternative quantity by a simple majority), it is usually inefficient.
- Under the assumptions made in this chapter, individual preferences are single-peaked. Therefore, by the median-voter theorem, the quantity chosen under the simple majority rule is the median of the distribution of the individuals' most preferred quantities: $G^1, G^2, \ldots, G^n$. With no loss of generality, let $G^1 \leq G^2 \leq \ldots \leq G^n$. If n is odd, then the median of

the distribution is the quantity $G^m = G^{\frac{n+1}{2}}$ and this quantity is chosen by the simple majority rule (G^m is the Condorcet winning alternative).

- Since G^m is the optimal quantity for the median voter m, and we assume that this quantity is affordable by his income, the necessary condition for optimality is satisfied:

$$MRS_m\left(G^m, M_m - \frac{G^m}{n}\right) = \frac{1}{n} \tag{1}$$

However, the condition that characterizes an efficient positive quantity of the public good G^e is the equality:

$$\sum_{i=1}^{n} MRS_i\left(G^e, M_i - \frac{G^e}{n}\right) = 1 \tag{2}$$

These different conditions usually imply that $G^m \neq G^e$.

- When the collective choice is determined by a dictatorial rule, that is, the collective decision is made by a certain individual d, the chosen quantity is usually different from the efficient one because the condition that characterizes the optimal bundle of the dictator is different from the necessary condition for the efficient quantity of the public good.

- The quantity chosen by the Borda rule, G^B, takes into account the relative ranking of all the alternatives by all voters and it attains the highest average ranking of all the individuals. This feature differs from the condition that characterizes an efficient quantity of the public good, (2) and, therefore, there is no reason to expect that $G^B = G^e$.

- The unanimity rule can choose an efficient quantity of the public good, provided that the differential prices of the public good are Lindahl prices (taxes). Usually, however, the use of this rule does not ensure efficiency and an efficient quantity of the public good does not require the use of the unanimity rule.

- In the game of voluntary (private) provision of a public good, the players are the n consumers, the strategy set of consumer i is the set $S_i = \{g_i : 0 \le g_i \le M_i\}$ and his payoff function is $U^i(g_1, \ldots, g_n) = f_i(g_i + \sum_{k \neq i} g_k) + (M_i - g_i)$.

In a Nash equilibrium $(g_1^*, \ldots, g_n^*)$ of this game, g_i^* is a solution to the problem:

$$\underset{g_i \geq 0}{Max} \; f_i\left(g_i + \sum_{k \neq i} g_k^*\right) + (M_i - g_i) \tag{3}$$

This solution therefore satisfies the necessary and sufficient conditions:

$$f_i'(G^*) \leq 1 \tag{6}$$

and

$$f_i'(G^*) = 1 \Leftarrow g_i^* > 0 \tag{7}$$

Therefore, when $n > 1$ and $G^e > 0$,

$$\sum_{i=1}^{n} MRS_i(G^*, M_i - g_i^*) = \sum_{i=1}^{n} f_i'(G^*) > 1 \tag{8}$$

This implies that the necessary condition for efficiency is not satisfied. Furthermore, the public good is under-provided because $G^* < G^e$. In such a case, the problem of inefficiency is referred to as the "free-rider" problem: every individual has an insufficient incentive to purchase the public good, because he enjoys the aggregate quantities of the public good purchased by other individuals.

10 Do individuals reveal their true preferences?

Given a set of alternatives, a collective choice rule (function) assigns a subset of alternatives to any given preference profile; the alternative or alternatives that are chosen. Until now we have assumed that the preference profiles of individuals represent their true preferences. This assumption implies that when collective choice rules are applied, individuals who participate in the choice reveal their true preferences. This chapter focuses on the question of whether it is possible to expect true revelation of preferences. In other words, is using the collective choice function an effective way to evoke a sincere report of preferences from the individuals participating in the collective choice? This question is interesting because it raises an additional aspect of collective choice that we have not yet addressed, namely, the strategic or game theoretic aspect. It is possible to consider the collective choice as a strategic game in which a player's set of strategies consists of all possible preference relations. One of the possible strategies of each player is the choice of his true preferences. Therefore, given collective choice rules that determine players' payoff functions, the question is whether the true preference profile is an equilibrium in the collective choice game.

Below we will clarify with the help of examples why the rule of simple majority + chairman, the sequential majority rule, and Borda's rule do not necessarily result in true revelation of preferences. Then we will examine a general result, the Gibbard–Satterthwaite theorem, which shows that any collective choice rule that is not dictatorial does not result in a revelation of true preferences.

With regard to the provision of a public good, the question of revelation of true preferences has special importance, because information about true preferences is essential in order for the government

Table 10.1

P_1	P_2	P_3
x	y	z
y	z	x
z	x	y

to determine the efficient quantity of the public good. In the second part of this chapter we will illustrate the problem for the simple case where society has to choose whether to produce or not to produce the public good. We will conclude by presenting a mechanism that reveals individuals' true preferences – the Clarke and Groves demand-revealing mechanism.

10.1 NON-TRUTHFUL REVELATION OF PREFERENCES
Below we will present three examples of different collective choice rules where there is an incentive to not reveal preferences truthfully. The existence of such an incentive means that the true preference profile is not a Nash equilibrium in the collective choice game. In this game individuals' strategies are the possible reported preferences (not necessarily the true preferences), the collective choice rule that transforms the revealed preference profile into a collective choice is given, and individuals have complete information about the choice rule and the (true) preference profile.

Example 10.1: The simple majority rule + chairman
The preferences of three individuals, $N = \{1, 2, 3\}$ with respect to three alternatives, $X = \{x, y, z\}$ are presented in Table 10.1 above (see Example 7.1). The collective choice rule is the simple majority rule; the choice is the Condorcet winner. If such a winner does not exist, the collective choice is based on the decision of individual 3, the chairman. In the case of the sincere preference profile of this example, there

Table 10.2

P_1'	P_2	P_3
y	y	z
z	z	x
x	x	y

Table 10.3

P_1	P_2	P_3
x	y	z
y	x	y
z	z	x

is no Condorcet winner and therefore z is chosen, the best alternative for the chairman. In this case individual 1 has an incentive not to reveal his preferences truthfully. In particular, it is preferable for him to report that his preference relation is P_1', see Table 10.2, because this false report results in y being chosen, which for individual 1 is preferable to z. ■

Example 10.2: The sequential majority rule
The preferences of three individuals, $N = \{1, 2, 3\}$ with respect to three alternatives, $X = \{x, y, z\}$ are presented in Table 10.3.

The collective choice rule is the sequential majority rule where alternatives y and z compete in the first stage and the winner competes against alternative x in the second stage. According to this decision rule, alternative y is chosen (verify). In such a case individual 1 has an incentive to not reveal his preferences truthfully; it is optimal for him to report P_1', see Table 10.4, because this false report results in x being chosen, which is optimal for him. ■

Table 10.4

P_1'	P_2	P_3
x	y	z
z	x	y
y	z	x

Table 10.5

Three individuals	Two individuals	Two individuals
z	y	x
y	x	w
x	w	z
w	z	y

Example 10.3: Borda's rule

The preferences of seven individuals, $N = \{1, 2, 3, 4, 5, 6, 7\}$ with respect to four alternatives, $X = \{x, y, z, w\}$ are presented in Table 10.5. The three columns of Table 10.5 represent the preference relations of three types of individual: three individuals of the first type and two individuals of the two remaining types.

The collective choice rule is the Borda rule and accordingly alternative x is chosen, winning with 20 points (verify). In such a case every individual whose preferences are represented in the middle column of the table has an incentive to not report his preferences truthfully. Specifically, reporting the insincere preference relation presented in the second column from the left in Table 10.6 is preferable, because this non-truthful revelation results in y being chosen with 17 points (verify), which is, in fact, optimal. ∎

Table 10.6

Three individuals	One individuals	One individuals	Two individuals
z	y	y	x
y	w	x	w
x	z	w	z
w	x	z	y

Now we turn to the generalization of these three examples and present the properties of the collective choice rule that ensure the existence of incentives for non-truthful preference revelation.

10.2 THE IMPOSSIBILITY THEOREM OF GIBBARD (1973)–SATTERTHWAITE (1975)

Denote by $\mathbf{P}^n$ the set of strict orderings on X and by $C(\mathbf{P}) = C(\mathbf{P}, X)$ the resolute collective choice function, $C(\mathbf{P})\colon \mathbf{P}^n \to X$. The preference profile $\mathbf{P}$ belongs to the set of possible profiles $\mathbf{P}^n$ and its i'th component is individual i's strict preference relation.

The collective choice function $C(\mathbf{P})$ is *Pareto-efficient* if whenever $x \in X$ is the best alternative for each individual, then $C(P_1, \ldots, P_n) = x$.

The collective choice function $C(\mathbf{P})$ is *monotonic* if whenever $C(P_1, \ldots, P_n) = x$ and for each individual i and for each alternative y, x is ranked strictly above y in the preference relation P_i' when this is the ranking between the two alternatives in P_i, then $C(P_1', \ldots, P_n') = x$.

The collective choice function $C(\mathbf{P})$ is *dictatorial* if there exists an individual i such that $C(P_1, \ldots, P_n) = x$ if, and only if, x is individual i's best alternative.

Theorem 10.1: If $|X| \geq 3$ and the resolute collective choice function $C(\mathbf{P})$ is Pareto-efficient and monotonic, then $C(\mathbf{P})$ is dictatorial.

Table 10.7

	Collective Choice	
$P_1 \ldots P_{t-1} P_t P_{t+1} \ldots P_n$		
$b \ldots b$	$a \; a \;\; \ldots a$	
$a \ldots a$	$b \; . \;\; \ldots .$	
.	. . . . .	
.	. . . . .	$\to a$
.	. . . . .	
. ....	. $b \;\; \ldots b$	

Table 10.8

	Collective Choice	
$P_1 \ldots P'_{t-1} P'_t P'_{t+1} \ldots P_n$		
$b \ldots b$	$b \; a \;\; \ldots a$	
$a \ldots a$	$a \; . \;\; \ldots .$	
.	. . . . .	
.	. . . . .	$\to b$
.	. . . . .	
.	. . $b \;\; \ldots b$	

Proof: (See Reny (2001))

Step 1

Consider any two alternatives in X, alternatives a,b, and a profile in which a is ranked highest and b lowest for every individual $i = 1, \ldots$ n. Pareto efficiency implies that the collective choice for this profile is a.

Now change individual 1's ranking by raising alternative b one position at a time. By monotonicity, the collective choice continues to be a as long as b is below a in 1's ranking. However, when b is finally ranked above a, monotonicity implies that the collective choice is still a or that it changes to b. If a is still the collective choice, then apply the same process to individual 2, then 3, etc. until for some individual t, the collective choice does change from a to b when a is ranked lower than b in t's ranking. Pareto efficiency ensures that such an individual t exists (verify). Tables 10.7 and 10.8 illustrate the profiles for just before and after individual t's ranking of b is raised above a.

Step 2

Consider now Tables 10.7′ and 10.8′. Table 10.7′ is derived from Table 10.7 (and Table 10.8′ is derived from Table 10.8) by moving alternative a to the bottom of individual i's ranking for $i < t$ and

Table 10.7'   Table 10.8'

$P_1 \ldots P_{t-1}\ P_t\ P_{t+1} \ldots P_n$	Collective Choice	$P'_1 \ldots P'_{t-1}\ P'_t\ P'_{t+1} \ldots P_n$	Collective Choice
$b\ \ldots b \quad a\ .\quad \ldots.$		$b\ \ldots b \quad b\ .\quad \ldots.$	
$.\quad \ldots. \quad b\ .\quad \ldots.$		$.\quad \ldots. \quad a\ .\quad \ldots.$	
$.\qquad .\quad .\ .$		$.\qquad .\quad .\ .$	
$.\qquad .\quad .\quad .$	$\to a$	$.\qquad .\quad .\quad .$	$\to b$
$.\qquad .\quad a\ \ldots a$		$.\qquad .\quad a\ \ldots a$	
$a\ \ldots a\quad .\ b\ \ldots b$		$a\ \ldots a\quad .\ b\ \ldots b$	

moving it to the second to last position in i's ranking for $i > t$. These changes do not affect the collective choices, as we will clarify below.

First, notice that the collective choice in Table 10.8' must be b due to monotonicity, because no individual's ranking of b relative to any other alternative changes from Table 10.8 to Table 10.8' and the collective choice in Table 10.8 is b. Also note that the only difference in the profiles presented in Tables 10.7' and 10.8' is individual t's ranking of alternatives a and b. Therefore, by monotonicity, the collective choice in table 10.7' must be either a or b because the collective choice in Table 10.8' is b. But if the collective choice is b, then by monotonicity, the collective choice in Table 10.7 must be b, which is a contradiction. Therefore the collective choice in Table 10.7' is a.

Step 3

Now consider alternative c, which is distinct from a and b. Owing to monotonicity, the collective choice corresponding to the profile presented in Table 10.9 must be a, because this profile can be obtained from the Table 10.7' profile without altering the ranking of a relative to any other alternative in any individual's ranking.

Step 4

Now consider the profile of rankings in Table 10.10, derived from the Table 10.9 profile by interchanging the ranking of alternatives a and

Table 10.9

P_1	P_{t-1}	P_t	P_{t+1}	P_n	Collective Choice
.	.	a	.	.	
.	.	c	.	.	
.	.	b	.	.	→ a
c	... c	.	c	c	
b	... b	.	a	... a	
a	... a	.	b	... b	

Table 10.10

P_1	P_{t-1}	P_t	P_{t+1}	P_n	Collective Choice
.	.	a	.	.	
.	.	c	.	.	
.	.	b	.	.	→ a
c	... c	.	c	c	
b	... b	.	b	... b	
a	... a	.	a	... a	

b for individuals $i > t$. Owing to monotonicity, the collective choice in Table 10.10 must be a or b, because the collective choice in Table 10.9 is a and because the change in ranking for individuals $i > t$ is the only difference between the profiles in Tables 10.9 and 10.10. But the collective choice in Table 10.10 cannot be b, because alternative b is ranked below c in every individual's Table 10.10 ranking (and monotonicity would then imply that the collective choice would remain b even if c was ranked highest by every individual, which contradicts Pareto efficiency). Therefore the collective choice in Table 10.10 is a.

Step 5

Notice that an arbitrary profile of rankings with a ranked the highest by individual t can be obtained from the profile in Table 10.10 without lowering the ranking of a relative to any other alternative in any individual's ranking. Hence, monotonicity implies that whenever a is ranked the highest by individual t, the collective choice must be a. In other words, one may consider individual t a dictator for alternative a. Note that because a was chosen arbitrarily, we have shown that there is a dictator for a for each alternative a in the set X. But there cannot be distinct dictators for distinct alternatives. Therefore there is a single dictator for all alternatives. **Q.E.D.**

Denote by $\mathbf{P}_{-i}$ the profile of all strict orderings of the individuals except for the preference relation P_i,

$$\mathbf{P}_{-i} = (P_1, \ldots, P_{i-1}, P_{i+1}, \ldots, P_n)$$

The resolute collective choice function $C(P)$ is *strategy-proof* or *non-manipulable* if for every individual i, every profile $\mathbf{P}$ in $\mathbf{P}^n$ and for every strict ordering P'_i,

$$[C(\mathbf{P}) \neq C(\mathbf{P}_i', P_{-i})] \rightarrow [C(\mathbf{P})P_i C(\mathbf{P}_i', P_{-i})]$$

Individual i thus does not have an incentive to report P'_i when his true preference relation is P_i. Note that such a non-truthful report leads to a less desirable collective choice for him relative to the collective choice made when he reports that his (true or sincere) preferences are P_i.

The collective choice function is *onto* if every alternative in the range of the function is the image of some element in the domain of the function, that is, every alternative is chosen for some profile.

Theorem 10.2: If the resolute collective choice function $C(P)$ is onto and strategy-proof, then $C(P)$ is Pareto-efficient and monotonic.

Proof: Let us assume that $C(\mathbf{P}) = a$ and that for every alternative b, the strict ordering P_i' ranks a above b as long as the strict preference relation P_i ranks a above b. To prove that monotonicity is satisfied, we must show that $C(P_i', \mathbf{P}_{-i}) = a$. Let us assume on the contrary that $C(P_i', \mathbf{P}_{-i}) = b \neq a$. It follows from this assumption, due to the strategy proofness property, that alternative a is ranked above alternative b according to the preference relation P_i, that is:

$$C(\mathbf{P}) = a \, P_i \, b = C(P_i', \mathbf{P}_{-i})$$

But since the ranking of a does not fall when P_i changes to P_i', a is also ranked above b according to the preference relation P_i', that is:

$$C(\mathbf{P}) = a \, P_i' \, b = C(P_i', \mathbf{P}_{-i})$$

But this violates the strategy-proofness property of $C(\mathbf{P})$. Therefore it must be that:

$$C(P_i', \mathbf{P}_{-i}) = C(\mathbf{P}) = a$$

Now let us assume that $C(\mathbf{P}) = a$ and that for every individual i and for every alternative b, the strict ordering P_i' ranks a above b as long as the strict ordering P_i ranks a above b. Since it is possible to switch from the profile $\mathbf{P} = (P_1, \ldots, P_n)$ to the profile $\mathbf{P}' = (P_1', \ldots, P_n')$ by changing all individuals' preference relations from P_i to P_i' one at a time, and since we showed that the collective choice must remain the same when these changes occur, it must be the case that $C(\mathbf{P}) = C(\mathbf{P}')$. In other words, the collective choice function $\mathbf{C}$ is monotonic.

Let us choose an alternative a in X. By assumption, the choice function is onto and therefore there exists a profile $\mathbf{P}$ in $\mathbf{P}^n$ such that $C(\mathbf{P}) = a$. The monotonicity property implies that a is still the collective choice when alternative a becomes the best alternative for each individual. Monotonicity also implies that the collective choice must remain a regardless of how individuals rank the alternatives below a. Consequently, as long as a is ranked first by every individual, the collective choice is a. Since a is chosen arbitrarily, C is Pareto-efficient. **Q.E.D.**

The impossibility theorem of Gibbard–Satterthwaite follows directly from Theorem 10.1 and Theorem 10.2.

Theorem 10.3: If $|X| \geq 3$ and the resolute collective choice function $C(\mathbf{P})$ is onto and strategy-proof, then $C(\mathbf{P})$ is dictatorial.

Theorem 10.3 implies that under the general assumptions of this section, any collective choice function that is not dictatorial is not strategy-proof, that is, it does not result in a true revelation of preferences. The Gibbard–Satterthwaite theorem is a central result in the field of social choice and its importance is comparable to that of Arrow's impossibility theorem. See Reny (2001) for more on the close connection between these two impossibility theorems. Moreover, the Gibbard–Satterthwaite theorem has served as a substantial incentive for developing the extensive literature dealing with mechanism design, namely, the designing of a decentralized mechanism of collective choice that results in a game whose non-cooperative equilibrium, Nash equilibrium, brings about a desired (efficient) allocation of resources.

10.3 REVELATION OF PREFERENCES AND THE EFFICIENT PROVISION OF A PUBLIC GOOD – THE DICHOTOMOUS CASE

The question of true revelation of preferences has special importance with regard to the provision of a public good, because information about true preferences is essential in order for the government to successfully determine the efficient quantity of the public good. This discussion will be condensed in comparison to the extensive discussion of the previous section. We will present the problem of true preference revelation and its solution in the simple dichotomous case in which n individuals choose between producing or not producing a specific quantity of a public good. Quantity of the public good G is therefore equal to 0 or 1. Let us assume that the cost to provide the public good is equal to c and that the relative share of individual i in funding the public good is equal to t_i. When G = 1 the total cost for individual i is therefore equal to $t_i c$. When $G = 0$ the total cost for individual i is equal to 0. An additional simplifying assumption is that individuals' preferences between providing the public good and not providing it are represented by the function:[1]

$$U^i(G) = \begin{cases} r_i - t_i c & G = 1 \\ 0 & G = 0 \end{cases}$$

where r_i is the reservation price of individual i. Henceforth we will call the difference, $v_i = r_i - t_i c$, individual i's **net value** of provision of the public good. Notice that under these assumptions, providing the public good is efficient ($G = 1$ is the efficient quantity of the public good) if $\sum_{i=1}^{n} U^i(1) = \sum_{i=1}^{n} (r_i - t_i c) > 0$ (verify). It is possible to base the choice between two quantities of the public good on the following choice mechanism: Each individual is asked to reveal his net value of provision of the public good and the public good is provided ($G = 1$) if the sum of the net values reported by the individuals is non-negative. We will denote by s_i the net value reported by individual i. The report of individual i is honest or truthful when $s_i = v_i = r_i - t_i c$. Even under the simplifying assumptions of the current collective choice setting, the proposed mechanism does not necessarily provide an incentive for truthful revelation of preferences and, therefore, it does not ensure an efficient provision of the public good. For example, let us assume that t_i is fixed and the net value of individual 1 of providing the public good is positive, $(r_1 - t_1 c) > 0$. In such a case, individual 1 has an incentive to report that his utility from the public good is very high because a non-truthful report does not influence his payoff, whether the public good is provided, $G = 1$, or not provided, $G = 0$, but he can ensure that his preferred outcome is chosen ($G = 1$). It is clear that a non-truthful report of this type can lead to an inefficient quantity of the public good, in other words, the public good is provided despite the fact that its provision is inefficient. Conversely, let us assume

---

[1] We assume that individuals' utilities for the public good and for private consumption (see Chapter 9) are quasi-linear.

that the utility of individual 1 from the public good being provided is negative, $(r_1 - t_1 c) < 0$. In such a case, individual 1 has an incentive to report a very low utility of the provided public good, since such a non-truthful report does not influence his payoff, whether $G = 1$ or $G = 0$, but he can ensure that his preferred outcome is chosen $(G = 0)$. Also in this case, it is clear that a non-truthful report of this type can result in an inefficient quantity of the public good, namely, the public good is not provided, despite the fact that such resource allocation is inefficient.

In the simple dichotomous case described above, it is possible to ensure that every individual will report his net value honestly such that the efficient quantity of the public good is provided. Nevertheless, as we clarify below, it is not possible to ensure resource-allocation efficiency (efficient allocation of the public and private goods). We proceed therefore to the presentation of mechanisms that reveal the true individual preferences.

10.3.1 The Groves–Clarke revelation mechanism

One mechanism for revealing preferences of individuals is defined in the following way:

(1) Each agent reports his net value s_i of provision of the public good.

(2) The public good is provided $(G = 1)$ if $\sum_{i=1}^{n} s_i \geq 0$ and it is not provided if $\sum_{i=1}^{n} s_i < 0$.

(3) If the public good is provided, each individual receives a payment equal to the sum of the net values that are reported by the other individuals, $\sum_{j \neq i} s_j$ (when the sum is positive, individual i receives the payment. When the sum is negative, individual i gives the payment).

Let us clarify why each individual will truthfully report his net value of provision of the public good (recall that the net value of individual i is v_i). More specifically, we want to show that for every individual i who participates in the public-good provision game, the strategy $s_i = v_i$ is a dominant strategy, that is, sincere revelation of the net value is optimal, regardless of how the other individuals report. Agent i's payoff function is:

$$U^i(s_1, \ldots, s_n) = \begin{cases} v_i + \sum_{j \neq i} s_j & \text{if} \quad s_i + \sum_{j \neq i} s_j \geq 0 \\ 0 & \text{if} \quad s_i + \sum_{j \neq i} s_j < 0 \end{cases}$$

Suppose that $v_i + \sum_{j \neq i} s_j > 0$. In such a case individual i can ensure that the public good will be provided if he reports that $s_i = v_i$. If $v_i + \sum_{j \neq i} s_j < 0$, then individual i can ensure that the public good will not be provided, if he reports that $s_i = v_i$. In any case, truthful revelation of the net value is an optimal strategy. Notice that there never is an incentive to misrepresent one's net value, regardless of how the other players reveal their preferences. The information-gathering mechanism essentially has been modified so that each individual now faces the collective decision problem instead of the individual decision problem, and therefore he has an incentive to reveal his preferences truthfully.

However, this mechanism that reveals individuals' preferences has a significant drawback; it carries a potentially high cost due to the fact that the sum of payments to individuals can be very large. The question can be asked whether there exists a mechanism that carries no costs, namely a mechanism for which the sum of payments imposed (positive or negative) is equal to zero. In general, no such mechanism exists, but it is possible to design a mechanism such that the payments will always be negative. In other words, there is a mechanism which results in true revelation of preferences whereby individuals must pay a "tax," but they will never receive payments. The allocation of public and private goods will not be Pareto-efficient because of these wasted tax payments, but at least the public good will be provided if, and only if, its provision is efficient.

We now turn to a mechanism that involves only taxation. We start by presenting a more general mechanism than the mechanism just described. The general mechanism can be described in the following way:

(1) Every individual reports his net value s_i of the provision of the public good.

(2) The public good is provided $(G = 1)$ if $\sum_{i=1}^{n} s_i \geq 0$ and it is not provided $(G = 0)$ if $\sum_{i=1}^{n} s_i < 0$.

(3') If the public good is provided, every individual receives a payment equal to $\sum_{j \neq i} s_j + h_i(\mathbf{S}_{-i})$, where $\mathbf{S}_{-i}$ is a vector of the reports of all the individuals with the exception of individual i and $h_i(\mathbf{S}_{-i})$ is the additional payment to $\sum_{j \neq i} s_j$, which is dependent only on the strategies of the other individuals.[2]

Since the additional payment $h_i(\mathbf{s}_{-i})$ is independent of the strategy reported by individual i, individual i's incentive to reveal his preferences honestly is not affected. Therefore this more general mechanism results in truthful revelation of individuals' preferences. In other words, for every individual i that plays this game, strategy $s_i = v_i$ is a dominant strategy.[3]

By means of an appropriate choice of the function h_i, it is possible to significantly reduce the extent of payments by the participants. We close this chapter with the presentation of a specific function h_i that has very interesting properties. This specific function is defined in the following way:

$$
h_i(\mathbf{s}_{-i}) = \begin{cases} -\sum_{j \neq i} s_j & \text{if} \quad \sum_{j \neq i} s_j \geq 0 \\ 0 & \text{if} \quad \sum_{j \neq i} s_j < 0 \end{cases}
$$

---

[2] See Groves (1973).

[3] Individual i's new payoff function is:

$$
U^i(s_1, \ldots, s_n) = \begin{cases} v_i + \sum_{j \neq i} s_j + h_i(s_{-i}) & \text{if} \quad s_i + \sum_{j \neq i} s_j \geq 0 \\ 0 & \text{if} \quad s_i + \sum_{j \neq i} s_j < 0 \end{cases}
$$

Verify, on the basis of the same considerations presented above, that the general mechanism does indeed result in the revelation of individuals' true preferences.

Such a choice of h_i leads to a mechanism in which the tax imposed on the individuals is known as the Clarke tax.[4] Given this mechanism, the new payoff function of individual i is:

$$
U^i(s_1, \ldots, s_n) = \begin{cases}
v_i & \text{if } \sum_i s_i \geq 0 \text{ and } \sum_{j \neq i} s_j \geq 0 & \text{(Case 1)} \\[2mm]
v_i + \sum_{j \neq i} s_j & \text{if } \sum_i s_i \geq 0 \text{ and } \sum_{j \neq i} s_j < 0 & \text{(Case 2)} \\[2mm]
- \sum_{j \neq i} s_j & \text{if } \sum_i s_i < 0 \text{ and } \sum_{j \neq i} s_j \geq 0 & \text{(Case 3)} \\[2mm]
0 & \text{if } \sum_i s_i < 0 \text{ and } \sum_{j \neq i} s_j < 0 & \text{(Case 4)}
\end{cases}
$$

According to this mechanism:

(i) The individual never receives a positive payment, but he may receive a negative payment, that is, he may pay a tax.

(ii) The tax is imposed on individual i only if the net value that he reports changes the collective decision (see Cases 2 and 3).

(iii) The tax imposed on individual i is equal to the sum of the damages caused to other individuals due to the change in the collective decision resulting from the report of individual i (see Cases 2 and 3).

(iv) The tax imposed on any individual is never higher than the value of the collective decision for him.

Notice that the sum of the tax imposed on individuals cannot be returned to them, because such a transfer may change the individuals' incentives to reveal their preferences truthfully.

The Clarke–Groves demand-revelation mechanism has three primary disadvantages:

(i) The mechanism does not result in a Pareto-efficient allocation, because it entails imposing a tax that is not returned to the individuals. This means that there exists an alternative allocation of resources in which the individuals consume the efficient quantity of the public good, but the private consumption of at least one individual can be increased.

4   See Clarke (1971).

(ii) The mechanism effectivity hinges on the restrictive assumption that the individuals' utility is quasi-linear.

(iii) The mechanism is immune to manipulation by other individuals, but it is not necessarily immune to manipulation by coalitions of individuals.

Example 10.4

Let us assume that $n = 3$, $c = 300$, $t_1 = t_2 = t_3 = 1/3$, $r_1 = r_2 = 50$, and $r_3 = 250$.

Therefore, we have $v_1 = v_2 = -50$ and $v_3 = 150$. In Nash equilibrium $(s_1^*, s_2^*, s_3^*) = (-50, -50, 150)$ and $s_1^* + s_2^* + s_3^* > 0$, and therefore the mechanism chooses to provide the public good. The Clarke tax imposed on individual 1 is 0 because his report does not change the collective decision. Similarly, the Clarke tax imposed on individual 2 is also 0. However, individual 3's report changes the collective decision; while $s_1 + s_2 < 0$ we have $s_1 + s_2 + s_3 > 0$, and therefore the payment he receives is equal to $(s_1 + s_2) = -100$. In other words, the Clarke tax imposed on individual 3 is equal to 100. In conclusion, let us clarify how the mechanism based on the Clarke tax operates. Consider, for example, individual 1. Given that $s_2^* = -50$ and $s_3^* = 150$, it is not optimal for individual 1 to deviate from his sincere report, $s_1^* = -50$. Reporting a higher net value would not change the collective decision and therefore his utility would not change. Reporting a net value smaller than (-50) but larger than (-100) also would not change the collective decision and therefore his utility would not change. Reporting a net value smaller than (-100) would change the collective decision, the public good would not be provided, and thus individual 1 would pay a Clarke tax equal to $-50 + 150 = 100$ and his utility would decrease from (-50) to (-100). Therefore, it is not optimal for individual 1 to deviate from his true report of $s_1^* = -50$. It is straightforward to see, using similar arguments, that it is also optimal for individual 2 and individual 3 to report their true net values of provision of the public good.

Individual	Cost of the public good $t_i c = (1/3)300$	Reservation price of the public good r_i	Net value of the public good $v_i = r_i - t_i c$	Clarke tax
1	100	50	−50	0
2	100	50	−50	0
3	100	250	150	100

■

10.4 EXERCISES

Material included in section 10.2 is based on an article by Reny (2001).
Material included in section 10.3 is based on section 8.23 in Varian's
(1992) book.
The following questions are intended to clarify the demand-revealing
mechanism of Groves–Ledyard.

Question 10.1
In the following table information is given regarding the preferences
of three individuals with respect to the provision of a public good that
costs 240.

Individual	Cost of the public good $t_i c = (1/3)240$	Reservation price of the public good r_i	Net value of the public good $v_i = r_i - t_i c$	Clarke tax
1	80	180	100	?
2	80	150	70	?
3	80	0	−80	?

1. Sometimes an individual who causes a change in the collective choice
   by reporting his preferences is called a pivotal individual. Who are the
   pivotal individuals in this example when the decision regarding provision of the public good is made using Clarke's demand-revealing
   mechanism?
2. "A Clarke tax is imposed on the pivotal individuals." Discuss.
3. Calculate the Clarke tax imposed on each individual.

4. Explain why a sincere revelation of preferences would no longer be a Nash equilibrium of the game if the Clarke tax imposed on individual 1 were transferred to individual 2.

Answer

1. Individual 1 is the only pivotal individual.
2. The claim is true.
3. A Clarke tax of 10 is imposed on individual 1. A Clarke tax of 0 is imposed on individuals 2 and 3.
4. By definition, the tax imposed on individual 1 is equal to the sum of the damages incurred by individual 2 and individual 3 as a result of his decision, when individual 1 is pivotal. If the tax imposed on individual 1 is transferred to individual 2, then individual 2 has an incentive to increase the tax imposed on individual 1. Individual 2 will accomplish this by not reporting his preferences truthfully.

Question 10.2

"A Clarke tax is not a successful tax for funding the public good because it is likely to cause a government deficit." Discuss.

Answer

A Clarke tax may cause a deficit, but it may also cause a balanced budget or a budget surplus. For example, see Question 10.1. The success of this tax is not measured by its ability to fund, but rather by its ability to create incentives that cause individuals to report their preferences sincerely.

Question 10.3

Assume that the decision to provide a particular public good from which three individuals benefit is made with the aid of the demand-revealing mechanism suggested by Clarke. Is it possible that the Clarke tax may create a budget surplus even when no individual is required to participate in funding the good, that is, when $t_1 = t_2 = t_3 = 0$?

Answer

The example below shows that a Clarke tax may create a budget surplus, even when no individual is required to participate in the funding of the good. As in Question 10.1, let us assume that the cost of the public good is 240. By assumption, $t_1c = t_2c = t_3c = 0$. The reservation price and the net value of the individuals are given in the following table:

Individual	Cost of the public good $t_ic = 0$	Reservation price of the public good r_i	Net value of the public good $v_i = r_i - t_ic$	Clarke tax
1	0	701	701	700
2	0	100	100	99
3	0	−800	−800	0

In this case the public good is provided, a Clarke tax of 700 is imposed on individual 1, a Clarke tax of 99 is imposed on individual 2, and a Clarke tax of 0 is imposed on individual 3 (verify). The sum of the tax is equal to 799. The Clarke tax therefore creates a budget surplus of 559 (799 − 240).

Question 10.4

The following matrix describes four individuals' net value for constructing a lighthouse. Assume that $t_1 = t_2 = t_3 = t_4 = 0$.

Individual 1	Individual 2	Individual 3	Individual 4
300	−200	−250	200

Assuming that the collective decision to prove the lighthouse is made using the Clarke's demand-revealing mechanism, choose the ("partnership") game that individual 1 would prefer.

1. A game in which the two other players are individuals 2 and 4.
2. A game in which the two other players are individuals 2 and 3.
3. A game in which the other players are individuals 2, 3, and 4.
4. A game in which the two other players are individuals 3 and 4.

Answer

The game in which the other players are individuals 2 and 4 is the preferred game for individual 1. The outcome of the game is that the lighthouse is constructed and a Clarke tax of 0 is imposed on individual 1. As a result, individual 1's utility is 300. His net value from each of the alternative games is lower (verify).

Question 10.5

Assume that the cost of constructing a lighthouse is 150. The individual monetary values of constructing the lighthouse are r_1, r_2, and r_3. The individuals declare the amounts s_1, s_2, and s_3 that they are willing to pay in order to construct the lighthouse. The lighthouse is constructed if the sum of the offers is greater than or equal to 150. In this instance, each individual pays the amount that he declares. Which of the following claims is true?

1. In Nash equilibrium the government budget is necessarily balanced.
2. Nash equilibrium is necessarily efficient.
3. If $r_1 + r_2 + r_3 > 150$, then in Nash equilibrium the lighthouse is necessarily constructed.
4. If $r_1 + r_2 + r_3 < 150$, then the lighthouse may be constructed in Nash equilibrium, but not necessarily.

Answer

The payoff function of individual i is:

$$U^i(s_1, s_2, s_3) = \begin{cases} r_i - s_i & s_1 + s_2 + s_3 \geq 150 \\ 0 & s_1 + s_2 + s_3 < 150 \end{cases}$$

From this we have two cases:

Case 1: If $r_1 + r_2 + r_3 \geq 150$, then there are an infinite number of Nash equilibria (s_1^*, s_2^*, s_3^*). In equilibrium either $s_1^* + s_2^* + s_3^* = 150$ and the lighthouse is constructed or $s_1^* + s_2^* + s_3^* = 0$ and the lighthouse is not constructed (verify). In case 1, the government budget is balanced.

Case 2: If $r_1 + r_2 + r_3 < 150$, then in equilibrium we have (s_1^*, s_2^*, s_3^*), where $s_1^* = s_2^* = s_3^* = 0$ (verify) and the lighthouse is not constructed. In case 2, the government budget is balanced.

In both cases the government budget is balanced and therefore claim 1 is correct.

In case 1 it is possible that Nash equilibrium is inefficient, that is, $r_1 + r_2 + r_3 \geq 150$ but $s_1^* + s_2^* + s_3^* = 0$, and therefore claim 2 is not correct.

In case 1 it is possible that the lighthouse will not be constructed and therefore claim 3 is incorrect.

In case 2 the lighthouse is never constructed and therefore claim 4 is incorrect.

10.5 SUMMARY

- The collective choice function C(**P**) is *Pareto-efficient* if whenever $x \in X$ is the best alternative for each individual, then $C(P_1, \ldots, P_n) = x$.
- The collective choice function C(**P**) is *monotonic* if whenever $C(P_1, \ldots, P_n) = x$ and for each individual i and for each alternative y, x is ranked strictly above y in the preference relation P_i' when this is the ranking between the two alternatives in P_i, then $C(P_1', \ldots, P_n') = x$.
- The collective choice function C(**P**) is *dictatorial* if there exists an individual i such that $C(P_1 \ldots, P_n) = x$ if, and only if, x is individual i's best alternative.
- **Theorem 10.1:** If $|X| \geq 3$ and the resolute collective choice function C(**P**) is Pareto-efficient and monotonic, then C(**P**) is dictatorial.
- The resolute collective choice function C(**P**) is *strategy-proof* or *non-manipulable* if for every individual i and for every profile **P** in $\mathbf{P}^n$ and for every strict ordering P_i', $[C(\mathbf{P}) \neq C(P_i', \mathbf{P}_{-i})] \rightarrow [C(\mathbf{P}) \, P_i \, C(\mathbf{P}_i', \mathbf{P}_{-i})]$
- The collective choice function is *onto* if every alternative in the range of the function is the image of some alternative in the domain of the function, that is, every alternative is chosen for some profile.
- **Theorem 10.2:** If the resolute collective choice function C(**P**) is onto and strategy-proof, then C(**P**) is Pareto-efficient and monotonic.

- **Theorem 10.3:** If $|X| \geq 3$ and the resolute collective choice function $C(\mathbf{P})$ is onto and strategy-proof, then $C(\mathbf{P})$ is dictatorial.

- In the context of dichotomous provision of a public good, $G = 0$ or $G = 1$, and assuming that individuals' preferences are represented by quasi-linear utility functions, we presented mechanisms for revealing the true preferences of individuals. In particular, we discussed the demand-revealing mechanisms of Clarke and Groves.

- Demand-revealing mechanisms for public goods have three primary disadvantages:

  First, the mechanisms are predicated on very strong assumptions of individuals' preferences; individuals' utilities are quasi-linear. Second, the mechanisms reveal the individuals' true demand for the public good, but they do not lead to an efficient allocation of resources. The reason for this is that their use carries with it a cost; either there is a need to pay a "subsidy" to individuals or there is a need to impose "taxes" on individuals and not to make use of the tax. Third, the mechanisms are strategy-proof to individuals acting alone, but not necessarily strategy-proof to coalitions of individuals.

Part III Identical Preferences, Different Decisional Skills

11 Which rule is better: the expert rule or the simple majority rule? Decisional errors in dichotomous choice and Condorcet's jury theorem

So far we have been concerned with various problems that were due mainly to the heterogeneity in individual preferences. However, various problems associated with the aggregation of individual decisions also arise when individuals share identical preferences, but have to make decisions given their different decisional capabilities. The problem of aggregating individual decisions under an uncertain dichotomous choice setting had already been studied in the eighteenth century and in recent years it has attracted continuous renewed interest. The last two chapters are devoted to various aspects of this problem.

In the social context, the move from individual to social preferences or from individual to social choice hinges on the applied aggregation rule. When individuals who share identical preferences operate in an uncertain environment, the problem of preference aggregation is no longer relevant, but the issue of choice aggregation is still pertinent. In an uncertain environment individuals may have identical or different decisional skills, but in any case they may err and make incorrect decisions. In this context, therefore, the aggregation problem takes the following form: What is the most appropriate collective decision rule for implementing the common objective of the individual decision makers? In this chapter we focus on the case of homogenous individuals who share identical decisional skills and on the case of (possibly different) unknown skills, and compare the performance of two collective decision rules: the simple majority rule and the expert rule – the rule based on the decision of a single individual, the most skillful individual. In the last chapter, we extend the framework and focus on the more general question of the optimal collective decision rule.

11.1 THE EXPERT RULE VS. THE SIMPLE MAJORITY RULE: THE CASE OF THREE IDENTICAL DECISION MAKERS

Consider a group of three individuals $(n = 3)$ that has to choose one of the two alternatives a and b, $X = \{a,b\}$. Since individual preferences are identical, one of the two alternatives is preferred by all of them, but in the current setting, the identity of that alternative, "the correct alternative" or "the more preferred alternative" is unknown. In particular, the selection of an alternative may have uncertain (future) consequences that depend on the realized state of nature. Hence, there is uncertainty regarding the answer to the question of which of the two alternatives will result in a better outcome for the individuals. That is, it is not clear which alternative better conforms to the common interest of the individuals. Suppose that the three individuals have equal ability to identify the more preferred alternative. This ability is represented by the probability p to identify and choose the preferred alternative. Henceforth we assume that $p > 1/2$ and that the decisional skills of the individuals are independent. In this case the individual decisional skills are represented by the vector $\mathbf{p} = (p,p,p)$. Assuming that the possibility of abstention from decision (voting) does not exist, $(1 - p)$ is the probability that an individual makes an incorrect decision. When the individuals are equally skilled, none of them can be considered as the only expert, but each of them can be viewed as an expert.

On the one hand, if the group decision is made by a single expert, that is, if the group applies the expert rule f^e, that is the collective decision coincides with the decision of one of its members, then the probability $\pi(f^e, \mathbf{p})$ that the group makes a correct decision is equal to the probability that the expert (in fact, one of the three experts) decides correctly, $\pi(f^e, \mathbf{p}) = p$. On the other hand, if the collective decision is made democratically by applying the simple majority rule f^m, that is, if the group decision coincides with the majority decision, then the probability $\pi(f^m, \mathbf{p})$ that the group makes a correct decision is equal to the probability that a majority chooses the correct alternative, $\pi(f^m, \mathbf{p}) = p^3 + 3p^2(1 - p)$.

Proposition 11.1: In a group that consists of three equally skilled individuals, the simple majority rule is preferred to the expert rule.

Proof

$$\pi(f^m, \mathbf{p}) - \pi(f^e, \mathbf{p}) = p^3 + 3p^2(1 - p) - p$$
$$= p^2(3 - 2p) - p$$
$$= p(2p - 1)(1 - p) \geq 0$$

Q.E.D.

This simple claim constitutes the basis of the argument that in certain circumstances, democratic decision making based on simple majority rule is superior to non-democratic collective decision making that does not enable all the individuals (voters, potential decision makers) to take part in the collective decision-making process. Notice that the proof of the claim rests on the assumption that the decisional skill of every individual is higher than the skill of an individual who makes random decisions tossing a fair coin, and on the assumption that the individual decisions are independent.

11.2 THE EXPERT RULE VS. THE SIMPLE MAJORITY RULE: THE CASE OF THREE DECISION MAKERS WITH UNKNOWN DECISIONAL SKILLS

We have proved above that if individual decisional skills are equal, then the simple majority rule is superior to the expert rule. Such superiority is not self-evident when the individuals differ in their skills (see the example in Section 11.3). When decisional skills are different and known, the choice between the two rules requires information on decisional skills. Such information is usually not available or difficult to get. The question therefore arises whether it is possible to determine which rule is superior even when individual decisional skills are unknown. The following proposition establishes the superiority of the simple majority rule relative to the expert rule when individual skills are unknown. In this case, when the collective decision is based on the decision of a single individual, the "expert," there is an equal probability that the "expert" is the individual with the highest decisional skill p_1, the intermediate skill p_2 or the lowest skill p_3. Again, with no loss of generality, we assume that $p_1 \geq p_2 > p_3 > 1/2$. This assumption implies that although individual decisional skills differ, due to the absence of information regarding these skills, the selection of any individual as the expert yields the same expected decisional skill, $\overline{p} = \dfrac{p_1 + p_2 + p_3}{3}$.

Proposition 11.2: In a three-member group with unknown decisional skills, the simple majority rule is preferred to the expert rule.

Proof: The probability that the group makes the correct decision when it applies the expert rule is equal to $\pi(f^e, \mathbf{p}) = \overline{p} = \dfrac{p_1 + p_2 + p_3}{3}$. The probability that the group makes the correct decision when it applies the simple majority rule is equal to

$$\pi(f^m, \mathbf{p}) = p_1 p_2 p_3 + p_1 p_2 (1 - p_3) + p_1 (1 - p_2) p_3 + (1 - p_1) p_2 p_3.$$

Notice that

$$\pi(f^m, p_1, p_2, p_3)$$
$$> \frac{1}{3}\pi(f^m, 1/2, p_2, p_3) + \frac{1}{3}\pi(f^m, p_1, 1/2, p_3)$$
$$+ \frac{1}{3}\pi(f^m, p_1, p_2, 1/2)$$

But

$$\pi(f^m, 1/2, p_i, p_j)$$
$$= p_i p_j + \frac{1}{2}p_i(1 - p_j) + \frac{1}{2}p_j(1 - p_i) = \frac{1}{2}p_i p_j$$

Hence, the right-hand side of the above inequality is equal to

$$\frac{1}{3}\left[\frac{1}{2}(p_2\,p_3)+\frac{1}{2}(p_1+p_3)+\frac{1}{2}(p_1+p_2)\right]$$

$$=\frac{1}{3}(p_1+p_2+p_3)=\overline{p}=\pi(f^e,\mathbf{p})$$

That is,

$$\pi(f^m,\,p_1,\,p_2,\,p_3) > \pi(f^e,\mathbf{p})$$

Q.E.D.

11.3 CONDORCET'S JURY THEOREM

The following two assertions appear in the classic work of the French philosopher and mathematician Condorcet (1785), in the context of uncertain collective dichotomous choice, where a group faces two alternatives, but the identity of the alternative which is preferred for all group members is uncertain.

1 *The probability that a group applying the simple majority rule chooses the preferred alternative ("the correct alternative") is higher than the probability that one of the group members chooses that alternative.*

2 *The choice of the preferred alternative becomes certain when the number of group members converges to infinity.*

The discovery of Condorcet's work by Black (1958) resulted in the derivation of alternative sufficient conditions to the validity of the above two claims. The simplest and best-known such condition that was proposed by Black appears in the so-called Condorcet's jury theorem, which generalizes Proposition 11.1.

Proposition 11.3: Condorcet's jury theorem: In a group of n decision makers, where n is odd, with identical decisional skills p, if skills are independent and the individuals are competent in the sense that $p > 1/2$, then:

1. The simple majority rule is preferred to the expert rule.

2. When the number of decision makers n converges to infinity, the probability of making a correct collective decision converges to 1.

Proof

1. When individual decisional skills are identical, the simple majority rule f^m is the optimal collective decision rule, as we shall see in the next chapter (Corollary 12.4). In particular, the simple majority rule f^m is preferred to the expert rule f^e. That is,

$$\pi(f^m, \mathbf{p}) = \sum_{j=(n+1)/2}^{n} \binom{n}{j} p^j (1 - p)^{n-j} > p = \pi(f^e, \mathbf{p})$$

2. By the strong law of large numbers, the relationship between the number of individuals who make a correct decision and the number of all individuals n converges to p when n converges to infinity. Since $p > 1/2$, this means that in this case the probability of obtaining a correct collective decision when the group applies the simple majority rule converges to 1. In other words,

$$\lim_{n \to \infty} \pi(f^m, \mathbf{p}) = \lim_{n \to \infty} \sum_{j=(n+1)/2}^{n} \binom{n}{j} p^j (1 - p)^{n-j} = 1$$

Q.E.D.

It can be easily verified that, in general, part 1 of the above proposition is not valid, even when all individuals are competent, that is, when

$$p_1 \geq p_2 \geq p_3 \geq \ldots \geq p_n > 1/2$$

For example, suppose that $\mathbf{p} = (p_1, p_2, p_3) = (0.9, 0.6, 0.6)$. In this case

$$\pi(f^m, \mathbf{p}) = p_1 p_2 p_3 + p_1 p_2 (1 - p_3) + p_1 (1 - p_2) p_3$$
$$+ (1 - p_1) p_2 p_3 = 0.792 < \pi(f^e, \mathbf{p}) = 0.9$$

That is, the expert rule is preferred to the simple majority rule. However, when $\mathbf{p} = (p_1, p_2, p_3) = (0.8, 0.7, 0.7)$, part 1 of the proposition is valid because $\pi(f^m, \mathbf{p}) = 0.826 > 0.8 = \pi(f^e, \mathbf{p})$.

An interesting question is: How can Condorcet's jury theorem be extended to the case where individual decisional skills are not identical? In the next section, three possible extensions of Condorcet's jury theorem are presented (without proof). The first extension generalizes Proposition 11.2, and the two other extensions generalize the second part of Condorcet's theorem.

11.4 EXTENSIONS OF CONDORCET'S JURY THEOREM

11.4.1 The superiority of the simple majority rule when the decisional skills of the n voters are unknown

As in Section 11.2, let us assume that when individual decisional skills are unknown and the collective decision is based on the decision of a single individual ("the expert"), there is equal probability that the skill of that "expert" is equal to $p_i, i = 1, \ldots, n$. This assumption implies that although individual decisional skills differ, in light of the absence of information about these skills, the selection of any individual as the expert ensures that his expected decisional skill is $\bar{p}$, $\bar{p} = \sum_{i=1}^{n} p_i$. Again, we assume that the individuals are competent, $p_1 \geq p_2 \geq p_3 \geq \ldots \geq p_n > 1/2$, and that their decisional skills are independent.

Proposition 11.4: In an n-member group with unknown decisional skills (n is an odd number larger than 1), the simple majority rule is preferred to the expert rule.

Proof: See Ben Yashar and Paroush (2000).
Proposition 11.4 is significant both normatively and from the positive point of view of decision theory; it explains why the use of simple majority rule is appropriate and so common in a world where information on individual decisional skills is difficult to obtain.

11.4.2 The superiority of the simple majority rule when the decisional skills of the n voters are different

The first extension of the asymptotic part in Condorcet's theorem (part 2) allows diversity in the individual decisional skills.

Proposition 11.5: In an n-member group, if $\overline{p}$ is fixed, individual decisional skills are independent and $\overline{p} > 1/2$, then $\lim_{n \to \infty} \pi(f^m, \mathbf{p}) = 1$.

Proof: See Owen, Grofman and Feld (1989).

The second extension of the asymptotic part of Condorcet's theorem also allows heterogeneity of decisional skills, but is not based on the assumption that the average skill $\overline{p}$ is fixed. Instead, it requires that individual decisional skills are sufficiently higher than 1/2 (the skill of a fair coin).

Proposition 11.6: In an n-member group, if there exists ε, $\varepsilon > 0$, such that the decisional skill of every individual satisfies the inequality $p_i \geq 1/2 + \varepsilon$, then $\lim_{n \to \infty} \pi(f^m, \mathbf{p}) = 1$.

Proof: See Paroush (1998).

There are other extensions of Condorcet's jury theorem. In particular, several attempts have been made to generalize the theorem assuming that individual decisional skills are dependent. See Berg (1993), Fey (2003) or Ladha (1993), (1995). Condorcet's theorem has also been studied in a more general setting where costs of applying the simple majority rule and the expert rule are taken into account. The following section is devoted to the possibility of extending the theorem to such a wider setting.

11.5 IS CONDORCET'S THEOREM VALID WHEN DECISIONAL SKILLS ARE DETERMINED ENDOGENOUSLY?

So far we have assumed that the individual decisional skills are fixed. This assumption is perhaps plausible in the context of juries. But in many economic contexts it is not plausible, because skills can often be affected, for example, by investment in human capital. When decisional skills are determined endogenously and the costs of investment in individual decisional skills are taken into account, Condorcet's jury theorem is no longer valid. This claim is proven below, assuming that decisional skills are controlled by a central planner who determines the investment in the decisional quality of the individuals. The proof is based on a simple counter-example, where the group includes three identical decision makers. In this extended setting, Condorcet's theorem is not valid because the use of the simple majority rule reduces the investment in the individual decisional skills relative to the investment in the decisional skill of a single individual, the expert.

11.5.1 The extended model: identical endogenous decisional skills

In addition to the assumptions presented in Section 11.1, let us assume that the common decisional skill p is a control variable determined by the amount of investment in human capital c, such that $p(c)$ is a monotone increasing function in c with positive and declining marginal productivity, that is, $p'(c) > 0$ and $p''(c) < 0$. In addition, let $p(0) = 1/2$ and $p(c \to \infty) \to 1$. Denote by B the net utility of a correct decision (choice of the preferred alternative). The expected utility of the group $R(B,n,p(c),c)$ depends therefore on the net utility of making a correct decision B, on the number of individuals who take part in making the collective decision n, on the production function of decisional skills $p(c)$, and on the investment in human capital in every individual who takes part in making the collective decision.

11.5.2 Centrally determined decisional skills

When there is a single decision maker, $n = 1$, let c_1 denote the optimal investment in his human capital. When the group includes three members, $n = 3$, let c_3 denote the optimal investment in the human capital of each of the three decision makers. In the first case where $n = 1$,

$$c_1 = \arg\max\left[R(B, 1, p(c), c) = Bp(c) - c\right] \tag{1}$$

If c_1 is an interior solution, then it satisfies the following equality:

$$p'(c_1) = \frac{1}{B} \tag{2}$$

In the second case where $n = 3$,

$$c_3 = \arg\max \left[\begin{array}{l} R(B, 3, p(c), c) \\ = B\left[(p(c))^3 + 3(p(c))^2(1 - p(c))\right] - 3c \end{array} \right] \tag{3}$$

If c_3 is an interior solution, then it satisfies the following equality:

$$p'(c_3) = \frac{1}{B} \cdot \frac{1}{2p(c_3)(1 - p(c_3))} \tag{4}$$

The first-order conditions (2) and (4) and the assumptions $p'(c) > 0$ and $p''(c) < 0$ imply that $c_1 > c_3$ (verify) and therefore $p(c_1) > p(c_3)$. It is possible then that the use of the simple majority rule reduces the probability of making a correct choice by each of the three individuals relative to the expert's probability of making a correct choice. In turn, it is possible that the expert rule results in higher performance relative to the simple majority rule.

Example 11.1

Suppose that $B = 6$ and $p(c) = 1 - \frac{1}{2}e^{-2c}$.

By the first-order condition (2) for an interior solution of c_1, one gets that $c_1 = 0.8958$.

By the first-order condition (4) for an interior solution of c_3, one gets that $c_3 = 0.3815$.

Hence,

$$R(B, 1, p(c_1), c_1) = Bp(c_1) - c_1$$

$$= 6(0.9166) - 0.8958 = 4.6038 > R(B, 3, p(c_3), c_3)$$

$$= B\left[(p(c_3))^3 + 3(p(c_3))^2(1 - p(c_3))\right] - 3c_3)$$

$$= 6\left[(0.7669)^3 + 3(0.7669)^2(0.2331)\right] - 3(0.3815)$$

$$= 6(0.8622) - 3(0.3815)$$

$$= 4.0292$$

∎

The example illustrates that when a central planner determines the quality of the decision makers by setting the investment in their human capital and the group applies the simple majority rule, an increase from $n = 1$ to $n = 3$ can reduce the expected utility of the group. Furthermore, such an increase in the number of decision makers can reduce the probability of selecting the preferred alternative from 0.9166 to 0.8622.

$$\left[(p(c_3))^3 + 3(p(c_3))^2(1 - p(c_3)) \right] = 0.8622$$

The example establishes that an increase in the number of decision makers accompanied by adjustment in the investment in human capital does not necessarily result in an increase in the probability that the correct alternative is selected. Indeed the simple majority rule improves the quality of collective decision making when individual decisional skills are identical, but in the extended model, the investment in the expert (the single individual who makes the collective decision) is larger than the investment in the three individuals whose decisions are the input of the simple majority rule. Consequently their decisional skills are lower than that of the expert, and so it is possible that the quality of the collective choice is reduced when the group applies the simple majority rule instead of the expert rule. In other words, Condorcet's jury theorem is not valid when individual decisional skills are determined endogenously by a central planner.

When skills are determined endogenously in a decentralized way by the decision makers and not by a central planner, Condorcet's theorem is also not necessarily valid (see Question 11.8). In this case, every individual who takes part in the collective decision determines the investment in his human capital c, which determines his decisional skill p. Since an individual's utility hinges not only on his skill, but also on the skills of the other individuals, the individual decision becomes strategic and, therefore, it makes sense to study individual decision making by resorting to game theory.

11.6 IS CONDORCET'S THEOREM VALID WHEN INDIVIDUAL DECISIONS ARE INSINCERE?

So far we have assumed implicitly that the individuals behave (vote) sincerely while taking part in the collective decision. In particular, an individual decision maker choosing between alternatives a and b behaves in the same sincere way when he is an expert who determines the collective choice and when he is just one member of the group that uses the simple majority rule. This assumption is plausible because, by assumption, all the individuals are interested in the selection of the "correct alternative" (the individual preferences are identical), and, therefore, it seems that no individual has an incentive and ability to affect the collective choice by insincere manipulative voting that harms the other individuals. But this intuitive assumption is not valid; that is, the individuals may certainly have an incentive to behave strategically in an insincere way. We present below an example illustrating the existence of such incentives to insincere voting. We will then clarify that such incentives do not exist in the context of the present chapter when a committee applies the simple majority rule. Condorcet's jury theorem is therefore valid in such a case even when strategic voting is allowed. In the more general setting of asymmetric alternatives, which is studied in the next chapter, strategic voting may undermine the validity of Condorcet's theorem and its extensions, which are based on the assumption of sincere voting. This possibility was first presented in Austen-Smith and Banks (1996).

11.6.1 Strategic considerations and insincere voting[1]

Consider a two-member committee where individual 1's decisional skill is $p_1 < 1$ and individual 2's decisional skill is $p_2 = 1$. Suppose that the committee applies the following collective decision rule. When the two individuals share the same decision, the rule chooses the agreed-upon alternative. Otherwise, that is, when the individuals' decisions differ, the rule chooses alternative a. In this case, individual 1 has an incentive to disregard his true (sincere) decision and always support the selection of alternative b. To illustrate this incentive,

---

[1] A comprehensive analysis of strategic voting in the context of uncertain dichotomous choice appears in Ben-Yashar and Milchtaich (2007). The examples presented below are based on those presented in their study.

Table 11.1

Decision of individual 1	Decision of individual 2	Collective choice under sincere voting	Strategic voting of individual 1	Collective choice under insincere voting of individual 1
a	*a*	*a*	*b*	*a*
a	*b*	*a*	*b*	*b*
b	*a*	*a*	*b*	*a*
b	*b*	*b*	*b*	*b*

let us consider all the decision profiles of the individuals and the corresponding collective committee decision under sincere voting, see the first three columns in Table 11.1.

Notice that under the second decision profile, see line 2 in the table, the collective choice is incorrect. If individual 1 adopts the insincere voting strategy of always voting for alternative *b*: see column 4 in the table, the collective decision is always the correct choice: see column 5. This extreme example demonstrates the possibility of advantageous strategic insincere voting.

11.6.2 Condorcet's theorem and strategic considerations
When the committee applies the simple majority rule and the assumptions of Condorcet's Jury Theorem (Proposition 11.3) are satisfied, no individual has an incentive to deviate from his sincere decision. This means that Condorcet's theorem is valid even when individuals can vote strategically (insincerely).[2] This claim is illustrated below in the case of a three-member committee with equally capable members whose decisional skills are equal to p, $p < 1$. Consider the decision profiles of the three individuals and the collective decision of

---

[2] Note that the possibility of strategic voting by coalitions of individuals is disregarded.

a committee that applies the simple majority rule; see the first four columns in Table 11.2.

The decisions of the committee under strategic and sincere voting differ only in two individual decision profiles; see lines 6 and 7 in the table. Any deviation from sincere voting by any individual cannot improve his situation (as well as the situation of the other committee members). This is demonstrated by assuming that the insincere strategy adopted by individual 1 is the constant choice of alternative a, regardless of his sincere decision; see column 5 in the table. The corresponding collective choice by the simple majority rule is presented in column 6 of the table. The probability that the decision of the committee is correct and that under sincere voting we obtain one of the two decision profiles presented in line 6 or line 7 in the table is equal to $p^2(1 - p)$ (explanation: the two alternatives are symmetric, that is, the a-priori probability of each of them to be the correct choice is equal to $1/2$. Hence, the probability of obtaining b as a correct decision and the decision profile of line 6, (b, b, a), is equal to $\frac{1}{2}(p^2(1 - p))$. Similarly, the probability of obtaining b as a correct decision and the decision profile of line 7, (b, a, b), is the same. The probability of obtaining b as a correct decision in one of these two decision profiles is therefore equal to $p^2(1 - p)$). However, under strategic voting, the probability that the decision of the committee is correct and one of these two decision profiles is obtained is smaller and equal to $(1 - p)^2 p$ (explanation: the probability of obtaining a as a correct decision and the decision profile of line 6, (b, b, a), is equal to $\frac{1}{2}(1 - p)^2 p$). Similarly, the probability of obtaining a as a correct decision and the decision profile of line 7, (b, a, b), is the same. The probability of obtaining a as a correct decision in one of these two decision profiles is therefore equal to $(1 - p)^2 p$. This means that individual 1 does not have an incentive to deviate from his sincere voting and always vote for alternative a. In a similar way it can be shown that individual 1, and in fact any individual, does not have an incentive to always vote for alternative b or choose any other insincere voting strategy. This reasoning

Table 11.2

Decision of individual 1	Decision of individual 2	Decision of individual 3	Collective choice under simple majority and sincere voting	Strategic voting of individual 1	Collective choice under simple majority and insincere voting of individual 1
a	a	a	a	a	a
a	a	b	a	a	a
a	b	a	a	a	a
a	b	b	b	a	b
b	a	a	a	a	a
b	b	a	b	a	a
b	a	b	b	a	a
b	b	b	b	a	b

is also valid when the number of committee members is larger than three.

When the committee applies the simple majority rule and the alternatives are symmetric, no individual has an incentive to deviate from his sincere voting, even when decisional skills are heterogeneous. The extensions of Condorcet's jury theorem corresponding to this case are therefore valid when individuals are allowed to vote strategically. We will not present the proof of this claim. However we conclude this chapter with a clarification of why no individual has an incentive to deviate from his sincere voting when the committee includes three members, $p_1 = p_2 = p < 1$ and $p_3 = 1$.

Consider the possible decision profiles of the three individuals and the corresponding majority decision; see the first four columns in Table 11.3. Note that a mistaken decision is obtained in two decision profiles; see lines 2 and 6 of the table. Any individual's deviation from his sincere voting is not advantageous (either to him or to the other committee members). To illustrate this assertion, let us assume that the strategy adopted by individual 1 is a constant choice of alternative a disregarding his sincere decision; see column 5 in Table 11.3. The collective decision by simple majority is presented in column 6. Notice that in this case an incorrect collective choice is also obtained in two decision profiles; see lines 2 and 7 of the table. The first decision profile described in line 2 that results in an incorrect decision is identical under sincere and insincere voting. The probability of an incorrect decision and the emergence of the second decision profile, presented on line 7 when individual 1 votes strategically, is equal to $p(1 - p) \cdot 1$. This probability is larger than $(1 - p)^2 \cdot 1$, the probability of an incorrect decision and the emergence of the second decision profile presented on line 6 when individual 1 votes sincerely. Since $p(1 - p) > (1 - p)^2$, individual 1 has no incentive to change his sincere voting and always support alternative a.[3]

---

[3]   Note that when the two alternatives are not symmetric, as will be discussed in the general setting of the next chapter, and the a-priori probability of alternative a is

Table 11.3

Decision of individual 1	Decision of individual 2	Decision of individual 3 (the expert)	Collective choice under simple majority and sincere voting	Strategic voting of individual 1	Collective choice under simple majority and insincere voting of individual 1
a	a	a	a	a	a
a	a	b	a	a	a
a	b	a	a	a	a
a	b	b	b	a	b
b	a	a	a	a	a
b	b	a	b	a	a
b	a	b	b	a	a
b	b	b	b	a	b

Similarly, it can be shown that individual 1 and every other individual do not have an incentive to constantly vote for alternative b or choose any other insincere voting strategy.

11.7 EXERCISES

The proof of the extension of Condorcet's jury theorem to the case where decisional skills are unknown, Proposition 11.4, appears in Ben Yashar and Paroush (2000). The proof of the second extension of the second asymptotic part of Condorcet's theorem, Proposition 11.6, appears in Paroush (1998).

11.1 The expert rule vs. the simple majority rule: The case of three identical decision makers

Question 11.1

Suppose that individual decisional skills are known. How can the assumption $p > 1/2$ be justified?

Answer

When individual decisional skills are known and $p < 1/2$, the alternative chosen by an individual can be considered as the alternative the group should not choose. If the individual selects alternative a, the group will interpret it as a recommendation to choose alternative b. If the individual selects alternative b, the group interprets it as a recommendation to choose alternative a. Such an attitude to the individual's decision ensures that in fact his decisional skill is equal to $(1 - p) > 1/2$.

Question 11.2

Assuming that the three individuals are equally competent, what is the value of p that ensures a maximal advantage of the simple majority rule over the expert rule?

sufficiently larger than the a-priori probability of alternative b, it is definitely possible that individual 1 has an incentive to vote insincerely and always support alternative a. In this case, Condorcet's theorem and its extensions are not valid, as shown by Austen-Smith and Banks (1996).

Answer

The answer to this question is obtained from the solution to the problem:

$$\underset{p}{\text{Max}} \, A(p) = \pi(f^m, \mathbf{p}) - \pi(f^e, \mathbf{p})$$
$$= p^3 + 3p^2(1 - p) - p = 3p^2 - 2p^3 - p$$

The first-order condition to an interior solution of the problem is the equality:

$$\frac{\mathrm{d}A}{\mathrm{d}p} = 6p - 6p^2 - 1 = 0$$

The solution of this quadratic equation implies that the maximal advantage of the simple majority rule over the expert rule is obtained when p = 0.788 (verify). In this case,

$$\text{Max}\,A(p) = \pi(f^m, \mathbf{p}) - \pi(f^e, \mathbf{p}) = 3p^2 - 2p^3 - p = 0.097$$

That is, the use of the simple majority·rule increases by about 10% the probability that the group makes the correct decision.

Question 11.3

Discuss and give your opinion on the following claim: "When the decisions of two individuals are totally dependent on the decision of the third individual (the leader), that is, when these individuals always choose the same alternative chosen by the third individual, Proposition 11.1 is not valid."

Answer

The claim is correct. In such a case of complete dependence, the probability of making a correct decision is equal to p, both under the expert rule and under the simple majority rule.

11.2 The expert rule vs. the simple majority rule: The case of three decision makers with unknown decisional skills

Question 11.4

What is the basic difference between the expert rule in the context of identical individuals and the expert rule in the context of individuals whose decisional skills are unknown?

Answer

When individuals are equally skilled, a collective decision based on the decision of a single individual means that the decision rule is indeed an expert (in the weak sense) rule, although the identity of the expert is inconsequential because decisional skills are identical. When individuals are heterogeneous, a collective decision based on the decision of a single individual is not necessarily an expert rule, because the probability that the decisional skill of the "expert" is the highest is equal only to 1/3.

11.3 Condorcet's jury theorem

Question 11.5

Why is Condorcet's theorem called Condorcet's jury theorem?

Answer

Condorcet's theorem is meaningful in a jury context because in this setting the assumptions of the theorem are plausible: The decision of the jury is dichotomous; the jury members share identical preferences, and, therefore, there exists a correct or a preferred alternative; and finally, the decisional skills of the jury members are imperfect.

The decision of the jury is dichotomous: to acquit or convict the accused. The decision makers share a common objective: to reveal the truth, that is, make the correct decision – convict the accused if he is guilty or acquit him if he is innocent. Nevertheless, the decision makers may err; that is, the jury does not necessarily make the correct decision.

Question 11.6

What is the significance of Condorcet's theorem and its extensions?

Answer

Condorcet's theorem and its extensions clarify under what conditions the simple majority rule is superior to the expert rule, and when it is justified to increase the number of decision makers (voters). These results are significant because they provide a possible formal rationalization of democratic decision making that is based on simple majority, without restricting the number of participants in the decision-making process.

11.4 Extensions of Condorcet's jury theorem

Question 11.7

What are the reasons for the superiority of simple majority rule over the expert rule?

Answer

By Condorcet's theorem (Proposition 11.3), the reasons for the superiority of simple majority rule over the expert rule are: (i) independence of individual decisions; (ii) the fact that the decision makers are qualified (the probability that an individual makes the correct choice is larger than $1/2$); (iii) the equality of individual decisional skills.

By the extension of the first part of Condorcet's theorem (Proposition 11.4), the reasons for the superiority of simple majority rule over the expert rule are: (i) independence of individual decisions; (ii) the fact that the decision makers are qualified (the probability that an individual makes the correct choice is larger than $1/2$); (iii) the fact that individual decisional skills are unknown, which implies equality of the probabilities that the individuals serve the expert's role and determine the collective decision.

11.5 Is Condorcet's theorem valid when decisional skills are determined endogenously?

Question 11.8

Suppose that an individual who takes part in the collective decision making decides on the investment in his own human capital, c, that determines his decisional skill, $p(c)$. Since the benefit of every individual hinges on his skill, but also on the skills of the other individuals, his decision making is strategic. It therefore makes sense to study the individuals' decision making, applying the methodology of game theory. Assume that the collective benefit from choosing the preferred alternative, B, is equally shared by all the individuals (regardless of whether they take part or not in the collective decision making).

a. What is the condition that characterizes optimal investment in human capital, c^*, when the group applies the expert rule $(n = 1)$?

b. What is the condition that characterizes optimal investment in the human capital of three individuals, (c^{**}, c^{**}, c^{**}), in a symmetric Nash equilibrium, when the group applies the simple majority rule and $n = 3$?

c. Prove that when $B = 6$ and $p(c) = 1 - \frac{1}{2}e^{-2c}$, the probability of making the correct choice is reduced if the group applies the simple majority rule instead of the expert rule.

Answer

a. Let A denote the individual's benefit from a correct choice, $A = B/3$. Since $c^* = \arg\max\,[R(A, 1, p(c), c] = Ap(c) - c]$, if c^* is an interior solution, then it satisfies the equality: $p'(c^*) = \frac{1}{A}$.

b. When $n = 3$, the individuals are players in a non-cooperative game and the payoff function of individual i, $i = 1,2,3$, is

$$u^i(c_1, c_2, c_3)$$
$$= A[p(c_1)p(c_2)\,p(c_3) + p(c_1)p(c_2)(1 - p(c_3))$$
$$+ p(c_1)(1 - p(c_2)(p(c_3) + (1 - p(c_1))p(c_2)p(c_3)] - c_i$$

Since the game is symmetric, there exists a symmetric Nash equilibrium where

$$c^{**} = \arg\max \left[A \left[\begin{array}{l} p(c)(p(c^{**})^2 + 2(p(c)(p(c^{**})(1 - p(c^{**})) \\ + p(c^{**})^2(1 - p(c)) \end{array} \right] \right] - c$$

c^{**} is characterized by the equality:

$$p'(c^{**}) = \frac{1}{A} \cdot \frac{1}{2p(c^{**})(1 - p(c^{**}))}$$

c. By the condition of part (a), $c^* = 0.3465$ and therefore the probability that the correct alternative is chosen by the expert is equal to 0.75. By the condition in part (b), $c^* = 0$. Hence, the probability of making the correct collective choice under the simple majority rule is reduced to 1/2.

11.6 Is Condorcet's theorem valid when individual decisions are insincere?

Question 11.9

Explain why the proof of Condorcet's theorem is based on the implicit assumption that the individuals vote sincerely.

Answer

When sincere voting is assumed, an individual who chooses between the two alternatives a and b behaves in the same way when he is the expert who determines the collective decision and when he is one of the members of a group that applies the simple majority rule. Identical behavior in these two cases implies that we can use the same decisional skills (the individual probabilities of making the correct choice) in the expression specifying the probability of a correct collective choice under the expert rule and in the expression specifying the probability of a correct collective choice when the group applies the simple majority rule.

Question 11.10

Clarify the two basic causes for the existence of an incentive to insincere voting.

Answer

There are two causes for the existence of an incentive to insincere voting.

One factor is the individual's awareness that when the group applies the simple majority rule, his voting is of critical significance only in tie situations. In these situations his vote is pivotal; it determines which of the two alternatives a and b is chosen.

The second factor is the individual's awareness that a tie situation reveals information on the "signals" of some of the other voters, and as a result the individual is advantageous when he disregards the private "signal" that he gets.

Question 11.11

Discuss and give your opinion on the following claim: "When individuals differ in their decisional skills and the group uses the simple majority rule, strategic insincere voting of coalitions is possible" (use the example presented in Table 11.3).

Answer

The claim is correct. The coalition that includes individuals 1 and 2 can improve the situation of every member if individual 1 adopts the insincere strategy of always voting for alternative a and individual 2 adopts the insincere strategy of always voting for alternative b. In such a case, the decision of the committee is always correct.

11.8 SUMMARY

- In the context of the uncertain dichotomous choice model, we first presented the following two results:

Proposition 11.1: In a group that consists of three equally skilled individuals, the simple majority rule is preferred to the expert rule.

Proposition 11.2: In a three-member group with unknown decisional skills, the simple majority rule is preferred to the expert rule.

- Condorcet's jury theorem generalizes Proposition 11.1.

Proposition 11.3 (Condorcet's jury theorem): In a group of n decision makers, where n is odd, with identical decisional skills p, if skills are independent and the individuals are competent in the sense that $p > 1/2$, then:

1. The simple majority rule is preferred to the expert rule.
2. When the number of decision makers n converges to infinity, the probability of making a correct collective decision converges to 1.

- The first extension of Condorcet's theorem generalizes Proposition 11.2.

Proposition 11.4: In an n-member group with unknown decisional skills (n is an odd number larger than 1), the simple majority rule is preferred to the expert rule.

- The last two results are two extensions of Condorcet's theorem to the case of n individuals with different decisional skills.

Proposition 11.5: In an n-member group, if $\bar{p}$ is fixed, individual decisional skills are independent and $\bar{p} > 1/2$, then $\lim_{n \to \infty} \pi(f^m, \mathbf{p}) = 1$.

Proposition 11.6: In an n-member group, if there exists ε, $\varepsilon > 0$, such that the decisional skill of every individual satisfies the inequality $p_i \geq 1/2 + \varepsilon$, then $\lim_{n \to \infty} \pi(f^m, \mathbf{p}) = 1$.

- In the last two sections of this chapter, we presented two limitations of Condorcet's theorem:

1. We first proved that the theorem cannot be generalized to the case where individual decisional skills are endogenously determined by a central planner.

2. We then presented an example where equilibrium voting is insincere. This example raises doubts regarding the validity of Condorcet's theorem when group decision making is conceived as a strategic game in which individual behavior is obtained in (Nash) equilibrium. The example and its implication are obtained despite the fact that, in the game theoretic model, conflicts among the individuals' interests do not exist (the individuals share identical preferences).

12 The optimal decision rule under uncertain dichotomous choice

In the simple context of dichotomous choice, the simple majority rule and the expert rule are just two of the possible collective decision-making rules. The main question on which this chapter focuses is the following: What is the optimal collective decision rule from the point of view of individuals who share the same preferences, but differ in their decision-making capabilities? We first identify the optimal decision rule in the general context of uncertain dichotomous choice, then focus on its characteristics in special cases. In particular, we clarify under what circumstances the optimal decision rule is the simple majority rule or the expert rule. The last part of the chapter is devoted to a short discussion of some possible extensions of the model.

As in the model presented in the preceding chapter, we assume that the size of the group is fixed and the decisional skills of the individuals are independent. Nevertheless, the dichotomous decision-making model we present is more general because it allows variability in individual decisional skills, asymmetry in the individual utility in case of making a correct decision in the two possible states of nature, and asymmetry in the priors of the states of nature. The general model and the main results of this chapter are presented in Nitzan and Paroush (1982), (1985).

12.1 DICHOTOMOUS DECISION MAKING – THE MODEL

Consider a group of individuals $N = \{1, \dots, n\}$ (a team of experts, a committee, a board of managers) that faces a choice between two alternatives, a and b (approve or not an investment project, admit or not a candidate, acquit or convict an accused person). The number of members in the group N is fixed and equal to n, $|N| = n$. The choice of individual i between the alternatives a and b is represented by the decision variable x_i that is equal to 1 or to -1. $x_i = 1$ means that the individual chooses alternative a. $x_i = -1$ means that he chooses alternative b. Notice that in the dichotomous model the possibility of abstention is not allowed. The decisions of the group members are represented by a decision profile $x = (x_1, \ldots, x_n)$. This profile specifies the actual decisions of all group members. Let Ω denote the set of all possible profiles.

In the uncertain dichotomous choice model, there are two possible states of nature, and in each of them the correct choice is one of the two alternatives a and b. For simplicity, denote by 1 the state of nature in which a is the correct alternative that should be chosen, and by -1 the state of nature where b is the correct choice. Let us clarify the meaning of the term *correct alternative*. We denote by $B(a; 1)$ the utility from choosing a in state of nature 1. $B(a; -1)$ denotes the utility from a in state of nature -1. In an analogous way, $B(b; 1)$ and $B(b; -1)$ denote, respectively, the utility from choosing b in states of nature 1 and -1. Given state of nature 1, alternative a is the correct alternative if $B(a; 1) > B(b; 1)$. Given state of nature -1, alternative b is the correct alternative if $B(b; -1) > B(a; -1)$. The common preferences of the individuals are thus represented by the payoff matrix B

$$B(a; 1) \quad B(b; 1)$$
$$B(a; -1) \quad B(b; -1)$$

Let α and $(1 - \alpha)$, $0 \leq \alpha \leq 1$, denote respectively the a-priori probabilities of realization of states of nature 1 and -1. In other words, α and $(1 - \alpha)$ are the a-priori probabilities that a and b are the correct alternatives.

The decisional skill of individual i is represented by the probability of making the correct decision given the state of nature. We assume that this probability is equal in the two states of nature and denote it by p_i, that is, $p_i = \Pr(a; 1) = \Pr(b; -1)$. This means that the decisional skill of the individual can be represented by a single parameter. We also assume that the probability of making an incorrect decision is equal to $(1 - p_i)$, the individual probabilities of making a correct decision are independent, and that $p_i > 1/2$. The vector $p = (p_1, \ldots, p_n)$ represents therefore the individual decisional skills. With no loss of generality, we assume that if $i < j$, then $p_i \geq p_j$. This means that individual 1 can be referred to as the expert and individual n is the least competent.

The collective decision making is based on the individual decisions. In fact it involves the aggregation of the actual individual decisions. In the dichotomous setting, the collective decision rule f assigns to any possible profile of individual decisions $x = (x_1, \ldots, x_n)$ one of the two alternatives a and b. Formally, f is a function from the set of all possible profiles Ω to the set $\{1, -1\}$. $f(x) = 1$ means that, given the profile x, the group N that applies the rule f chooses alternative a. $f(x) = -1$ means that, given the profile x, the group N that applies the rule f chooses alternative b. We denote by F the set of all possible collective decision rules.

The problem on which this chapter focuses is the identification of the collective decision rule that maximizes the expected utility of the group (every member of the group). To define the objective function in our problem, we have to introduce the conditional probabilities of making a correct collective decision in the two possible states of nature. For this purpose, we partition the set of all possible profiles into two subsets; one subset, $X(a; f)$, includes the profiles where the collective decision rule f selects alternative a. The other subset, $X(b; f)$, includes the profiles where the collective decision rule f selects alternative b. That is,

$$X(a; f) = \left\{ x \in \Omega : f(x) = 1 \right\} \quad \text{and} \quad X(b; f) = \left\{ x \in \Omega : f(x) = -1 \right\}.$$

Under a given collective decision rule f, the probability that the group makes a correct decision in state of nature 1, where a is the correct decision, is equal to $\pi(f : 1) = \Pr\left\{ x \in X(a; f) : 1 \right\}$. In an analogous way, given the decision rule f, the probability that the group makes a correct decision in state of nature -1, where b is the correct decision, is equal to $\pi(f : -1) = \Pr\left\{ x \in X(b; f) : -1 \right\}$. Since f

chooses one of the two alternatives, $\Pr\{x \in X(b; f) : 1\} = 1 - \pi(f : 1)$ and $\Pr\{x \in X(a; f) : -1\} = 1 - \pi(f : -1)$.

The problem on which we focus is the identification of the collective decision rule that maximizes the expected utility of every individual, E. Specifically, given the decision profile x, the a-priori probability α, the payoff matrix B and the decisional skills of the individuals, $p = (p_1, \ldots, p_n)$, the problem is:

$$\max_{f \in F} \quad E(f : x, p_1, \ldots, p_n, \alpha, B)$$

where

$$E = B(a; 1)\pi(f : 1)\alpha + B(b; 1)[1 - \pi(f : 1)]\alpha$$
$$+ B(b; -1)\pi(f : -1)(1 - \alpha) + B(a; -1)[1 - \pi(f : -1)](1 - \alpha)$$
$$= B(1)\pi(f : 1)\alpha + B(-1)\pi(f : -1)(1 - \alpha)$$
$$+ [B(b; 1)\alpha + B(a; -1)(1 - \alpha)]$$

Note that $B(1) = B(a; 1) - B(b; 1)$ is the net utility from making a correct decision in state of nature 1, and $B(-1) = B(b; -1) - B(a; -1)$ is the net utility from making a correct decision in state of nature -1.

12.2 THE OPTIMAL DECISION RULE

Denote by f^* the optimal collective decision rule, that is, the solution of the above problem. Theorem 12.1 presents the main result of this chapter.

Theorem 12.1

$$f^* = sign\left(\sum_{i=1}^{n} \beta_i x_i + \gamma + \delta\right)$$

where

$$sign\, t = \begin{cases} 1 & t > 0 \\ -1 & t > 0 \end{cases}, \beta_i = \ln\frac{p_i}{1 - p_i},$$

$$\gamma = \ln\frac{\alpha}{1 - \alpha} \text{ and } \delta = \ln\frac{B(1)}{B(-1)}$$

Proof: For any decision profile x in Ω, let us partition the individuals in the group N into $A(x)$ and $B(x)$, such that $i \in A(x)$ if $x_i = 1$ and $i \in B(x)$ if $x_i = -1$. Denote, respectively, by $g(x:1)$ and by $g(x:-1)$ the conditional probabilities of obtaining the profile x in states of nature 1 and -1. That is,

$$g(x:1) = \prod_{i \in A(x)} p_i \prod_{i \in B(x)} (1 - p_i) \quad \text{and} \quad g(x:-1) = \prod_{i \in B(x)} p_i \prod_{i \in A(x)} (1 - p_i)$$

Given a collective decision rule f,

$$\pi(f:1) = \sum_{x \in X(a;f)} g(x:1) \quad \text{and} \quad \pi(f:-1) = \sum_{x \in X(b;f)} g(x:-1)$$

By the definition of the expected utility E, the following inequalities are a sufficient condition for the optimality of f^* :

$$X(a;f) = \left\{ x : x \in \Omega \,\&\, B(1)g(x:1)\alpha > B(-1)g(x:-1)(1-\alpha) \right\}$$

$$= \left(x : x \in \Omega \,\&\, \frac{B(1)\alpha}{B(-1)(1-\alpha)} \prod_{i \in A(x)} p_i \prod_{i \in B(x)} (1 - p_i) \right.$$

$$\left. > \prod_{i \in B(x)} p_i \prod_{i \in A(x)} (1 - p_i) \right)$$

$$= \left(x : x \in \Omega \,\&\, \frac{B(1)\alpha}{B(-1)(1-\alpha)} \prod_{i \in A(x)} \frac{p_i}{(1 - p_i)} > \prod_{i \in B(x)} \frac{p_i}{(1 - p_i)} \right)$$

$$= \left(x : x \in \Omega \,\&\, \sum_{i \in A(x)} \beta_i + \gamma + \delta > \sum_{i \in B(x)} \beta_i \right)$$

$$= \left(x : x \in \Omega \,\&\, \sum_i \beta_i x_i + \gamma + \delta > 0 \right)$$

$$X(b;f^*) = \Omega - X(a;f^*) = \left(x : x \in \Omega \,\&\, \sum_i \beta_i x_i + \gamma + \delta < 0 \right)$$

and, therefore,

$$f^* = sign\left(\sum_{i=1}^{n} \beta_i x_i + \gamma + \delta \right)$$

Q.E.D.

12.2.1 Qualified weighted majority rule

The optimal decision rule is a qualified weighted majority rule. A decision rule is a *qualified weighted majority rule* f_q, if one of the alternatives is chosen only when its (normalized) weighted advantage relative to the other alternatives exceeds the special qualified majority q. When the weight assigned to individual i is w_i, the weighted advantage of alternative a is equal to $\sum_{i=1}^{n} w_i x_i$ and the weighted advantage of alternative b is equal to $-\sum_{i=1}^{n} w_i x_i$. The normalized weighted advantage of alternative b relative to alternative a is therefore equal to $-\sum_{i=1}^{n} w_i x_i / \sum_{i=1}^{n} w_i$. A qualified weighted majority rule which is biased in favor of alternative a is thus defined as follows:

$$f_q(x) = \begin{cases} -1 & -\sum_{i=1}^{n} w_i x_i / \sum_{i=1}^{n} w_i \geq q \\ 1 & otherwise \end{cases}$$

By Theorem 12.1, we obtain that when $(\gamma + \delta)$ is positive, the rule f_q is biased in favor of alternative a and the optimal qualified majority q^* required for the selection of alternative b is equal to $(\gamma + \delta)/ \sum_{i=1}^{n} \beta_i$. That is,

Corollary 12.1: The optimal decision rule f^* is a weighted qualified majority rule f_{q^*}, such that $q^* = (\gamma + \delta)/ \sum_{i=1}^{n} \beta_i$.

The two parameters γ and δ determine the desirable bias in favor of one of the alternatives. The parameter γ specifies the asymmetry between the a-priori probabilities of the two states of nature. The parameter δ specifies the asymmetry between the net utilities obtained when making a correct decision in the two states of nature. Notice that the optimal rule f_{q^*} is not a degenerate qualified majority rule unless $\beta' < \gamma + \delta < \sum_{i=1}^{n} \beta_i$, where $\beta' = \min \beta_i$. If $\gamma + \delta > \sum_{i=1}^{n} \beta_i$, then $q^* > 1$, that is, for any decision profile x, $f_{q^*}(x) = 1$. Put differently, in such a case alternative a is always chosen. If $\gamma + \delta < \beta'$, then the qualified majority is meaningless. That is, $f^* = sign(\sum_{i=1}^{n} \beta_i x_i)$ (verify).

12.2.2 Qualified majority rule

When the individual decisional skills are identical, the optimal decision rule is a (non-weighted) qualified majority rule. This common
rule is defined as follows:

f_k, $k > 1/2$, is a *qualified majority rule* biased in favor of alternative
a if

$$f_k(x) = \begin{cases} -1 & N(b) \geq kn \\ 1 & otherwise \end{cases}$$

where $N(b) = |B(x)|$ is the number of individuals who choose alterna-
tive b. The qualified majority rule gives an advantage to alternative
a, and it enables a minority of more than $(1 - k)n$ individuals to prevent the selection of alternative b, which is preferred by a majority
of fewer than kn individuals. By Theorem 12.1, one can obtain that
when $(\gamma + \delta)$ is positive, the rule f_k is biased in favor of alternative
a and the optimal qualified majority k^* required for the selection of
alternative b is equal to

$$k^* = \frac{1}{2}[1 + r^*] = \frac{1}{2}\left[1 + \frac{\gamma + \delta}{\beta n}\right]$$

Corollary 12.2: If individual decisional skills are identical, then the
optimal decision rule f^* is a qualified majority rule f_{k^*} where

$$k^* = \frac{1}{2}[1 + r^*] = \frac{1}{2}\left[1 + \frac{\gamma + \delta}{\beta n}\right].$$

Proof: Let $\beta_0 = \gamma + \delta$. Notice that

$$2\beta[k^*n - N(b)] = 2n\beta\left[\frac{1}{2}\left(1 + \frac{\beta_0}{\beta n}\right) - \frac{N(b)}{n}\right]$$

$$= \beta\left[n - 2N(b) + \frac{\beta_0}{\beta}\right]$$

$$= \beta\left[N(a) - N(b) + \frac{\beta_0}{\beta}\right]$$

$$= \beta[N(a) - N(b)] + \beta_0$$

Hence,

$$2[k^*n - N(b)] = N(a) - N(b) + \frac{\beta_0}{\beta}$$

Clearly,

$$k^*n - N(b) \leq 0 \Leftrightarrow N(b) \geq k*n$$
$$\Leftrightarrow N(a) - N(b) + \frac{\beta_0}{\beta} \leq 0$$
$$\Leftrightarrow N(b) - N(a) \geq \frac{\beta_0}{\beta}$$
$$-\left(\sum_{i=1}^{n} x_i\right)/n \geq \frac{\beta_0}{n\beta}$$

We have therefore obtained that

$$N(b) \geq k*n \Leftrightarrow -\left(\sum_{i=1}^{n} x_i\right)/n \geq \frac{\beta_0}{n\beta} = \frac{\gamma + \delta}{n\beta} = r^*$$

that is,

$$k^* = \frac{1}{2}[1 + r^*] = \frac{1}{2}\left[1 + \frac{\gamma + \delta}{\beta n}\right]$$

In other words, $f^* = f_{k^*}$ **Q.E.D.**

The use of qualified majority rules is very common. In particular, this is true with respect to the 2/3 or 3/4 majority rules. Two extreme such rules are hierarchy and polyarchy. A collective choice rule is called the hierarchy rule or *hierarchy* if it is a qualified majority rule f_{k^h} such that $k^h = 1$. When the rule is hierarchy, the choice of alternative b requires unanimity. A collective choice rule is called *polyarchy* if it is a qualified majority rule f_{k^p} such that $k^p = 1/n$. When the rule is polyarchy, the choice of alternative b requires the minimal support of a single individual.[1]

---

[1]   On the comparison between hierarchies and polyarchies, see Sah and Stiglitz (1988) and Ben Yashar and Nitzan (2001a).

12.3 THE OPTIMAL DECISION RULE IN THE SYMMETRIC CASE

12.3.1 Weighted majority rule

A collective decision rule is called a *weighted majority rule* if $f(x) = sign\left(\sum_{i=1}^{n} w_i x_i\right)$, where w_i is the weight assigned to individual i. By Theorem 12.1 the following result is obtained:

Corollary 12.3:[2] When there is symmetry between the states of nature, $\gamma + \delta = 0$, the optimal collective decision rule is the weighted majority rule

$$f^* = sign\left(\sum_{i=1}^{n} \beta_i x_i\right)$$

12.3.2 Simple majority rule

A collective decision rule is called a *simple majority rule* if

$$f(x) = f^m(x) = sign\left(\sum_{i=1}^{n} x_i\right)$$

By Corollary 12.3 we obtain:

Corollary 12.4: When there is symmetry between the states of nature, $\gamma + \delta = 0$, and the individual decisional skills are identical, the optimal collective decision rule is the simple majority rule

$$f^* = f^m = sign\left(\sum_{i=1}^{n} x_i\right)$$

12.3.3 The expert rule

A collective decision rule is called the *expert rule* if $f(x) = f^e(x) = x_1$. Recall that, with no loss of generality, we have assumed that $i < j$ implies that $p_i \geq p_j$. Hence individual 1 is the expert. By Corollary 12.3 we obtain:

---

[2]   This is the main result in Nitzan and Paroush (1982) and in Shapley and Grofman (1984).

Corollary 12.5: When there is symmetry between the states of nature, $\gamma + \delta = 0$, the expert rule is optimal if, and only if, $\beta_1 > \beta_2 + \cdots + \beta_n$.

(Question 12.11 generalizes this corollary to the case of m experts.)

12.4 EXTENSIONS

The uncertain dichotomous choice model can be extended in different directions. Some of these possible extensions are described briefly below. For applications of Arrow's impossibility theorem to judgment aggregation, see Dietrich (2006, 2007), Dietrich and List (2007), and List and Petit (2002).

12.4.1 Dependence of decisional skills on the state of nature

The decisional skill of an individual may depend on the state of nature. In such a case the skill is not represented by the probability of making the correct decision p_i, but by two probabilities: the probabilities of making a correct choice in states of nature 1 and 2. The generalization of Theorem 12.1 to this case is presented in Ben Yashar and Nitzan (1997).

12.4.2 Dependent decisions

Individual decisional skills may be statistically dependent. Such dependence can be due to different reasons, such as social pressure, persuasion, exchange of information among the individuals, or the existence of a leader or leaders in the group of decision makers. Theorem 12.1 is based on the assumption of independent individual decisional skills. A discussion of the general case of dependent individual skills appears in Ladha (1993, 1995) and in Chapter 6 of Nitzan and Paroush (1985).

12.4.3 The number of decision makers is not fixed

Usually, different collective decision rules have different costs. In particular, the cost of a decision rule that uses more decision makers is higher. For this reason, the expert rule might be considerably cheaper than simple majority rule. On the other hand, a rule that utilizes more qualified decision makers (who have higher decisional skills) is usually more expensive. The identification of the optimal decision rule in this chapter disregards such cost considerations, the costs of the applied collective decision rules. A discussion of the extended case where such costs of different rules are taken into account (whether due to the different number of individuals used by the rule or due to the different decisional quality of the individuals used by the rule) can be found in Chapter 3 of Nitzan and Paroush (1985) or in Ben Yashar and Nitzan (2001b), Gradstein, Nitzan and Paroush (1990) and Paroush and Karotkin (1989).

12.4.4 Decisional skills are not fixed

Individual decisional skills need not be exogenous, as we have assumed so far.

Sometimes, the individuals determine in a decentralized manner the extent of investment in their own skills. In such a case, their decisions may depend on the information and beliefs regarding the decisional skills of the other individuals. Alternatively, investment in the human capital of the individuals and in turn in their decisional skills might be determined by a central planner (Ministry of Education, Ministry of Industry Trade and Labour). Endogenous determination of individual decisional skills in the context of optimal decision making is studied in Ben-Yashar and Nitzan (1998), (2001b) and in Nitzan and Paroush (1980).

12.4.5 Partial information on decisional skills

The optimal decision rule presented in Theorem 12.1 depends on the parameters of the problem on which we focus and, in particular, on the decisional skills of the individuals. These skills have been assumed to be known, although quite often information on these skills is very hard to get and skill estimation can be difficult. A more plausible assumption is that individual decisional skills are only partly known. The question is what can be said about the optimal collective decision rule, assuming that there is only such partial information on the individual decisional skills. Chapter 5 in Nitzan and Paroush (1985) and the studies by Ben Yashar and Paroush (2000) and Berend and Harmse (1993) focus on this issue.

12.4.6 Sequential decision

In the model of this chapter, the number of individuals who take part in the collective decision is given exogenously. We have already noted above that this number can be determined endogenously. But in both cases the number of active decision makers is not a random variable. The model can be extended to the case of sequential collective decision making. In this case, the group size n is a random variable. The implications of this extension on the optimal collective decision rule are discussed in Chapter 8 of Nitzan and Paroush (1985) and in Koh (2005).

12.4.7 More than two alternatives

In many cases, the collective decision is dichotomous. The significance of the dichotomous model and the possibility of extending it to the case of multiple alternatives are discussed in Chapter 9 of Nitzan and Paroush (1985). A generalization of Theorem 12.1 to this more general case appears in Ben Yashar and Paroush (2001).

12.5 EXERCISES

Note: Reading Nitzan and Paroush (1982) may help with some of the following questions.

12.1 Dichotomous decision making – the model

Question 12.1

What is the number of collective decision rules that are available to the group N?

Answer

$$|F| = 2^{2^n}.$$

Question 12.2

Discuss the following claim: "The correct choice cannot be the same alternative in the two states of nature."

Answer

This situation is possible. However, in this case the collective decision problem is inconsequential; the group has to always choose the correct alternative under the two states of nature.

Question 12.3

What are the particular assumptions of the uncertain dichotomous choice model that give rise to the setting of Condorcet's Theorem (Theorem 11.3)?

Answer

The setting of Condorcet's Jury Theorem requires the following assumptions:

a. There is symmetry between the alternatives in the sense that $\alpha = 1/2$.
b. There is symmetry between the alternatives in the sense that

$$B(a; 1) - B(b; 1) = B(a; -1) - B(b; -1),$$

That is, the net benefit from a correct decision is independent of the state of nature.
c. Individual skills are homogeneous.
d. The number of individuals is odd.

Question 12.4

Under what circumstances is it likely that alternatives a and b are asymmetric in the sense that $B(a; 1) - B(b; 1) \neq B(a; -1) - B(b; -1)$?

Answer

Such asymmetry is plausible when one of the alternatives is reversible and the other is irreversible. For example, suppose that a is the imposition of the death penalty on the accused and b is his acquittal.

Question 12.5

Under what circumstances is it likely that alternatives a and b are asymmetric in the sense that $\alpha \neq 1/2$?

Answer

Such asymmetry is plausible when one alternative is "some change in the status quo" and the other alternative is "maintaining the status quo". The reason is that the status quo is commonly considered as representing the successful collective effort to ensure the selection of the socially correct alternative.

12.2 The optimal decision rule

12.2.1 Qualified weighted majority rule

Question 12.6

Prove Corollary 12.1. That is, prove that the optimal decision rule f^* is a weighted qualified majority rule f_{q^*}, such that $q^* = (\gamma + \delta) / \sum_{i=1}^{n} \beta_i$.

Answer

$$f^* = sign \left(\sum_{i=1}^{n} \beta_i x_i + \gamma + \delta \right)$$

That is, given a decision profile x,

$$f^*(x) = \begin{cases} -1 & \sum_{i=1}^{n} \beta_i x_i + \gamma + \delta < 0 \\ 1 & \sum_{i=1}^{n} \beta_i x_i + \gamma + \delta > 0 \end{cases}$$

or

$$f^*(x) = \begin{cases} -1 & \sum_{i=1}^{n} \beta_i x_i < -(\gamma + \delta) \\ 1 & \sum_{i=1}^{n} \beta_i x_i > -(\gamma + \delta) \end{cases}$$

or

$$f^*(x) = \begin{cases} -1 \\ 1 \end{cases} \quad \left\{ \begin{array}{l} -\sum_{i=1}^{n} \beta_i x_i / \sum_{i=1}^{n} \beta_i > (\gamma + \delta)/ \sum_{i=1}^{n} \beta_i = q^* \\ otherwise \end{array} \right.$$

Question 12.7

Discuss the following claim: "If there is asymmetry between the two states of nature, then it is impossible that the optimal decision rule is a (non-qualified) weighted majority rule."

Answer

The claim is incorrect. It is possible that $\gamma + \delta > 0$, that is, there exists asymmetry between the two states of nature, yet $\gamma + \delta < \beta' = min\beta_i$. In such a case the qualification is meaningless, that is, $f^* = sign(\sum_{i=1}^{n} \beta_i x_i)$, $q^* \sum_{i=1}^{n} \beta_i < \beta'$ and, therefore, $sign\left(\sum_{i=1}^{n} \beta_i x_i + \gamma + \delta \right) = sign\left(\sum_{i=1}^{n} \beta_i x_i + q^* \sum_{i=1}^{n} \beta_i \right) = sign\left(\sum_{i=1}^{n} \beta_i x_i \right)$.

Question 12.8

Discuss the following claim: "The optimal rule is a (non-qualified) weighted majority rule if, and only if, there is no asymmetry between the two states of nature, that is, $\alpha = 1/2$ and $B(1) = B(-1)$."

Answer

The claim is incorrect. In the previous question, we have seen that it is possible that the optimal decision rule is a (non-qualified) weighted majority rule even when the two states of nature are asymmetric. Furthermore, the optimal rule is a (non-qualified) weighted majority rule when $\gamma + \delta = 0$, that is, when $\alpha B(1) = (1 - \alpha)B(-1)$ and not necessarily when $\alpha = 1/2$ and $B(1) = B(-1)$.

12.2.2 Qualified majority rule

Question 12.9

Discuss the following claim: "Under the optimal qualified majority rule, the majority k^* required for the selection of alternative b is monotone increasing in $\beta_0 = \gamma + \delta$ and in the number of individuals n."

Answer

The claim is incorrect. It is easy to verify that the derivative of k^* with respect to $\beta_0 = \gamma + \delta$ is always positive, but it is negative with respect to n when $\beta_0 = \gamma + \delta > 0$.

12.3 The optimal decision rule in the symmetric case

Question 12.10

Discuss the following claim: "If the optimal rule is the simple majority rule, then the individual decisional skills are identical."

Answer

The claim is incorrect. It is possible that individual decisional skills differ; in turn, the optimal individual weights $\beta_1, \ldots, \beta_n$ are different (see Corollary 12.3) and still the optimal rule is the simple majority rule. In such a case the different optimal individual weights ensure that any simple majority coalition wins – the coalition secures the choice of the alternative desired by its members. For example, suppose that $n = 3$ and $(\beta_1, \beta_2, \beta_3) = (0.3, 0.4, 0.5)$. It is easy to verify that in this case any two-member coalition wins. In other words, this system of weights defines the simple majority rule that can be defined equivalently by the system of equal weights.

Question 12.11

Assuming that the alternatives are symmetric, what is the necessary and sufficient condition for the dependence of the optimal weighted majority rule only on the decisions of the m, $m < n$, most skillful individuals?

Answer

Let $\beta^*(m) = \min\limits_{x_1, \ldots, x_m} \left[(\sum\limits_{i=1}^{m} \beta_i x_i) : \sum\limits_{i=1}^{m} \beta_i x_i \geq 0 \right]$. Hence, $f^*(x) = sign(\sum\limits_{i=1}^{m} \beta_i x_i)$, where m is the minimal number of individuals

that satisfies the inequality: $\beta^*(m) > \sum\limits_{i=m+1}^{n} \beta_i$. It can be verified that
when $m < n$, the optimal weighted majority rule is based only on the
decisions of the most skillful individuals, because in this case, for
any profile of decisions x, $sign(\sum\limits_{i=1}^{n} \beta_i x_i) = sign(\sum\limits_{i=1}^{m} \beta_i x_i)$.

12.6 SUMMARY

• In the general uncertain dichotomous choice model, on which we
have focused in this chapter, we have assumed, as in Chapter 11, that
the size of the group is fixed and the exogenously given individual
decisional skills are independent. This model is more general because
it allows skill heterogeneity, asymmetry in the individual utilities
from making a correct choice in the two states of nature and asymmetry in the a-priori probabilities of the two states of nature.

• The optimal collective decision rule f^* maximizes the expected
utility of every individual E, given the decision profile x, the a-priori
probabilities of the two states of nature α and $(1 - \alpha)$, the payoff matrix
B,

$B(b; 1)$ $B(a; 1)$
$B(b; -1)$ $B(a; -1)$

and the decisional skills of the individuals, $p = (p_1, \ldots, p_n)$. This rule
is the solution to the problem:

$$\max_{f \in F} \; E(f : x, p_1, \ldots, p_n, \alpha, B)$$

• **Theorem 12.1**

$$f^* = sign\left(\sum_{i=1}^{n} \beta_i x_i + \gamma + \delta\right)$$

where

$$\delta = \ln\frac{B(1)}{B(-1)}, \, \gamma = \ln\frac{\alpha}{1-\alpha}, \, \beta_i = \ln\frac{p_i}{1-p_i}, \; sign\,t = \begin{cases} 1 & t > 0 \\ -1 & t < 0 \end{cases}$$

$B(1) = B(a; 1) - B(b; 1)$ is the net utility of making a correct decision in state of nature 1 and $B(-1) = B(b; -1) - B(a; -1)$ is the net utility of making a correct decision in state of nature -1.

- A decision rule is a *qualified weighted majority rule* f_q if one of the alternatives is chosen only when its (normalized) weighted advantage relative to the other alternative exceeds the special qualified majority q. When the weight assigned to individual i is w_i, the weighted advantage of alternative a is equal to $\sum_{i=1}^{n} w_i x_i$ and the weighted advantage of alternative b is equal to $-\sum_{i=1}^{n} w_i x_i$. The normalized weighted advantage of alternative b relative to alternative a is therefore equal to $-\sum_{i=1}^{n} w_i x_i / \sum_{i=1}^{n} w_i$. A qualified weighted majority rule which is biased in favor of alternative a is thus defined as follows:

$$f_q(x) = \begin{cases} -1 & -\sum_{i=1}^{n} w_i x_i / \sum_{i=1}^{n} w_i \geq q \\ 1 & otherwise \end{cases}$$

- **Corollary 12.1:** The optimal decision rule f^* is a weighted qualified majority rule f_{q^*}, such that $q^* = (\gamma + \delta) / \sum_{i=1}^{n} \beta_i$.

The two parameters γ and δ determine the desirable bias in favor of one of the alternatives. The parameter γ specifies the asymmetry between the a-priori probabilities of the two states of nature. The parameter δ specifies the asymmetry between the net utilities obtained when making a correct decision in the two states of nature.

- f_k, $k > 1/2$, is a qualified majority rule biased in favor of alternative a if

$$f_k(x) = \begin{cases} -1 & N(b) \geq kn \\ 1 & otherwise \end{cases}$$

where $N(b) = |B(x)|$ is the number of individuals who choose alternative b.

• **Corollary 12.2:** If individual decisional skills are identical, then the optimal decision rule f^* is a qualified majority rule f_{k^*} where

$$k^* = \frac{1}{2}[1 + r^*] = \frac{1}{2}\left[1 + \frac{\gamma + \delta}{\beta n}\right]$$

• A collective decision rule is called a *weighted majority rule* if $f(x) = sign\left(\sum_{i=1}^{n} w_i x_i\right)$, where w_i is the weight assigned to individual i.

• **Corollary 12.3:** When there is symmetry between the states of nature, $\gamma + \delta = 0$, the optimal collective decision rule is the weighted majority rule

$$f^* = sign\left(\sum_{i=1}^{n} \beta_i x_i\right)$$

• A collective decision rule is called a *simple majority rule* if

$$f(x) = f^m(x) = sign\left(\sum_{i=1}^{n} x_i\right)$$

• **Corollary 12.4:** When there is symmetry between the states of nature, $\gamma + \delta = 0$, and the individual decisional skills are identical, the optimal collective decision rule is the simple majority rule

$$f^* = f^m = sign\left(\sum_{i=1}^{n} x_i\right)$$

• A collective decision rule is called the *expert rule* if $f(x) = f^e(x) = x_1$.

• **Corollary 12.5:** When there is symmetry between the states of nature, $\gamma + \delta = 0$, the expert rule is optimal if and only if $\beta_1 > \beta_2 + \cdots + \beta_n$.

Bibliography

Arrow, K. J., *Social Choice and Individual Values*, 2nd edn, New Haven: Yale University Press, 1963.

Austen-Smith, D. and J. S. Banks, 'Information Aggregation, Rationality and the Condorcet Jury Theorem,' *American Political Science Review*, 90(1), 1996, 34–45.

Austen-Smith, D. and J. S. Banks, *Positive Political Theory I: Collective Preferences*, Michigan: University of Michigan Press, 1998.

Baharad, E. and S. Nitzan, 'Ameliorating Majority Decisiveness Through Expression of Preference Intensity,' *American Political Science Review*, 96(4), 2002, 745–54.

Baharad, E. and S. Nitzan, 'The Borda Rule, Condorcet Consistency and Condorcet Stability,' *Economic Theory*, 22(3), 2003, 685–8.

Baharad, E. and S. Nitzan, 'Approval Voting Reconsidered,' *Economic Theory*, 26(3), 2005a, 619–28.

Baharad, E. and S. Nitzan, 'The Inverse Plurality Rule – An Axiomatization,' *Social Choice and Welfare*, 25(1), 2005b, 173–8.

Baharad, E. and S. Nitzan, 'On the Selection of the same Winner by all Scoring Rules,' *Social Choice and Welfare*, 26(3), 2006, 579–601.

Baharad, E. and S. Nitzan, 'Scoring Rules: An Alternative Parameterization,' *Economic Theory*, 30(1), 2007a, 187–90.

Baharad, E. and S. Nitzan, 'The Cost of Implementing the Majority Principle: The Golden Voting Rule,' *Economic Theory*, 31(1), 2007b, 69–84.

Baigent, N., 'Metric Rationalization of Social Choice Functions According to Principles of Social Choice,' *Mathematical Social Sciences*, 13, 1987, 59–65.

Barthelemy, J. P. and B. Monjardet, 'The Median Procedure in Cluster Analysis and Social Choice Theory,' *Mathematical Social Sciences*, 1, 1981, 235–67.

Ben-Yashar, R. and I. Milchtaich, 'First and Second Best Voting Rules in Committees,' *Social Choice and Welfare*, 29(3), 2007, 453–86.

Ben-Yashar, R. and S. Nitzan, 'The Optimal Decision Rule for Fixed-size Committees in Dichotomous Choice Situations: The General Result,' *International Economic Review*, 38(1), 1997, 175–87.

Ben-Yashar, R. and S. Nitzan, 'Quality and Structure of Organizational Decision making,' *Journal of Economic Behavior and Organization*, 36, 1998, 521–34.

Ben-Yashar, R. and S. Nitzan, 'The Robustness of Optimal Organizational Architectures: A note on Hierarchies and Polyarchies,' *Social Choice and Welfare*, 18(1), 2001a, 151–63.

Ben-Yashar, R. and S. Nitzan, 'The Invalidity of Condorcet Jury Theorem under Endogenous Decisional Skills,' *Economics of Governance*, 2, 2001b, 143–52.

Ben-Yashar, R. and J. Paroush, 'A non-asymptotic Condorcet Jury Theorem,' *Social Choice and Welfare*, 17, 2000, 189–99.

Ben-Yashar, R. and J. Paroush, 'Optimal Decision Rules for Fixed-size Committees in Polychotomous Choice Situations,' *Social Choice and Welfare*, 18(4), 2001, 737–46.

Berend, D. and J. E. Harmse, 'Expert Rule versus Majority Rule under Partial Information,' *Theory and Decision*, 35, 1993, 179–97.

Berg, S., 'Condorcet's Jury Theorem, Dependency among Voters,' *Social Choice and Welfare*, 10, 1993, 87–95.

Bergstrom, T., Blume, L. and Varian, H., 'On the Private Provision of Public Goods,' *Journal of Public Economics*, 29, 1986, 25–49.

Black, D., *The Theory of Committees and Elections*, Cambridge: Cambridge University Press, 1958.

Blau, J. H., 'Liberal Values and Independence,' *Review of Economic Studies*, 42, 1975, 395–402.

Campbell, D. and S. Nitzan, 'Social Compromise and Social Metrics,' *Social Choice and Welfare*, 3, 1986, 1–16.

Chamberlin, J., 'Provision of Collective Goods as a Function of Group Size,' *American Political Science Review*, 65, 1974, 707–16.

Chebotarev, P. U. and E. Shamis, 'Characterizations of Scoring Methods for Preference Aggregation,' *Annals of Operations Research*, 80, 1998, 299–332.

Clarke, E., 'Multipart Pricing of Public Goods,' *Public Choice*, 11, 1971, 17–33.

Condorcet, Marquiz de, 'Essay on the Application of Analysis to the Probability of Decisions Rendered by a Plurality of Voting,' in I. McLean and A. Urken (eds.), *Classics in Social Choice*, Ann Arbor: The University of Michigan Press, 1995 (original 1785).

Cornes, R. and T. Sandler, *The Theory of Externalities, Public Goods and Club Goods*, Cambridge: Cambridge University Press, 1986.

Dietrich, F., 'Judgment Aggregation: (Im)possibility Theorems,' *Journal of Economic Theory*, 126(1), 2006, 286–98.

Dietrich, F., 'A Generalized Model of Judgment Aggregation,' *Social Choice and Welfare*, 28(4), 2007, 529–65.

Dietrich, F. and C. List, 'Arrow's Theorem in Judgment Aggregation,' *Social Choice and Welfare*, Springer 29, 2007, 19–33.

Dodgson, C. L., *A Method of Taking Votes on More than Two Issues*, Third Pamphlet, 1876 (Reprinted in Black (1958) pp. 224–34).

Farkas, D. and S. Nitzan, 'The Borda Rule and Pareto Stability: A Comment,' *Econometrica*, 47, 1979, 1305–6.

Feldman, A., *Welfare Economics and Social Choice Theory*, Boston: Kluwer, 1984.

Fey, M., 'A Note on Condorcet Jury Theorem with Supermajority Voting Rules,' *Social Choice and Welfare*, 20, 2003, 27–32.

Fishburn, P. C., *The Theory of Social Choice*, Princeton: Princeton University Press, 1973.

Gibbard, A., 'Manipulation of Voting Schemes: A General Result,' *Econometrica*, 41, 1973, 587–601.

Gibbard, A., 'A Pareto-Consistent Libertarian Claim,' *Journal of Economic Theory*, 7, 1974, 388–410.

Gradstein, M. and S. Nitzan, 'Binary Participation and Incremental Provision of Public Goods,' *Social Choice and Welfare*, 7, 1990, 171–92.

Gradstein, M., S. Nitzan and J. Paroush, 'Collective Decision Making and the Limits on the Organization's Size,' *Public Choice*, 66, 1990, 279–91.

Groves, T., 'Incentives in Teams,' *Econometrica*, 41, 1973, 617–31.

Hammond, P. J., 'Equity, Arrow's Condition and Rawls' Difference Principle,' *Econometrica*, 44(4), 1976; 793–804.

Harel, A. and S. Nitzan, 'The Libertarian Resolution of the Paretian-Liberal Paradox,' *Journal of Economics*, 1987, 337–52.

Harsanyi, J. C., 'Cardinal Welfare, Individualistic Ethics and Interpersonal Comparisons of Utility,' *Journal of Political Economy*, 63, 1955, 309–21.

Kelly, J. S., *Social Choice Theory – An Introduction*, Berlin: Springer Verlag, 1988.

Kemeny, J. G., 'Mathematics without Numbers,' *Daedalus*, 88, 1959, 577–91.

Kemeny, J. G. and J. L. Snell, *Mathematical Models in the Social Sciences*, New York: Blaisdell, 1962.

Koh, W., 'Optimal Sequential Decision Architectures and the Robustness of Hierarchies and Polyarchies,' *Social Choice and Welfare*, 24(3), 2005, 397–411.

Ladha, K. K., 'Condorcet's Jury Theorem in Light of de Finetti's Theorem, Majority Rule with Correlated Votes,' *Social Choice and Welfare*, 10, 1993, 69–86.

Ladha, K. K., 'Information Pooling through Majority-Rule voting: Condorcet's Jury Theorem with Correlated Votes,' *Journal of Economic Behavior and Organization*, 26, 1995, 353–72.

Lehrer, E. and S. Nitzan, 'Some General Results on the Metric Rationalization for Social Decision Rules,' *Journal of Economic Theory*, 37(1), 1985, 191–201.

Lindahl, E., 'Just Taxation – A Positive Solution,' in R. A. Musgrave and A. T. Marshall (eds.), *Classics in the Theory of Public Finance*, London: Macmillan, 1958 (original 1919).

List, C. and P. Petit, 'Aggregating Sets of Judgments: An Impossibility Result,' *Economics and Philosophy*, 18, 2002, 89–110.

May, K., 'Independent Necessary and Sufficient Conditions for Simple Majority Decision,' *Econometrica*, 1952, 680–4.

Moulin, H., *The Strategy of Social Choice*, Paris: Ecole Polytechnique, 1981.

Mueller, D. C., *Public Choice III*, Cambridge: Cambridge University Press, revised edn, 2003.

Nash, J. F., 'The Bargaining Problem,' *Econometrica*, 18, 1950, 155–62.

Nitzan, S., 'Linear and Lexicographic Orders, Majority Rule and Equilibrium,' *International Economic Review*, 17(1), 1976, 213–19.

Nitzan, S., 'Some Measures of Closeness to Unanimity and Their Implications,' *Theory and Decision*, 13, 1981, 129–38.

Nitzan, S., 'The Vulnerability of Point Voting Schemes to Preference Variation and Strategic Manipulation,' *Public Choice*, 47(2), 1985, 349–70.

Nitzan, S., 'More on the Preservation of Preference Proximity and Anonymous Social Choice,' *Quarterly Journal of Economics*, 104(1), 1989, 187–90.

Nitzan, S., 'The Likelihood of Inefficiency, a Prisoners' Dilemma and Sub-optimality in Games of Binary Voluntary Provision of Public Goods,' *Social Choice and Welfare*, 11, 1994, 157–64.

Nitzan, S. and J. Paroush, 'Investment in Human Capital and Social Self Protection under Uncertainty,' *International Economic Review*, 21, 1980, 547–57.

Nitzan, S. and J. Paroush, 'Optimal Decision Rules in Uncertain Dichotomous Choice Situations,' *International Economic Review*, 23(2), 1982, 289–97.

Nitzan, S. and J. Paroush, *Collective Decision Making: An Economic Outlook*, Cambridge: Cambridge University Press, 1985.

Nitzan, S. and A. Rubinstein, 'A Further Characterization of Borda Ranking Method,' *Public Choice*, 36, 1981, 153–8.

Nurmi, H., *Voting Paradoxes and How to Deal with Them*, Berlin: Springer-Verlag, 1999.

Nurmi, H., *Voting Procedures under Uncertainty*, Berlin: Springer-Verlag, 2002.

Olson, M., *The Logic of Collective Action*, Cambridge, MA: Harvard University Press, 1965.

Ordeshook, P. C., *Game Theory and Political Theory: An introduction*, Cambridge: Cambridge University Press, 1986.

Owen, G., B. Grofman and S. Feld, 'Proving a Distribution Free Generalization of the Condorcet Jury Theorem,' *Mathematical Social Sciences*, 17, 1989, 1–16.

Paroush, J., 'Stay Away from Fair Coins: A Condorcet Jury Theorem,' *Social Choice and Welfare*, 15, 1998, 15–20.

Paroush, J. and D. Karotkin, 'Robustness of Optimal Majority Rules Over Teams with Changing Size,' *Social Choice and Welfare*, 6, 1989, 127–38.

Rawls, J. A., *Theory of Justice*, Oxford: Harvard University Press, 1971.

Reny, P. J., 'Arrow's Theorem and the Gibbard–Satterthwaite Theorem: A Unified Approach,' *Economics Letters*, 70(1), 2001, 99–105.

Richelson, J. T., 'A Characterization Result for the Plurality Rule,' *Journal of Economic Theory*, 19, 1978, 548–50.

Sah, R. K. and J. Stiglitz, 'Committees, Hierarchies and Polyarchies,' *The Economic Journal*, 98, 1988, 451–70.

Satterthwaite, M. A., 'Strategy Proofness and Arrow's Conditions,' *Journal of Economic Theory*, 10, 1975, 187–217.

Sen, A., *Collective Choice and Social Welfare*, San Francisco: Holden Day Inc., 1970.

Sen, A., 'Social Choice Theory: A Reexamination,' *Econometrica*, 45, 1977a, 53–89.

Sen, A., 'On Weights and Measures: Informational Constraints in Social Choice Analysis,' *Econometrica*, 45, 1977b, 1539–72.

Sen, A., 'Social Choice Theory,' in K. J. Arrow and M. Intriligator (eds), *Handbook of Mathematical Economics*, vol. III, Amsterdam: North Holland, 1986.

Shapley, L. and B. Grofman, 'Optimizing Group Judgmental Accuracy in the Presence of Interdependencies,' *Public Choice* 43, 1984, 329–43.

Varian, H. R., *Microeconomic Analysis*, 3rd edn, New York: W. W. Norton & Company, 1992.

Wriglesworth, J. L., *Libertarian Conflicts in Social Choice*, Cambridge: Cambridge University Press, 1985.

Yaari, M. E., 'Edgeworth, Shapley, Nash: Theories of Distributive Justice Re-Examined,' *Journal of Economic Theory*, 24, 1981, 1–39.

Young, H. P., 'An Axiomatization of Borda's Rule,' *Journal of Economic Theory*, 9, 1974, 43–52.

Author index

Subject index

Printed in the United States
by Baker & Taylor Publisher Services